Netscape Navigator 6

Introductory Concepts and Techniques

Gary B. Shelly
Thomas J. Cashman
Jeffrey J. Webb

COURSE
TECHNOLOGY
THOMSON LEARNING

COURSE TECHNOLOGY
25 THOMSON PLACE
BOSTON MA 02210

SHELLY
CASHMAN
SERIES®

Australia • Canada • Denmark • Japan • Mexico • New Zealand • Philippines • Puerto Rico • Singapore
South Africa • Spain • United Kingdom • United States

COURSE TECHNOLOGY

★

THOMSON LEARNING ™

COPYRIGHT © 2001 Course Technology, a division of Thomson Learning.
Printed in the United States of America

Asia (excluding Japan)
Thomson Learning
60 Albert Street, #15-01
Albert Complex
Singapore 189969

Japan
Thomson Learning
Palaceside Building 5F
1-1-1 Hitotsubashi, Chiyoda-ku
Tokyo 100 0003 Japan

Australia/New Zealand
Nelson/Thomson Learning
102 Dodds Street
South Melbourne, Victoria 3205
Australia

Latin America
Thomson Learning
Seneca, 53
Colonia Polanco
11560 Mexico D.F. Mexico

South Africa
Thomson Learning
Zonnebloem Building,
Constantia Square
526 Sixteenth Road
P.O. Box 2459
Halfway House, 1685
South Africa

Canada
Nelson/Thomson Learning
1120 Birchmount Road
Scarborough, Ontario
Canada M1K 5G4

UK/Europe/Middle East
Thomson Learning
Berkshire House
168-173 High Holborn
London, WC1V 7AA United Kingdom

Spain
Thomson Learning
Calle Magallanes, 25
28015-MADRID
ESPANA

PHOTO CREDITS: *Project 1, pages NN 1.2-3* 50s family, Courtesy of Corbis Images; Internet love graphic, Courtesy of Dynamic Graphics CD-ROM Image; woman, PhotoDisc Wired Business CD-ROM Image; control room, PhotoDisc Business & Technology CD-ROM Image; man, PhotoDisc Urban Lifestyles CD-ROM Image; children, PhotoDisc Business & Occupations CD-ROM Image; earth, Courtesy of Digital Stock Space & Space Flight CD-ROM Image; *Project 2, pages NN 2.2-3* all historical art elements, Courtesy of ArtToday.com, Inc. ©2000; *page NN 2.5* Internet graphics, Courtesy of Dynamic Graphics CD-ROM Image; *Project 3, page NN 3.5* computer graphic, Courtesy of Dynamic Graphics CD-ROM Image.

ISBN 0-7895-4647-7

1 2 3 4 5 6 7 8 9 10   BC   05 04 03 02 01

Netscape Navigator 6

Introductory Concepts and Techniques

C O N T E N T S

● **PROJECT 3**

**COMMUNICATING, SCHEDULING, AND CONTACT
MANAGEMENT WITH NETSCAPE**

● **APPENDIX**

NETSCAPE NAVIGATOR PREFERENCES

Preface

In the few short years since its birth, the World Wide Web, or Web for short, has grown beyond all expectations. During this time, Web usage has increased from a limited number of users to more than 200 million users worldwide, accessing Web pages on any topic you can imagine. Individuals, schools, businesses, and government all are taking advantage of this innovative way of accessing the Internet to provide information, products, services, and education electronically. Netscape Navigator 6 provides the novice as well as the experienced user a window with which to look into the Web and tap an abundance of resources.

rhi•noc•er•os

rĪ-'näs-r&s

noun

any o...ge he...

herbi......als of...

Objectives of This Textbook

Netscape Navigator 6: Introductory Concepts and Techniques is intended for use in a one-credit, three-to-five-week, course or in combination with other books in an introductory computer concepts or applications course. Specific objectives of this book are as follows:

- To teach students how to use Netscape Navigator 6 using the proven Shelly Cashman Series step-by-step, screen-by-screen pedagogy
- To expose students to various World Wide Web resources
- To acquaint student with the more popular search engines
- To show students how to do research using the World Wide Web
- To teach students how to communicate with other Internet users

The Shelly Cashman Approach

Features of the Shelly Cashman Series *Netscape Navigator 6: Introductory Concepts and Techniques* book include:

- **Step-by-Step, Screen-by-Screen, Instructions:** Each of the tasks required to complete a project is identified throughout the development of the project. The steps are accompanied by full-color screens.
- **Other Ways Boxes for Reference:** Netscape Navigator 6 provides a variety of ways to carry out a given task. The Other Ways boxes displayed at the end of most of the step-by-step sequences specify the other ways to do the task completed in the steps. Thus, the steps and the Other Ways box make a comprehensive reference unit.
- **More About Feature:** These marginal annotations provide background information that complements the topics covered, adding depth and perspective to the learning process.
- **A Wealth of World Wide Web Hands-on Exercises:** The Web is thoroughly integrated into students' Netscape Navigator 6 learning experience through the Online Practice Tests and Learning Games exercises.

Other Ways

1. On View menu click Reload
2. Press ALT+V, type R
3. Click Location field, press ENTER

More About

Help

Netscape offers a tutorial that explains the basics of the Internet, using the Netscape Web browser, and various tasks that can be performed over the Internet. Access the tutorial by clicking New to the Net Tutorial on the Help menu.

Organization of This Textbook

Netscape Navigator 6: Introductory Concepts and Techniques consists of three projects and an appendix. Each project ends with a large number of exercises to reinforce what students learn in the project. The projects and appendix are organized as follows:

Project 1 — Browsing the Web In Project 1, students are introduced to the Internet, World Wide Web, and Netscape Navigator 6. Topics include starting Netscape; browsing the World Wide Web using URLs and links; stopping and refreshing a Web page; using the History list; adding Web pages to the Bookmarks menu; displaying and removing Web pages from the Bookmarks menu; using My Sidebar; saving and printing a Web page; copying and pasting text from a Web page into WordPad; saving pictures from a Web page to disk; using the My Netscape feature; and accessing Netscape Help.

Project 2 — Web Search Tools and Research Techniques In Project 2, students are introduced to the seven types of Web pages that they will view on the Web, how to find information using Netscape's Internet Keyword System, Netscape Search, Google, AltaVista, and Yahoo!; and methods to evaluate a Web page. Topics include searching the Web using keywords or a directory; performing an advanced search; evaluating and recording relevant information about a Web source; creating maps; and creating a working bibliography that includes Web sources.

Project 3 — Communicating, Scheduling, and Contact Management with Netscape In Project 3, students learn how to communicate over the Internet using Netscape Mail, newsgroups, and Instant Messenger; how to get organized with Address Book and WebCalendar; and how to listen to music using Netscape Radio. Topics include reading, replying to, and deleting an e-mail message; composing and sending a new e-mail message; reading and posting a newsgroup article; subscribing and unsubscribing to a newsgroup; sending and replying to instant messages; creating and maintaining an address book and calendar; and listening to music using the browser.

Appendix A — Netscape Navigator Preferences Appendix A explains how to change the settings that control how Netscape looks, feels, and reacts to different situations.

End-of-Project Student Activities

A notable strength of the Shelly Cashman Series Web-browser books is the extensive student activities at the end of each project. Well-structured student activities can make the difference between students merely participating in a class and students retaining the information they learn. The following activities are included in this book.

- **What You Should Know** A listing of the tasks completed within a project together with the pages where the step-by-step, screen-by-screen explanations appear. This section provides a perfect study review for students.

- **Test Your Knowledge** A minimum of four pencil-and-paper activities designed to determine students' understanding of the material in the project. Included are true/false questions, multiple-choice questions, and short-answer activities. In addition, this section includes the Online Practice Tests and Learning Games exercises.

- **In the Lab** Several assignments per project require students to apply the knowledge gained in the project to solve problems on the Web and a computer.
- **Cases and Places** Up to seven unique case studies require students to apply their knowledge to real-world situations.

Shelly Cashman Series Teaching Tools

Two basic ancillaries accompany this textbook: Teaching Tools on CD-ROM (ISBN 0-7895-4661-2) and MyCourse.com. These ancillaries are free to adopters through your Course Technology representative or by calling one of the following telephone numbers: Colleges and Universities, 1-800-648-7450; High Schools, 1-800-824-5179; Private Career Colleges, 1-800-477-3692; Canada, 1-800-268-2222; and Corporations and Governments, 1-800-340-7450.

Teaching Tools

The comprehensive set of Teaching Tools for this textbook includes both teaching and testing aids. The contents of the Teaching Tools CD-ROM are listed below.

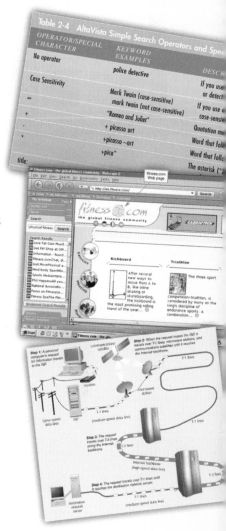

- **Instructor's Manual** The Instructor's Manual consists of Microsoft Word files that include the following for each project: project objectives; project overview; detailed lesson plans with page number references; teacher notes and activities; answers to the handwritten exercises; test bank (50 true/false, 25 multiple-choice, and 35 fill-in-the-blank questions per chapter); and figure references. The figures are available in the Figures in the Book ancillary. Using your word processing software, you can generate quizzes and exams.

- **Figures in the Book** Illustrations for every picture, table, and screen in the textbook are available in electronic form. Use this ancillary to present a slide show in lecture or to print transparencies for use in lecture with an overhead projector. If you have a personal computer and LCD device, this ancillary can be an effective tool for presenting lectures.

- **ExamView** ExamView is a state-of-the-art test builder that is easy to use. ExamView enables you to create printed tests, Internet tests, and computer (LAN-based) tests quickly. You can enter your own test questions or use the question test bank that accompanies ExamView. The question test bank is the same as the one in the Instructor's Manual.

- **Course Syllabus** Any instructor who has been assigned a course at the last minute knows how difficult it is to develop a course syllabus. For this reason, a one-credit hour, five-week course sample syllabus is included that can be customized easily to a course.

- **Interactive Labs** Eighteen hands-on Interactive Labs that take students from ten to fifteen minutes each to step through help solidify and reinforce mouse and keyboard usage and computer concepts. Student assessment is available in each Interactive Lab by means of a Print button.

MyCourse.com

MyCourse.com offers instructors and students an opportunity to supplement classroom learning with additional course content. You can use MyCourse.com to expand traditional learning by accessing and completing readings, tests, and other assignments through the customized, comprehensive Web site. For additional information, visit mycourse.com and click the Help button.

Shelly Cashman Online

Shelly Cashman Online is a World Wide Web service available to instructors and students of computer education. Visit Shelly Cashman Online at scseries.com. Shelly Cashman Online is divided into four areas:

- ● **Series Information** Shelly Cashman Series history and information.

- ● **Teaching Resources** Designed for instructors teaching from and using Shelly Cashman Series textbooks and software. This area includes password-protected instructor materials that can be downloaded, course outlines, teaching tools, and product catalog.

- ● **Community** Shelly and Cashman newsletters, Summer Institute, news, and more.

- ● **Student Center** Dedicated to students learning about computers with Shelly Cashman Series textbooks and software. This area includes cool links, data that can be downloaded, and much more.

Acknolwedgments

The Shelly Cashman Series would not be the leading computer education series without the contributions of outstanding publishing professionals. First, and foremost, among them is Becky Herrington, director of production and designer. She is the heart and soul of the Shelly Cashman Series, and it is only through her leadership, dedication, and tireless efforts that superior products are made possible. Becky created and produced the award-winning Windows series of books.

Under Becky's direction, the following individuals made significant contributions to these books: Doug Cowley, production manager; Ginny Harvey, series specialist; Ken Russo, senior Web and graphic designer; Mike Bodnar, associate production manager; Mark Norton, Web designer; Meena Moest, production editor; Michelle French, Christy Otten, Stephanie Nance, and Chris Schneider, graphic artists; Jeanne Black and Betty Hopkins, Quark experts; Lyn Markowicz, copyeditor and proofreader; Cristina Haley, indexer; Richard Keaveny, associate publisher; Jim Quasney, series consulting editor; Lora Wade, product manager; Erin Roberts, associate product manager; Erin Runyon, associate product manager; Francis Schurgot, Web product manager; Marc Ouellette, associate Web product manager; and Rachel VanKirk, marketing manager.

We hope you find using this book an exciting and rewarding experience.

Gary B. Shelly
Thomas J. Cashman
Jeffrey J. Webb

Netscape Navigator 6

Netscape Navigator 6

P R O J E C T

1

Browsing the Web

O B J E C T I V E S

You will have mastered the material in this project when you can:

- Define the Internet and the World Wide Web
- Describe hypermedia and browsers
- Explain a link
- Start Netscape Navigator
- Describe key Netscape Navigator features
- Enter a Uniform Resource Locator (URL)
- Click links to display Web pages
- Reload a Web page
- Use the Back and Forward buttons
- Create and remove bookmarks
- Use My Sidebar to access information
- Use Netscape's home page
- Save Web pages to disk
- Save a picture on a Web page to disk
- Paste text from a Web page into a WordPad document
- Print Web pages
- Display and customize the My Netscape page
- Use Netscape Help features
- Quit Netscape

Internet Timeline
Linking Networked Information

The year was 1957. Girls wore poodle skirts, and boys sported ducktails. Television sets were a novelty, and everyone liked Ike. Peace and prosperity reigned in the United States, and most people felt life was good, indeed. Against this idyllic American backdrop, Russia launched *Sputnik*, the first artificial Earth satellite, prompting fears of a Russian nuclear attack against the United States. In response, the Department of Defense was charged with developing a communications network that would remain operational in the event of a devastating attack.

The requirements for the system were simple: it had to be decentralized, which meant that information still could be transmitted, even if parts of the system were disabled. So, in 1969, ARPANET was born, the Pentagon's Advanced Research Projects Agency's precursor to the Internet. Four computers were networked that first year; two years later, 15 computers were networked. The following year, the number grew to 37 computers. So began what would become the Internet's exponential growth.

Nonmilitary users connected to ARPANET in the 1970s, and some networks offered to allow the public to connect to the system in the 1980s. The Department of Defense then decided to create another private network for its nonclassified information. The department moved its files to its new military side, MILNET, and left ARPANET in place. More and more networks added information to ARPANET, which earned the new name, Internet, to reflect this community of connected computers.

Internet
ARPANET 1970s
1960s
1950s

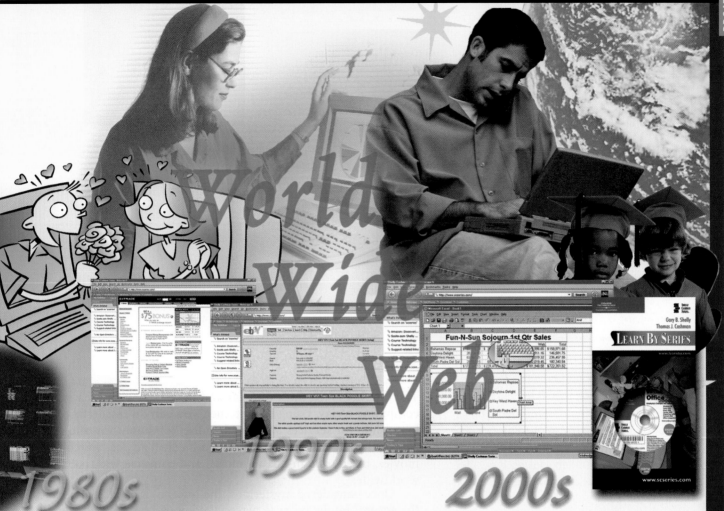

World Wide Web

1980s   1990s   2000s

In 1989, while working as a scientist at the European Laboratory for Particle Physics in Geneva, Switzerland, Tim Berners-Lee proposed the initial idea for the system that ultimately would evolve into the World Wide Web. He also set up the Internet's first Web server.

Today, the size of the Web is expanding at an exponential rate with millions of people using the Web worldwide.

This is an exciting time in the history of Internet access and Web browsing. Netscape Navigator is a popular Web browsing program that provides searching capabilities, allows you to link quickly to previously viewed Web pages via a History list, and keeps track of your favorite Web pages.

The unique structure of the Internet has spawned cutting-edge potential for the global economy. Worldwide marketing and distribution online offer a myriad of products and services. Internet businesses thrive in the twenty-first century as e-commerce transactions take place over secure electronic networks. With access to a computer, a network connection, and a means to pay for purchased goods, anyone can participate in e-commerce. In addition, the World Wide Web allows people everywhere to communicate via electronic mail; access the latest news, sports, and weather; conduct online banking and trading; enjoy multimedia entertainment; use travel-related services; telecommute; take Web-based courses; and seek employment.

In this project, you are introduced to the worldwide system of networks, the Internet; the software used to connect computers, called Transmission Control Protocol/Internet Protocol (TCP/IP) that provides networking services; and the World Wide Web, which is the collection of hyperlinks throughout the Internet that creates an interconnected network of links. The links enable you to access the location of the computer on which text, graphics, video, sound, and virtual reality are stored.

Upon completing the project, you will join the millions of individuals worldwide successfully sharing networked information.

Netscape Navigator 6

Browsing the Web

P R O J E C T

1

Introduction

The Internet is the most popular and fastest growing area in computing today. Using the Internet, you can do research, get a loan, shop for services and merchandise, job hunt, buy and sell stocks, display weather maps, obtain medical advice, watch movies, listen to high-quality music, and converse with people worldwide.

Once considered mysterious, the Internet is now accessible to the general public because personal computers with user-friendly tools have reduced its complexity. The Internet, with millions of connected computers, continues to grow with thousands of new users coming online every day. Schools, businesses, newspapers, television stations, and government services all can be found on the Internet. Service providers are popping up all over the country providing inexpensive access to the Internet from home; but just exactly what is the Internet?

The Internet

The **Internet** is a worldwide collection of networks (Figure 1-1), each of which is composed of a collection of smaller networks. A network is composed of several computers connected together to share resources and data. For example, on a college campus, the network in the student lab can be connected to the faculty computer network, which is connected to the administration network, and they all can connect to the Internet.

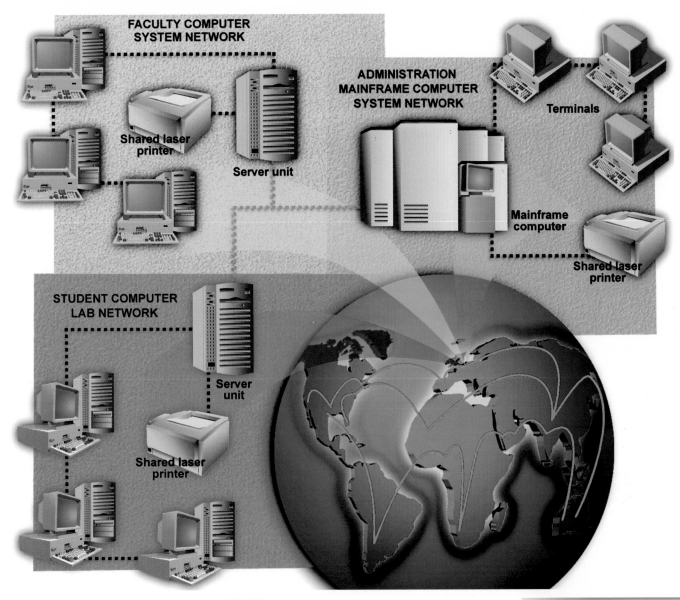

FIGURE 1-1

Networks are connected with high-, medium- and low-speed data lines that allow data to move from one computer to another (Figure 1-2 on the next page). The Internet has high-speed data lines that connect major computer systems located around the world, which form the **Internet backbone**. Other, less powerful computers, such as those used by local Internet service providers often attach to the Internet backbone using medium-speed data lines. Finally, the connection between your computer at home and your local Internet service provider, often called **the last mile**, employs low-speed data lines such as telephone. In many cases today, cable is replacing telephone lines over the last mile, which significantly improves access to information on the Internet.

More)About

The Internet

The Internet started as a government experiment for the military. The military wanted a communication means that would connect different computers running different operating systems. This method had to remain operational even if one or more of the computers became unavailable. From this experiment, a communication technique originated called Transmission Control Protocol/Internet Protocol, or TCP/IP.

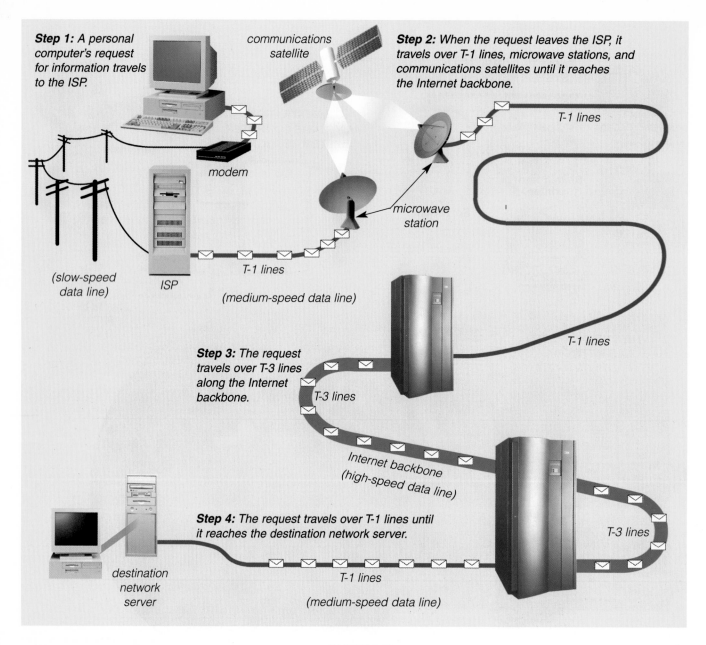

Step 1: A personal computer's request for information travels to the ISP.

communications satellite

Step 2: When the request leaves the ISP, it travels over T-1 lines, microwave stations, and communications satellites until it reaches the Internet backbone.

T-1 lines

modem

microwave station

(slow-speed data line)

ISP

T-1 lines

(medium-speed data line)

T-1 lines

Step 3: The request travels over T-3 lines along the Internet backbone.

T-3 lines

Internet backbone (high-speed data line)

Step 4: The request travels over T-1 lines until it reaches the destination network server.

destination network server

T-1 lines

(medium-speed data line)

T-3 lines

FIGURE 1-2

The World Wide Web

Computer systems have the capability to deliver information in a variety of ways, such as graphics, sound, video clips, animation, and, of course, regular text. On the Internet, this multimedia capability is available in a form called **hypermedia**, which is any variety of computer media, including text, graphics, video, sound, and virtual reality.

You access hypermedia using a **hyperlink**, or simply **link**, which is a special software pointer that points to the location of the computer on which the hypermedia is stored and to the hypermedia itself. A link can point to hypermedia on any computer connected to the Internet that is running the proper software. Thus, clicking a link on a computer in Los Angeles could display text and graphics located in New York.

The collection of links throughout the Internet creates an interconnected network called the **World Wide Web**, which also is referred to as the **Web**, or **WWW**. Each computer within the Web containing hypermedia that can be referenced with a link is called a **Web site**. Millions of Web sites around the world are accessible through the Internet.

Graphics, text, and other hypermedia available at a Web site are stored in a file called a **Web page**. Therefore, when you click a link to display a picture, read text, view a video, or listen to a song, you are viewing a Web page.

Figure 1-3 illustrates a Web page at the CBS Switchboard.com Web site. This Web page contains numerous links. For example, each underlined phrase in blue and the tabs below the title are links. Clicking a link, such as Find a Person in Figure 1-3, displays another Web page.

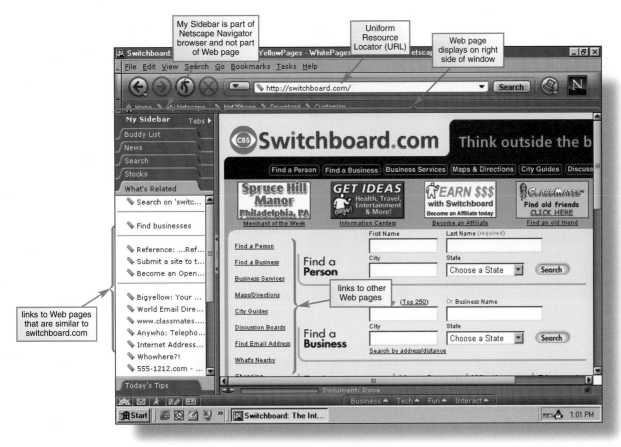

FIGURE 1-3

Uniform Resource Locator (URL)

Each Web page is identified by a special address called the Uniform Resource Locator. A **Uniform Resource Locator** or **URL** (pronounced *you are ell*) is important because it is the unique address of each Web page on the World Wide Web. The URL in Figure 1-3 is http://switchboard.com.

A URL often is composed of three parts (Figure 1-4 on the next page). The first part is the protocol. A **protocol** is a set of rules. Most Web pages use HyperText transport protocol. **Hypertext Transfer Protocol (HTTP)** describes the rules used to transmit Web pages electronically over the Internet. You enter the protocol in lowercase as http followed by a colon and two forward slashes (://). If you do not begin a URL with a protocol, Netscape will assume it is http, and automatically will append http:// to the front of the URL.

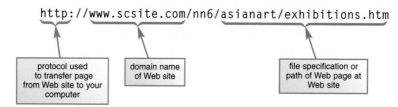

FIGURE 1-4

The second part of a URL is the domain name. The **domain name** is the Internet address of the computer on the Internet where the Web page is located. Each computer on the Internet has a unique address, called an **Internet Protocol address**, or **IP address**. The domain name identifies where to forward a request for the Web page referenced by the URL.

The last part of the domain name (com in Figure 1-4) indicates the type of organization that owns the Web site. For example, com indicates a commercial organization, usually a business or corporation. Educational institutions have edu at the end of the their domain names. Government entities use gov at the end of their domain names. Table 1-1 shows types of organizations and their extensions.

Table 1-1 Organizations and their Domain Name Extensions	
ORGANIZATION	*EXTENSION*
Commercial	.com
Educational	.edu
Government	.gov
Military	.mil
Major network support	.net
Organizations not covered above	.org
International	.int
Individual countries/states	Country/state code

The optional third part of a URL is the file specification of the Web page. The **file specification** includes the file name and possibly a directory or folder name. This information is called the **path**. If no file specification of a Web page is specified in the URL, a default Web page displays. This means you can display a Web page even though you do not know its file specification. The domain name of the Web site will display a default page.

You can find URLs that identify interesting Web sites in magazines or newspapers, on television, from friends, or even from just browsing the Web. In addition, for a list of excellent sites visit the Shelly Cashman Series Guide to the World Wide Web site at

    scsite.com/nn6/websites.htm

URLs of well-known companies and institutions usually contain the company's name and institution's name. For example, ibm.com is IBM Corporation, and purdue.edu is Purdue University.

HTML

HTML editing programs, such as FrontPage, Hotdog, and Hotmetal, make it easy to create Web pages without learning HTML syntax.

HyperText Markup Language

Web page authors use a special formatting language called **Hypertext Markup Language (HTML)** to create Web pages. Behind all the formatted text and eye-catching graphics on a Web page is plain text. Special HTML formatting codes and functions that control attributes such as font size, colors, and centering surround the text and picture references. Figure 1-5 shows part of the hyperText markup language used to create the Web page shown in Figure 1-3 on the previous page.

Though it looks somewhat cryptic, HTML is similar to a computer programming language. Using HTML, you can create your own Web pages and place them on the Web for others to see. Easier to use Web page development software, such as Microsoft's FrontPage and Netscape's Composer, have been developed to assist in creating Web pages.

Close button

HTML format codes

```
<HTML>
<HEAD>
<TITLE>Switchboard: The Internet Directory - YellowPages - WhitePages - Phone
<META name="keywords" content="YellowPages, Yellow Pages, White Pages, WhiteP
<META name="description" content="Switchboard is a leading provider of white
<META NAME="Switchboard" Content="Yellow Pages">
<META HTTP-EQUIV="Content-Type" content="text/html">
<Script Language="JavaScript">
<!--
        function verifyWP() {
      if (document.WPform.L.value == "") {
                alert("You must enter at least a Last Name.");
            document.WPform.L.focus();
            return false;
            }
        return true;
          }

        function verifyYP() {
                if ((document.YPform.C.value == "") && (document.YPfo
                      alert("You must enter a Category or Business
                      document.YPform.C.focus();
                      return false;
                      }

              if ((document.YPform.s.options[document.YPform.s.sele
```

FIGURE 1-5

Home Pages

No main menus or any particular starting points exist in the World Wide Web. Although you can reference any page on the Web when you begin, most people start with a specially designated page from a Web site called a home page. A **home page** is the introductory page for a Web site. All other Web pages for that site usually are accessible from the home page via links. In addition, the home page is the page that displays when you enter the domain name with no file specification, such as disney.com or cbs.com.

Because it is the starting point for most Web sites, designers try to make a good first impression and display attractive, eye-catching, specially formatted text and a variety of links to other pages at the Web site, as well as other interesting and useful Web sites.

Internet Browsers

Just as graphical user interfaces (GUIs), such as Microsoft Windows, simplify working with a computer by using a point-and-click method, a **browser**, such as Netscape Navigator (Netscape for short), makes using the World Wide Web easier by removing the complexity of having to remember the syntax, or rules, of commands used to reference Web pages at Web sites. A **browser** takes the URL associated with a link or the URL entered by the user, locates the computer containing the associated Web page, and then reads the HTML codes returned to display a Web page.

More About

Home Pages

A Web site may consist of many home pages. A computer used by faculty members or students for their hypertext documents would have many home pages – one for each person.

What Is Netscape Navigator?

Netscape Navigator (also called **Netscape**) is a Web browsing program that allows you to search for and view Web pages. Other applications that come with Netscape are Mail, Instant Messenger, Address Book, Calendar, and Composer.

The **Mail application** allows you to manage e-mail and newsgroups. The **Address Book application** can be used to maintain a personal address book. The **Calendar application** allows you to maintain a personal calendar of events. The **Instant Messenger application** can be used to send instantaneous messages to other Netscape users and also communicate in chat rooms. With the **Composer application,** you can create Web pages without any knowledge of HTML.

The Mail, Address Book, Calendar, and Instant Messenger applications use the Netscape server. Thus, you can access these applications from anywhere, provided you have a computer that has Netscape.

Starting Netscape

To start Netscape, the Windows desktop must display on the screen, and the Netscape icon must be on the desktop or Netscape must be on the Programs sub-menu. Perform the following steps to start Netscape using the Netscape icon.

 To Start Netscape

1 Point to the Netscape icon on the desktop (Figure 1-6).

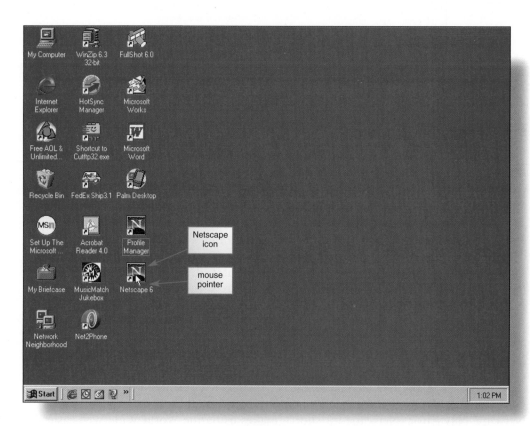

FIGURE 1-6

2 Double-click the Netscape icon.

The Netscape home page displays (Figure 1-7). This page may display differently on your computer. The Netscape home page changes often, providing continuous updates and information.

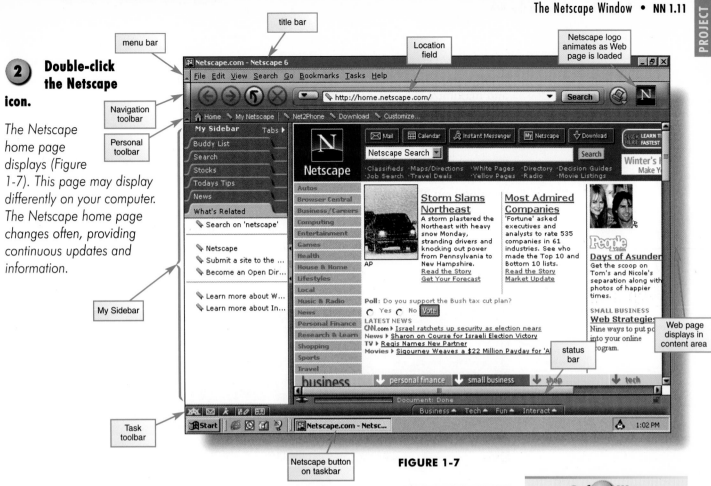

title bar

menu bar

Location field

Netscape logo animates as Web page is loaded

Navigation toolbar

Personal toolbar

My Sidebar

Task toolbar

Netscape button on taskbar

Web page displays in content area

status bar

FIGURE 1-7

Other Ways

1. On Start menu point to Programs, point to Netscape 6, click Netscape 6

Normally, when Netscape starts, the Netscape home page displays. Because it is possible to change the page that initially displays through the **Preferences command** on the Edit menu, the home page shown in Figure 1-7 may be different on your computer. For example, some schools and businesses have their own Web site home page display when starting Netscape. For information on how to change to a different home page, see Appendix A.

The Netscape Window

The **Netscape window** (Figure 1-7) consists of innovative features that make browsing the Internet easy. It contains a title bar, menu bar, Personal toolbar, Navigation toolbar, My Sidebar, content area where pages from the World Wide Web display, a scroll bar, a status bar, and a Task toolbar. Much of what you see in My Sidebar and the content area are links to popular Web sites.

TITLE BAR The title bar displays at the top of the Netscape window. As shown at the top of Figure 1-8a on the next page, the title bar includes the Control-menu icon on the left, the name of the window, and the Minimize, Restore (or Maximize), and Close buttons on the right. Double-click the Control-menu icon or click the Close button to close Netscape. Click the Minimize button to minimize Netscape. When you minimize an application, the window closes and the application displays as a button on the taskbar at the bottom of the screen. Click the Restore button to return the Netscape window to the size and position it occupied before being maximized. The Restore button changes to the Maximize button when the Netscape window is

More About

The Netscape Window

You can change the page that displays when you launch Netscape by clicking Edit on the menu bar, and then clicking Preferences on the Edit menu. You can choose to display the default Web page, the current Web page, or choose a page that you have saved to a file.

in a restored state. Click the Maximize button to maximize the Netscape window so it expands to fill the entire desktop. You also can double-click the title bar to restore and maximize the Netscape window. If the window is in a restored state, you can drag the title bar to move the window on the screen.

MENU BAR The **menu bar**, which is located immediately below the title bar, displays menu names (Figure 1-8a). Each **menu name** represents a menu of commands that you can use to perform actions, such as saving Web pages, copying and pasting, opening new Netscape windows, setting preferences, quitting Netscape, and so on. To display a menu, such as the File menu in Figure 1-8a, click File on the menu bar or press ALT+F. To invoke a command on the File menu, click the command name or type the shortcut keys shown to the right of the commands on the menu.

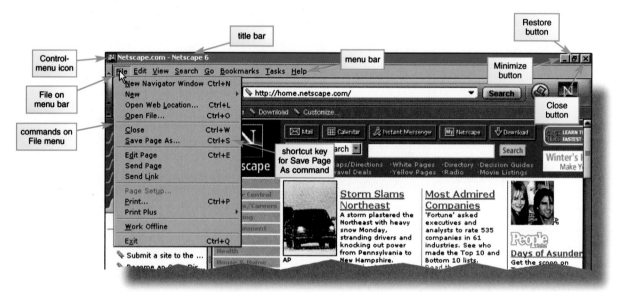

FIGURE 1-8a Title bar, menu bar, and File menu

PERSONAL TOOLBAR The **Personal toolbar** (Figure 1-8b) includes buttons that give you instant access to Web sites that are visited on a regular basis. If you click the **Home button** on the Personal toolbar, Netscape displays the home page in the content area (see Figure 1-7 on the previous page). Clicking **My Netscape** causes Netscape to load a customized Web page, one created by you with links to sites that are important to you. Clicking **Net2Phone** displays the Netscape Net2phone Web page, which allows you to make phone calls over the Internet, provided you sign up for the service.

Finally, to the far left on the Personal toolbar is a triangle called the Show/Hide button. When you click the **Show/Hide button**, it shows or hides the toolbar.

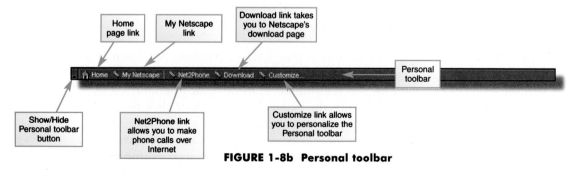

FIGURE 1-8b Personal toolbar

NAVIGATION TOOLBAR The **Navigation toolbar** (Figure 1-8c) contains buttons and the Location field that allow you to navigate quickly from one Web page to another. The **Back button** allows you to display the previous page. You use the **Forward button** to display a page that was viewed earlier, but after the current Web page. The Forward button is active only after backing up to display Web pages that you viewed earlier.

The **Reload button** reloads the Web page currently displaying in the content area. The Reload button can be useful when working with Web pages that are constantly changing. The **Stop button** stops the loading of a Web page. Use the Stop button if a Web page takes too long to load or you change your mind and don't want to view it.

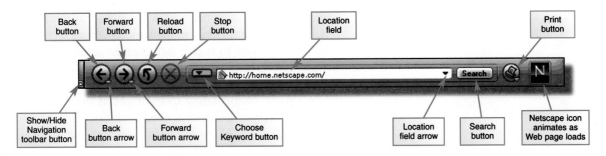

FIGURE 1-8c Navigation toolbar

In the middle of the Navigation toolbar is the Location field. The **Location field** holds the URL for the page currently shown in the content area. The URL updates automatically as you browse from page to page. If you know the URL of a Web page you want to visit, double-click the URL in the Location field, type the new URL, and press the ENTER key to display the corresponding page.

Besides entering a URL in the Location field, you can enter a general word and Netscape will attempt to display the desired Web page or point you in the right direction. For example, if you type, cisco, and press the ENTER key, Netscape displays the Cisco Systems home page (cisco.com). If you type a more general term, such as gifts, and press the ENTER key, Netscape displays links to Web pages where you can purchase gifts.

On the left side of the Location field is the Choose Keyword button. The **Choose Keyword button** allows you to enter phrases that help you find Web pages for which you are searching.

On the right side of the Location field is the **Location field arrow,** which allows you to revisit any Web site you visited over several sessions by clicking the page title in its list. Thus, unlike the Back button, which returns you to the previous page, the Location field arrow allows you to choose a Web site to redisplay from a list.

Use the **Search button** on the right side of the Navigation toolbar to pass the entry in the Location field to a search engine. With Netscape, if you enter a URL in the Location field, you press the ENTER key to display the corresponding page. If you type a word or series of words and click the Search button, then you initiate a search of the Web. A **search engine** searches the Web for pages that include the entry in the Location field. Search engines are discussed in Project 2.

To the right of the Search button is the Print button. The **Print button** prints the Web page currently displayed in the content area. Next to the Print button is the **Netscape icon,** which animates as a Web page is being loaded.

On the far left side of the Personal toolbar is the Show/Hide button for the Navigation toolbar. When you click the Show/Hide button, it shows or hides the toolbar.

The Personal Toolbar

You can change the home page by displaying a page and then dragging the URL to the Home button on the Personal toolbar.

MY SIDEBAR **My Sidebar** (Figure 1-9a) is a customizable frame in the Netscape browser that displays to the left of the content area. The term **frame** refers to any area on the screen that can contain a Web page. Figure 1-7 on page NN 1.11 displays two frames, one containing My Sidebar and one containing the content area. You use My Sidebar to quickly access items of interest, such as news, weather, and stock quotes. Each tab displays a different panel. Use the Tabs button to add, delete, and rearrange the sequence of the tabs in My Sidebar.

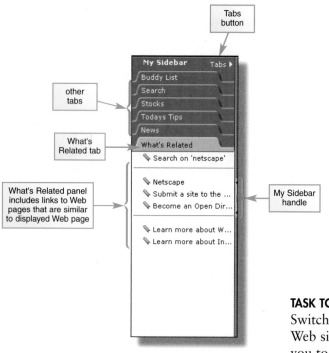

(a) My Sidebar

STATUS BAR The **status bar** (Figure 1-9b) is located immediately below the content area and includes messages and other information for the user. On the far left side of the status bar is the **Online/Offline button**, which allows you to toggle between being online and offline. Next to the Online/Offline button is the status indicator. The **status indicator** animates as Netscape loads a page. Immediately to the right of the status indicator, Netscape displays messages regarding its activities or the URL of the links to which the mouse pointer is pointing. At the far right of the status bar is the Security icon. If you click the **Security icon**, Netscape displays a Web page titled Netscape Personal Security Manager that allows you to make changes to the security level of the page you are viewing.

TASK TOOLBAR The **Task toolbar** (Figure 1-9c) includes the Task Switcher area and items you can click to display links to popular Web sites. The **Task Switcher area** contains five buttons that allow you to quickly start other Netscape applications, such as Netscape Navigator, Mail, Instant Messenger, Composer, and Address Book.

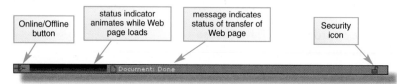

(b) Status bar

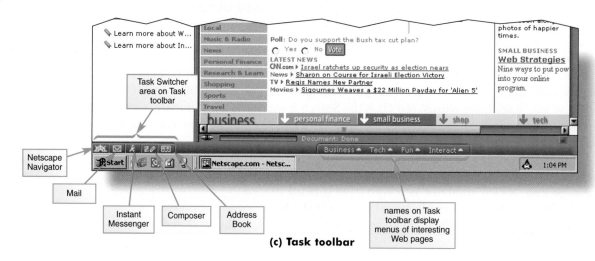

(c) Task toolbar

FIGURE 1-9

CONTENT AREA You view a Web page through the **content area** (see Figure 1-7 on page NN 1.11). At the right and sometimes at the bottom of the content area are scroll bars, scroll arrows, and a scroll box, which you can use to move up and down or left and right to reveal parts of the page not currently visible on the screen.

Browsing the World Wide Web

The most common way to browse the World Wide Web is to obtain the URL of a Web page you want to visit and enter it into the Location field on the Navigation toolbar. It is by visiting various Web sites that you can begin to understand the enormous appeal of the World Wide Web. The following steps show you how to contact a Web site provided by Web Art Publishing in Santa Fe, New Mexico and visit the Web page titled Asian Arts, which contains information and pictures of artwork from various countries in Asia. The URL for the Asian Art page is:

```
http://www.scsite.com/nn6/asianart.htm
```

You are not required to provide the leading http:// protocol or www when initially typing the URL in the Location field. Netscape will insert http:// and assume the www automatically, if you do not supply it. Thus, you can enter the above URL as:

```
scsite.com/nn6/asianart.htm
```

Perform the following steps to display the Asian Art Web page.

> ### More About
>
> ### The Netscape Display Area
>
> You can change the character fonts used in Web pages, the colors used to identify hyperlinks, and the appearance of toolbars, menus, and other items. Click Preference on the Edit menu and then use the Appearance category to make the desired changes. The Fonts subcategory controls font and type size; the Colors subcategory controls colors; and the Themes subcategory controls the appearance of the toolbars, buttons, menus, and other items.

Steps To Browse the Web by Entering a URL

1 **Double-click the URL in the Location field to select it.**

Netscape selects the current URL in the Location field (Figure 1-10). Because the mouse pointer is pointing at the Location field, a ScreenTip displays.

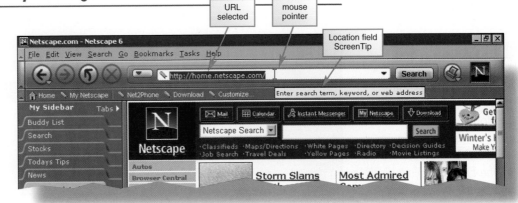

FIGURE 1-10

2 **Type** scsite.com/nn6/asianart.htm **as the new URL.**

The new URL displays in the Location field (Figure 1-11).

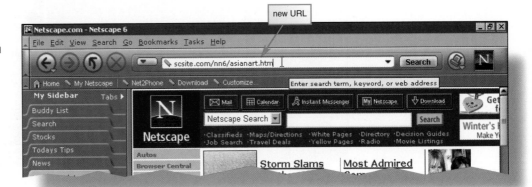

FIGURE 1-11

③ Press the ENTER key.

Netscape transfers the Web page http://www.scsite.com/ nn6/asianart.htm from the computer where it is located to your computer. The Stop button on the Navigation toolbar becomes active and the status indicator on the status bar and the Netscape icon begin to animate. A message providing information about the progress of the transfer displays on the status bar. The Web page displays in the content area (Figure 1-12). When the transfer is complete, a message displays on the status bar, indicating the transfer is complete.

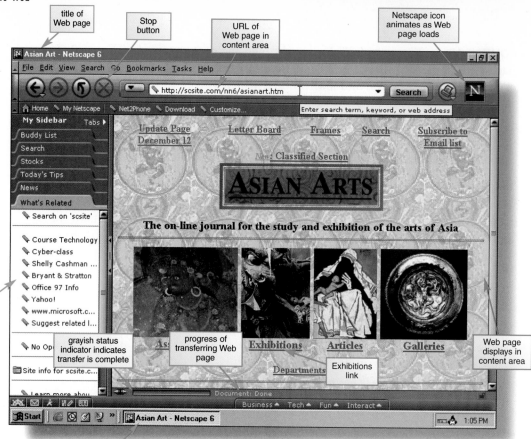

FIGURE 1-12

④ Point to the Exhibitions link.

The shape of the mouse pointer changes to a pointing hand to indicate the word Exhibitions is a link (Figure 1-13). The URL associated with the Exhibitions link displays on the status bar.

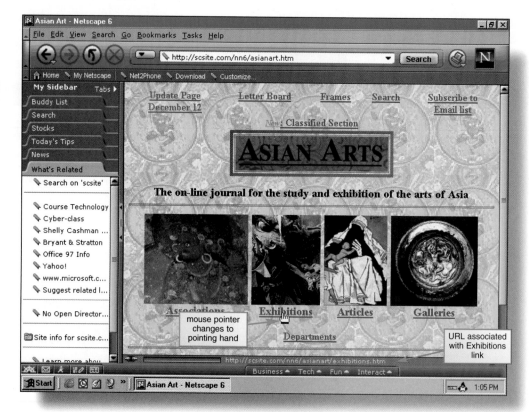

FIGURE 1-13

5 Click the Exhibitions link.

The Exhibitions page displays in the content area (Figure 1-14). A vertical scroll bar on the right side of the window indicates the page is larger than the content area. You will have to scroll down to view additional information and pictures.

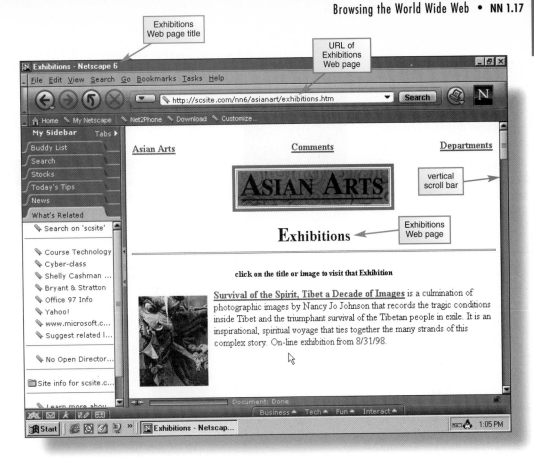

FIGURE 1-14

6 Scroll through the content area to display the link, The Splendors of Imperial China: Treasures from the National Palace Museum, Taipei, and then point to it.

The content area scrolls, the mouse pointer changes to a pointing hand icon, and the URL of the Web page associated with the link displays on the status bar (Figure 1-15). The picture at the right of the content area also is a link to the same page.

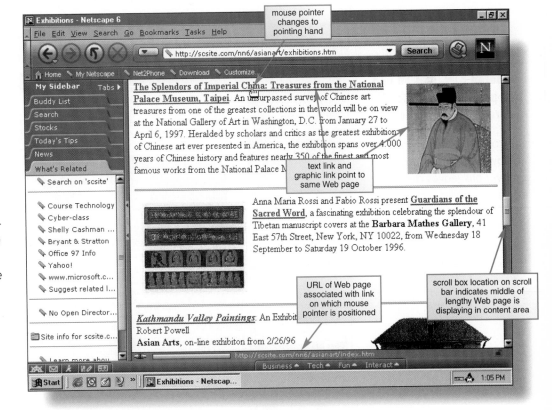

FIGURE 1-15

7 Click the link.

After a brief interval, The Splendors of Imperial China Web page displays (Figure 1-16). The Web page contains pictures and descriptions of the Chinese art located in the National Palace Museum in Taipei, China.

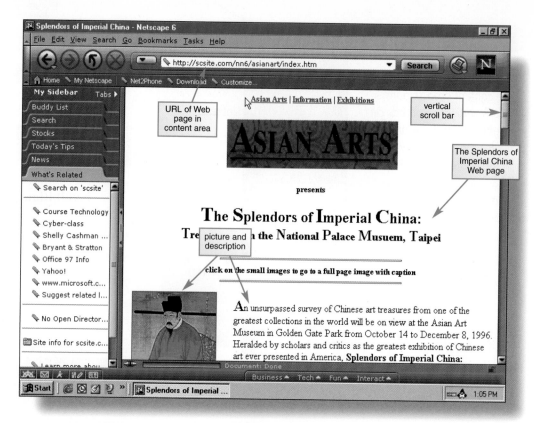

FIGURE 1-16

8 Scroll through the content area to view the three pictures numbered 8, 9, and 10 and then point to the center picture (picture number 9).

The content area scrolls to display the pictures of a stem cup, various leaves and flowers, and a globe vase (Figure 1-17). The pointing hand icon in the center picture indicates the picture with the title, Three leaves from Landscapes and Flowers, is a link.

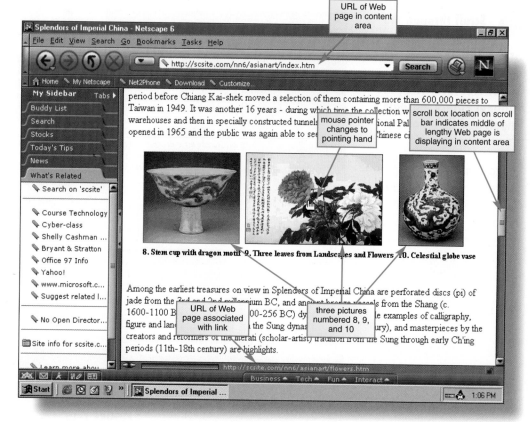

FIGURE 1-17

9 **Click the center picture. When the new Web page displays, scroll down to display the complete picture.**

A larger picture of number 9, Three leaves from Landscapes and Flowers, displays in the content area (Figure 1-18).

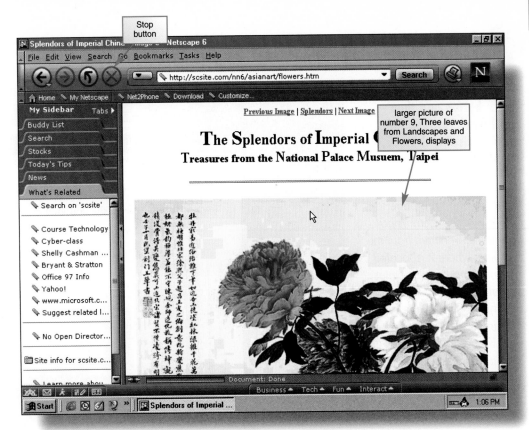

FIGURE 1-18

The preceding steps illustrate how simple it is to browse the World Wide Web. Displaying a page associated with a link is as easy as clicking a text or picture link.

Earlier, Step 2 involved typing a URL. If you type the wrong letter and notice the error before pressing the ENTER key, use the BACKSPACE key to erase all the characters back to and including the one that is wrong. If the error is easier to retype than correct, double-click the URL and retype it.

Stopping the Transfer of a Web Page

If a Web page you are trying to view is taking too long to transfer or if you clicked the wrong link, you may decide not to wait for it to finish transferring. The Stop button on the Navigation toolbar (Figure 1-18) allows you to stop the transfer of a page while the transfer is in progress. You will know the transfer is still in progress if the Netscape icon or status indicator is animated.

Reloading Pages

If you decide you want to refresh the Web page, you can reload the Web page using the **Reload button**. This is particularly useful with Web pages that dynamically change every few minutes, such as stock quotes, weather, and the news. The step on the next page shows how to use the Reload button to reload the Three leaves from Landscapes and Flowers Web page.

More About

Pictures

Some Web page authors note the size of an image to assist you in deciding to display or save the picture. If an image is several megabytes in size, you might decide not to select the link because of the time it would take to transfer the picture from the Web site to your display area.

To Reload a Web Page

1 **Click the Reload button and then scroll down through the page to display the complete picture.**

Netscape initiates a new transfer of the Web page http://www.scsite.com/nn6/ asianart/flowers.htm from the computer where it is located to your computer. The status indicator on the status bar and the Netscape icon begin to animate. The Three leaves from Landscapes and Flowers Web page redisplays in the content area (Figure 1-19).

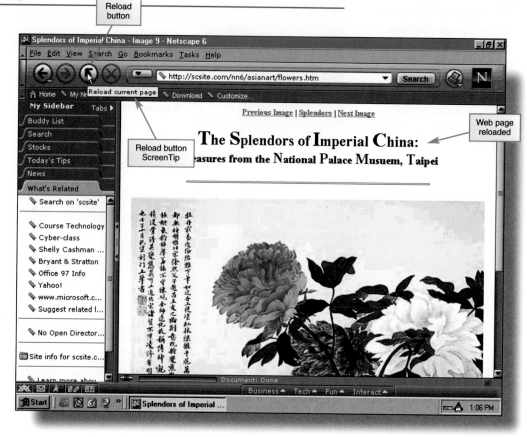

FIGURE 1-19

 **Other Ways**

1. On View menu click Reload
2. Press ALT+V, type R
3. Click Location field, press ENTER

More About

Redisplaying Web Pages

Displayed Web pages are stored in a special area on disk called a cache. If you request the same Web page again, Netscape will retrieve the page from the cache on your hard disk instead of having to contact the Web site again to retrieve the page. This can result in considerable time savings.

If the connection to the Web site where the page is located malfunctions and the page transfer does not finish, you can use the Reload button to request the page again.

Revisiting Web Pages

As you display different Web pages, Netscape keeps track of the ones you visit using four different lists. First, as you display Web pages, you can click the Back button arrow (Figure 1-20a) to display the names of the pages visited during the current session prior to the page displaying in the content area.

A second way to display all the pages visited during the current session is by clicking Go on the menu bar to display the **Go menu** (Figure 1-20b). A third method is to click the Location field arrow to display the URLs visited (Figure 1-20c) over the past few sessions.

The fourth list of visited sites is more permanent in that Netscape maintains the Web pages accessed over many sessions. This fourth list, called the History list, will be discussed shortly.

You quickly can determine if Web pages are listed on the Go menu by looking at the Back and Forward button on the Navigation toolbar. When Netscape first starts, both buttons are gray, or ghosted, which means they are inactive. As you display Web pages, the Back button becomes active. This lets you know that URLs of Web pages you have accessed are stored on the Go menu. If you use the Back button, then the Forward button becomes active.

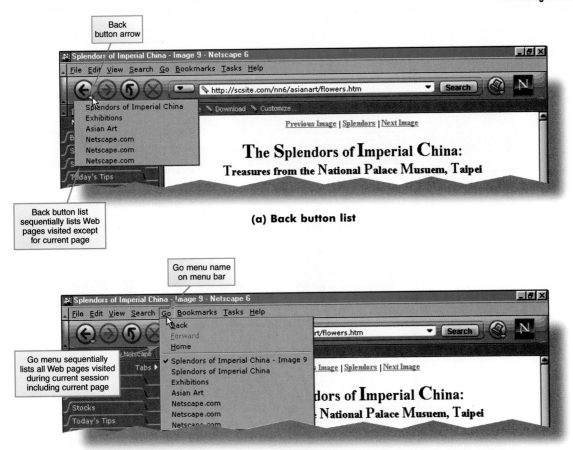

(a) Back button list

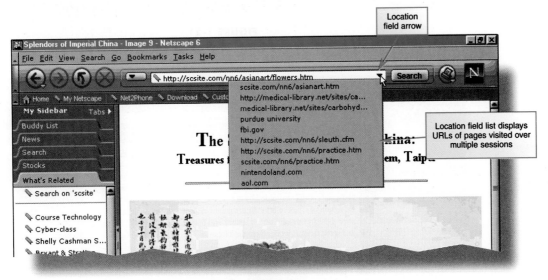

(b) Go menu

(c) Location field

FIGURE 1-20

Using the **Back button** and **Forward button** on the Navigation toolbar, you can travel back and forth quickly through the list on the Go menu, redisplaying the Web pages you have accessed during the current session. Perform the steps on the next page to move through the list on the Go menu using the Back and Forward buttons.

Steps **To Use the Back and Forward Buttons to Revisit Web Pages**

1 **Click the Back button.**

The Splendors of Imperial China Web page redisplays, and the arrow in the Forward button becomes active to indicate the Splendors of Imperial China Web page is not the last Web page visited this session (Figure 1-21).

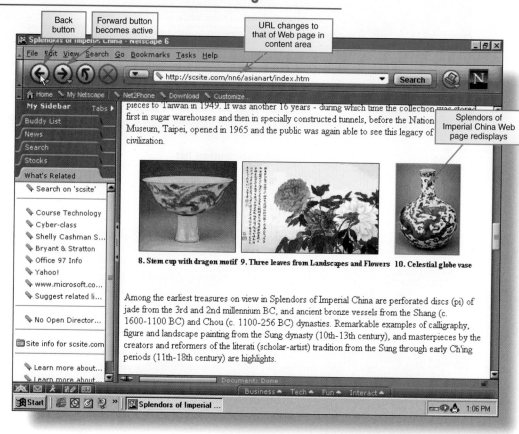

FIGURE 1-21

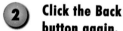
2 **Click the Back button again.**

The Exhibitions Web page redisplays (Figure 1-22).

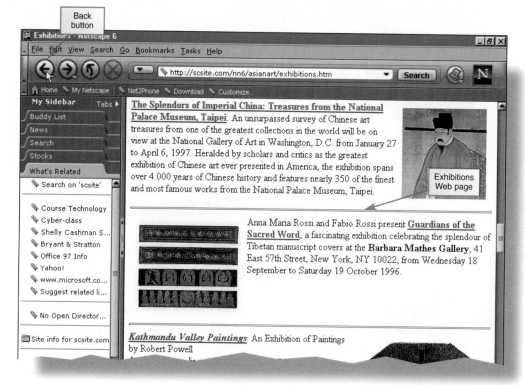

FIGURE 1-22

3 **Click the Forward button.**

The Splendors of Imperial China Web page displays again (Figure 1-23).

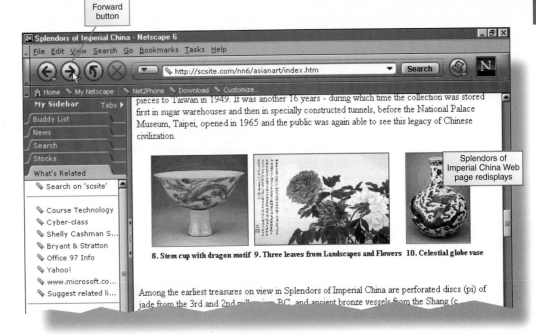

FIGURE 1-23

4 **Click the Forward button again.**

The Splendors of Imperial China - Image 9 Web page redisplays (Figure 1-24). The Forward button now is inactive, which indicates there are no additional pages to which you can move forward.

FIGURE 1-24

You can continue to page backward until you reach the beginning of the list on the Go menu. At that time, the Back button becomes inactive, which indicates that no additional pages to which you can move back are contained in the list. You can, however, move forward by clicking the Forward button.

Other Ways

1. On Go menu click Back or Forward
2. Back: press ALT+G, type B; forward: press ALT+G, type F

You can see that traversing the list of pages on the Go menu is easy using the Back and Forward buttons. Because many pages may display before the one you want to view, this method can be time-consuming, especially if you are connected to the Web with a modem.

Displaying a Web Page Using the Back Button List

It is possible to skip to any previously visited page by clicking its name in the Back button list. Thus, you can go to a previously visited page without redisplaying any intermediate pages, as shown in the following steps.

 To Display a Web Page Using the Back Button List

1 **Click the Back button arrow on the Navigation toolbar. When the Back button list displays, point to Asian Art.**

The Back button list displays a list of titles of Web pages you visited during this session beginning with the most recent (Figure 1-25).

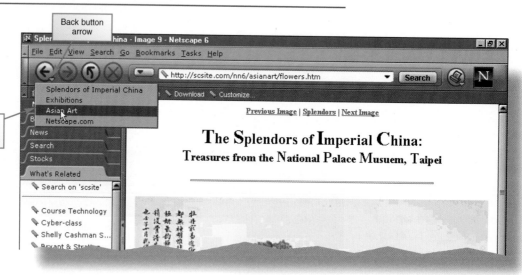

FIGURE 1-25

2 **Click Asian Art.**

Netscape redisplays the Asian Art Web page (Figure 1-26). Both the Back and Forward buttons are active, indicating there are Web pages to which you can move backward and forward.

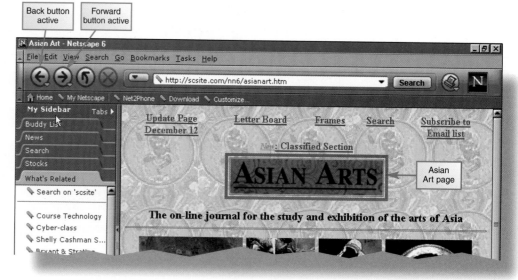

FIGURE 1-26

Other Ways

1. On Go menu click Web page name
2. Press ALT+G, click Web page name

If you have a small list of pages you have visited, or the Web page you wish to view is only one or two pages away, using the Back and Forward buttons to traverse the list probably is faster than displaying the Back button list and selecting the correct title. If you have visited a large number of pages, however, your list will be long, and it may be easier to use the Back button list or Go menu to select the exact page to redisplay.

Using the History List to Redisplay Web Pages

Netscape maintains another list of Web pages visited called the History list. The **History list**, which displays in the **History window**, is a list of Web pages visited over many sessions. You can use this list to redisplay Web pages you may have accessed weeks ago. The following steps show how to use the History list to redisplay Web pages.

More About

The History List

You can clear the History list by clicking Preferences on the Edit menu. When the Preferences dialog box displays, click the History subcategory under the Navigator category and then click the Clear History button. This dialog box also allows you to change the setting for the number of days Netscape keeps a Web page in the History list before deleting the page.

 To Use the History List to Redisplay Web Pages

1 Click Tasks on the menu bar. Point to Tools and then point to History on the Tools submenu.

The Tasks menu and Tools submenu display (Figure 1-27).

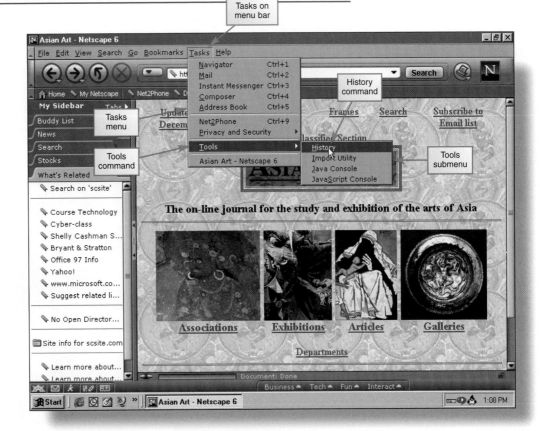

FIGURE 1-27

2 **Click History. When Netscape opens the History window, click the Title column heading in the upper-left corner of the window to sort the Web page titles into ascending sequence.**

The History list displays in the History window in alphabetical sequence sorted by Web page title (Figure 1-28). Your list may display different sites than those in the figure.

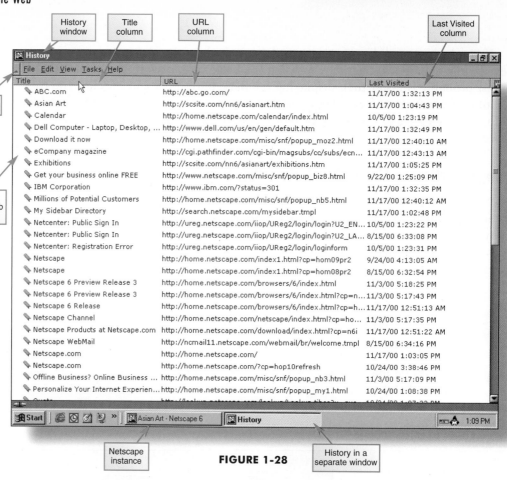

History window

Title column

URL column

Last Visited column

menu bar

History list sorted by Web page title

Netscape instance

FIGURE 1-28

History in a separate window

3 **In the Title column, double-click ABC.com: ABC TV's Official Site (or another title if you cannot locate it in the list).**

Netscape opens a new window and displays the ABC.com Web page (Figure 1-29).

4 **Click the Close button on the right side of the ABC TV home page title bar. When the History window displays, click the Close button on the right side of its title bar. If necessary, click the Asian Art button on the taskbar to display the Asian Art Web page.**

The Asian Art Web page displays as shown earlier in Figure 1-26 on page NN 1.24.

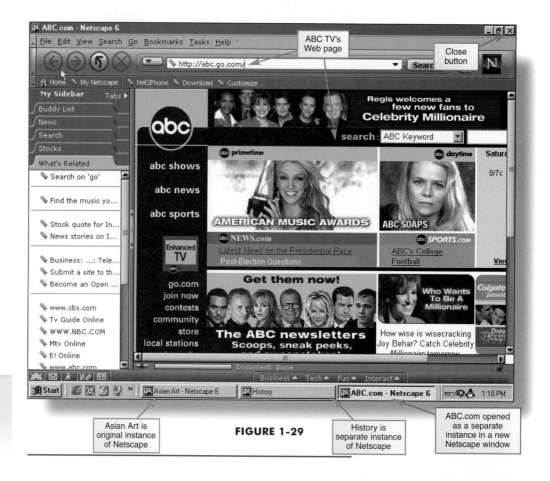

ABC TV's Web page

Close button

Asian Art is original instance of Netscape

FIGURE 1-29

History is separate instance of Netscape

ABC.com opened as a separate instance in a new Netscape window

Other Ways

1. Press CTRL+H
2. Press ALT+T, type T, type H

As shown on the taskbar in Figure 1-29, the History list displays in a new window as a separate instance of Netscape. Likewise, any Web page line in the History list you double-click displays as a separate instance of Netscape. This means that you can easily get back to the Web page you had on the screen when you initially clicked the History command by clicking the button on the taskbar with the Web page's title.

Once you display the History list, you can sort it in ascending or descending sequence on any of the three column titles (see Figure 1-28). Click a column title to sort the list on that column. Click the same column title again and Netscape will change the sequence of the sort.

You close the History window by clicking Close on the File menu or clicking the Close button on the right side of the title bar. The Edit menu in the History window provides several options, such as finding and deleting Web page titles in the History list.

Keeping Track of Your Favorite Web Pages

The bookmark feature of Netscape allows you to save the URLs of your favorite Web pages. A **bookmark** consists of the title of the Web page and the URL of that page. The title of the Web page is added to the Bookmarks menu. When you want to display a Web page you bookmarked earlier, you click Bookmarks on the menu bar.

If you place a bookmark under a **bookmark heading** (folder), then you click the folder to display its submenu. For example, in Figure 1-30 the mouse pointer is pointing to the Web page title Music & Video, which is on the submenu of the folder Best of the Web on the Bookmarks menu.

More About

Bookmark Titles

Netscape allows you to change the title that identifies a bookmark. Click Manage Bookmarks on the Bookmarks menu, right-click a bookmark in the Manage Bookmarks window, click Properties, and make changes in the Properties dialog box.

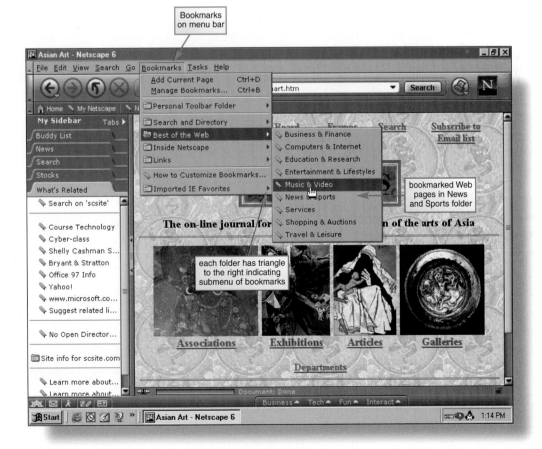

FIGURE 1-30

Think of the bookmark list as an electronic address book containing the title of Web pages that are important to you. You can add new bookmarks and remove bookmarks you no longer want. Figure 1-30 on the previous page shows a well-organized Bookmarks menu, with sets of bookmarks organized in appropriate folders. The following steps show how to add the Asian Arts Web page to the Bookmarks menu.

Steps To Add a Bookmark to the Bookmarks Menu

1 **With the Asian Art Web page in the content area, click Bookmarks on the menu bar, and then point to the Add Current Page command.**

The Bookmarks menu displays (Figure 1-31).

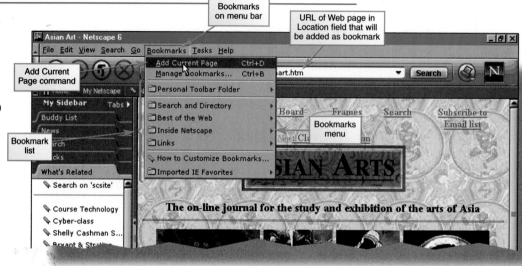

FIGURE 1-31

2 **Click Add Current Page.**

The Bookmarks menu disappears. The title of the Web page currently in the content area is added to the Bookmark list at the bottom of the Bookmarks menu.

3 **Click Bookmarks on the menu bar to verify that the page has been added to the Bookmark list.**

The Bookmarks menu displays, containing the newly added bookmark Asian Art (Figure 1-32).

FIGURE 1-32

1. Press CTRL+D

2. Press ALT+B, type A

When you add a bookmark, Netscape automatically adds it to the Bookmark list at the bottom of the Bookmarks menu. You can use the Manage Bookmarks command on the Bookmarks menu (Figure 1-31) to drag and drop the bookmark into a folder on the Bookmarks menu. The Manage Bookmarks command will be discussed shortly.

Using the Home Button to Display a Web Page

At any time, you can display the home page in the content area using the Home button on the Personal toolbar. Perform the following steps to display the Netscape home page (or the home page associated with your Netscape).

 Steps To Display the Home Page Using the Home Button

1 **Point to the Home button on the Personal toolbar (Figure 1-33).**

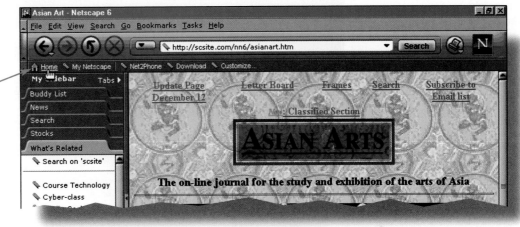

FIGURE 1-33

2 **Click the Home button.**

The Netscape home page displays in the content area and the URL for the home page displays in the Location field (Figure 1-34).

FIGURE 1-34

More *About*

Bookmarks

You can rearrange the order of your bookmarks by dragging a bookmark to another location in the Manage Bookmarks window and then releasing it.

Other **Ways**

1. On Go menu click Home
2. Press ALT+G, type H

Retrieving a Web Page Using a Bookmark

You can use Bookmarks on the menu bar to display favorite or frequently accessed Web pages quickly, without having to navigate through several unwanted pages. Using a bookmark to display a Web page is similar to using the History list to display a Web page. Perform the following steps to use the Bookmarks menu to display the Asian Art Web page.

Steps ### To Retrieve a Web Page Using a Bookmark

1 **Click Bookmarks on the menu bar and then point to Asian Art in the Bookmark list.**

The Bookmarks menu displays (Figure 1-35). The Asian Art bookmark is the last bookmark in the list.

FIGURE 1-35

2 **Click Asian Art.**

The Asian Art Web page displays in the content area, and its URL displays in the Location field (Figure 1-36).

FIGURE 1-36

Other **Ways**

1. Press CTRL+B, double-click Web page name
2. Press ALT+B, double-click Web page name

You have learned how to add a URL to the Bookmark list and how to retrieve that resource using the Bookmarks menu. Your Bookmark list will become an important asset, growing as you add new entries while exploring the World Wide Web.

Removing Bookmarks

The Manage Bookmarks command on the Bookmarks menu allows you to move bookmarks between folders or delete unwanted bookmarks or folders. Several reasons exist for removing a bookmark. With the World Wide Web changing every day, the URL that works today may not work tomorrow. Perhaps you just do not want a particular bookmark in your list anymore, or maybe the list is getting too big to be meaningful. The following steps show how to remove a bookmark from the Bookmark list.

 To Remove a Bookmark from the Bookmark List

1 **Click Bookmarks on the menu bar and then point to Manage Bookmarks.**

The Bookmarks menu displays (Figure 1-37).

FIGURE 1-37

2 **Click Manage Bookmarks. If necessary, scroll down to the bottom of the Bookmark list.**

The Manage Bookmarks window opens (Figure 1-38). The Manage Bookmarks window is organized into columns, beginning on the left with Name, URL, Custom Key-word, Description, Last Visited, Added On, and so on. To view column titles in their entirety, drag the borders between the column titles. The Name column lists the folders and the names of the Web pages.

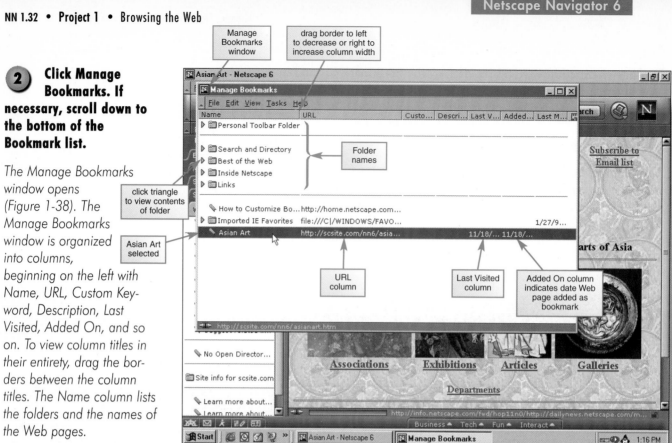

FIGURE 1-38

3 **Right-click Asian Art and point to Delete Bookmark on the pop-up menu.**

The pop-up menu displays (Figure 1-39).

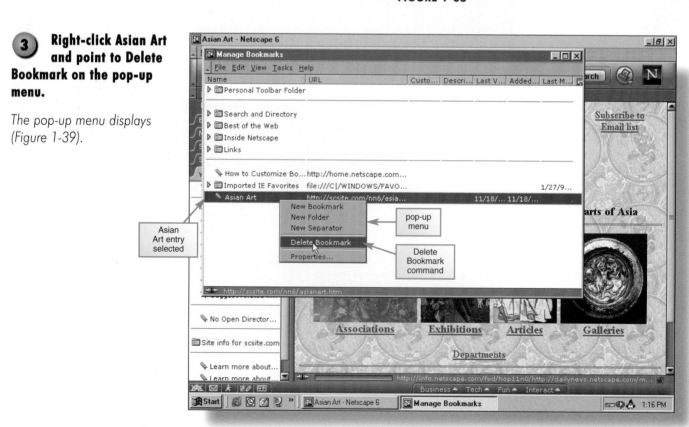

FIGURE 1-39

4 **Click Delete Bookmark. If a dialog box displays asking you to confirm the deletion, click the OK button.**

The Asian Art bookmark no longer displays as a bookmark (Figure 1-40).

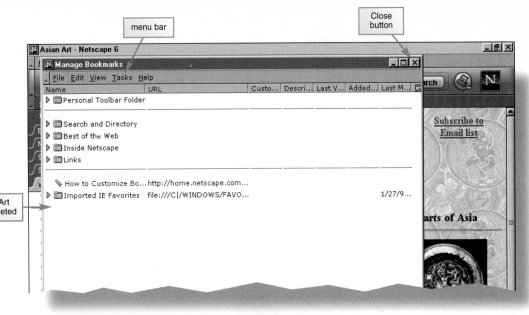

FIGURE 1-40

5 **Click the Close button on the right side of the Manage Bookmarks title bar.**

The Manage Bookmarks window closes.

6 **To verify that the bookmark has been removed, click Bookmarks on the menu bar.**

The Asian Art bookmark no longer displays on the Bookmarks menu (Figure 1-41).

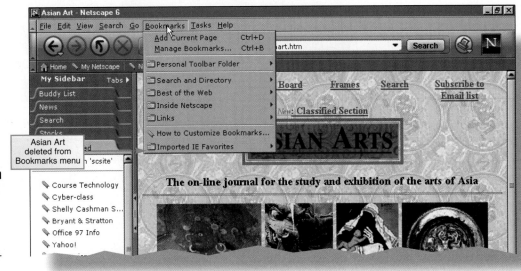

FIGURE 1-41

Other Ways

1. Press CTRL+B
2. Press ALT+B, type M

The functions in the Manage Bookmarks window make managing your bookmarks easy. Netscape provides many other advanced features for handling bookmarks. For example, through the pop-up menu (Figure 1-39) or New command on the File menu in the Manage Bookmarks window (Figure 1-40), you can create new folders and separators. You use **folders** to group similar Web pages in the Bookmark list. You use **separators** (horizontal lines) to make it easier to categorize folders and Web pages in the Bookmark list.

The Edit menu in the Manage Bookmarks window includes commands similar to those on any Edit menu, such as Undo, Redo, Cut, Copy, and Paste. A unique command on the Edit menu is the Properties command. The **Properties command** allows you to assign a keyword to a Web page in the Bookmark list. You then can enter the **keyword** in the Location field to display the bookmarked Web page, rather than clicking its name on the Bookmarks menu. The Properties command also allows you to edit the Web page name, the URL, add a description, and assign other characteristics to a bookmark.

When you install Netscape, it adds several folders of bookmarks to popular Web pages. If you don't want these folders of bookmarks, you can delete them as described in the previous set of steps.

Using Netscape's Home Page to Browse the World Wide Web

The Netscape home page (Figure 1-42) provides a starting point for browsing the World Wide Web. From Netscape's home page you can go virtually anywhere and do practically anything available on the Internet. The Netscape home page is updated often, so links that appear one day may be gone the next, having been replaced with new offerings.

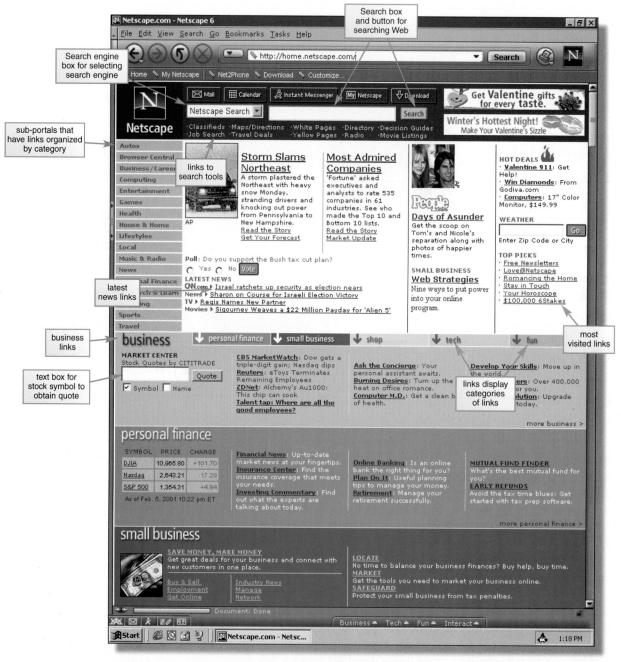

FIGURE 1-42

Netscape's home page is more than an ordinary Web page. It is a portal to the World Wide Web. A **portal** is a Web page designed to offer a variety of Web-related services from one, convenient location. If the Netscape home page does not display when you click the Home button on the Personal toolbar, enter the URL netscape.com.

Listed below are some of the services offered on the Netscape home page.

▶ Find out what's new and what's cool on the Web.
▶ Read the latest news, sports, and weather headlines.
▶ Place and reply to classified ads.
▶ Search for e-mail addresses, street addresses, and phone numbers of people and businesses.
▶ Play a variety of online games.
▶ Download shareware programs from a library of more than 40,000 software titles.
▶ Engage in community discussions with others who share your special interests.
▶ Search the World Wide Web for information.
▶ Shop from hundreds of online retailers.

Near the top of Netscape's home page in Figure 1-42 are links to searching for jobs, people, and directions, as well as links to shopping Web sites. Using Netscape's home page as your home base, you can access comprehensive and up-to-date information on practically any major topic — from business to computing to family interests to health matters to real estate to travel; read the latest news, sports, and weather headlines; shop from hundreds of online retailers; and search the World Wide Web for information. In essence, Netscape's home page gives you easy access to everything on the Internet. Other popular portals with similar links include Yahoo! (yahoo.com), Microsoft (msn.com), and America Online (aol.com).

Using My Sidebar

My Sidebar, which is located on the left side of the window, is separate from the content area where Web pages display. It contains tabs that allow you to organize links that you need to use all the time, such as the latest news, weather, stock quotes, address book, calendar, and much more. Netscape comes with some My Sidebar tabs already set up, but you can customize My Sidebar by adding, removing, and rearranging tabs. You click **customize** at the top of My Sidebar to customize its contents by choosing from hundreds of tabs.

Unless you close My Sidebar by clicking My Sidebar on the View menu, it is always open on the left side of the screen. When it is open, you can hide it so the content area is larger. You hide My Sidebar by clicking the **handle** on its right side (Figure 1-43 on the next page). If My Sidebar is hidden, you can show it by clicking the handle, which displays on the left side of the content area when My Sidebar is hidden.

You click a My Sidebar tab to display its panel with links related to the tab name. The contents of some My Sidebar panels, such as news, change as new stories develop. These panels are similar to miniature dynamic Web pages.

Using the What's Related Panel

A My Sidebar panel that changes each time you access a Web page is the What's Related tab. If you are viewing a page on movies, you can click the **What's Related tab** to display links to Web pages related to the Web page you are viewing. Thus, each time you view a new Web page, the links on the What's Related panel change. The steps on the next page show how to use the links in the What's Related panel after displaying the Internet Movie Database home page.

More About

My Sidebar

When you click Find More Tabs in the Customize Sidebar dialog box, the My Sidebar Directory window opens allowing you to choose tabs from several categories outside of the Netscape default categories.

Steps ## To Use Links on the What's Related Panel in My Sidebar

1 **Double-click the URL in the Location field on the Navigation toolbar. Type** imdb.com **as the new URL and then press the ENTER key. If necessary, click the My Sidebar handle to display My Sidebar, and then click the What's Related tab in My Sidebar.**

The Internet Movie Database home page displays in the content area, and the What's Related panel displays in My Sidebar (Figure 1-43).

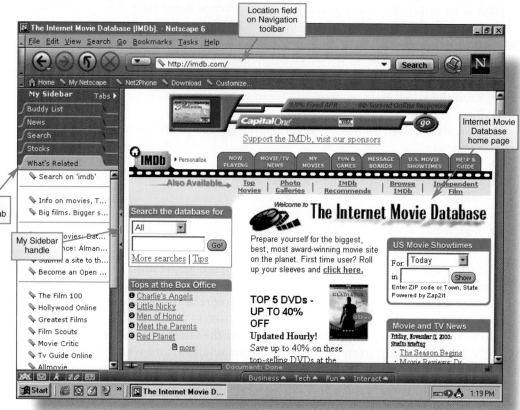

FIGURE 1-43

2 **Point to the Hollywood Online link (or a similar link) in the What's Related panel (Figure 1-44).**

FIGURE 1-44

Double-click the Hollywood Online link.

Netscape displays the Hollywood.com Web page (Figure 1-45). Netscape updates the What's Related panel with links to Web pages with more information about show business.

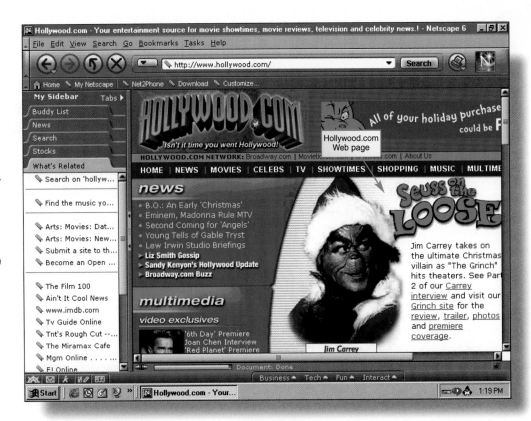 **When you have finished viewing the links, click the Back button to return to the Internet Movie Database home page.**

FIGURE 1-45

The What's Related panel in My Sidebar can be especially useful when you are trying to get varying opinions on a subject. After displaying a Web page, you can click the What's Related tab and then click one of the links to display a page on the same subject.

Using the Stocks Tab

Another popular panel on My Sidebar is Stocks. This panel allows you to enter a stock symbol or stock name and display a stock quote that is near real time (20-minute delay). The steps on the next page display the latest stock quote for America Online. The stock symbol is AOL.

To Use the Stocks Tab on My Sidebar

1 **Click the Stocks tab on My Sidebar.**

The Stocks tab displays on My Sidebar (Figure 1-46).

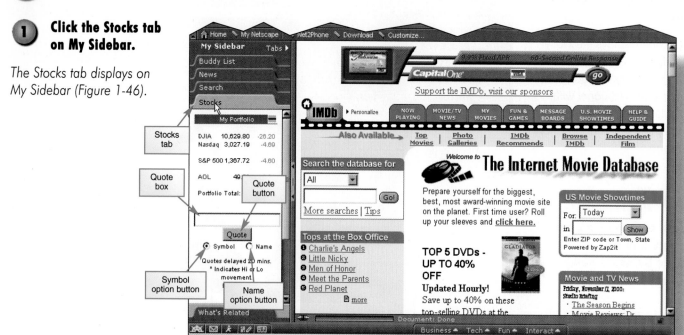

FIGURE 1-46

2 **With the Symbol option button selected, click in the Quote box. Type** aol **and then click the Quote button.**

The America Online Quote page displays, detailing the company's latest performance, including the latest stock quote and other relevant information (Figure 1-47).

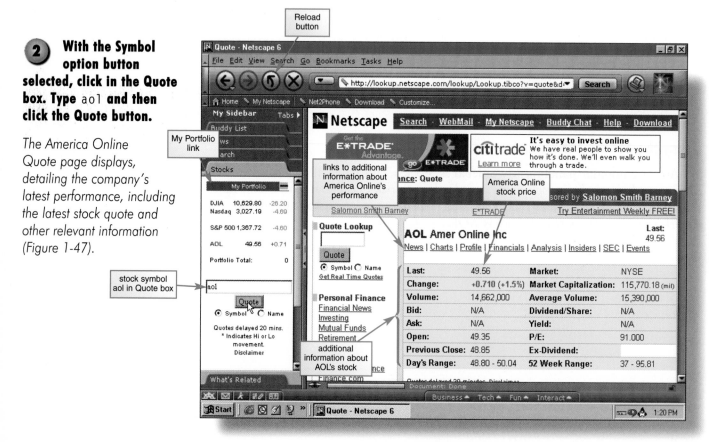

FIGURE 1-47

Once you display the America Online Quote page, you can click the Reload button on the Navigation toolbar to refresh the page. Each time you click the Reload button, the latest America Online stock information displays.

You can see from Figure 1-47 that the Quote page contains much more information than just the latest stock quote. For example, the Volume, Day's Range, 52-Week Range, and a 1-Year chart display on the Quote page. At the top of the Quote page are several links that offer additional valuable company information.

If you are a stock investor or an interested party, you can begin to see the potential of the World Wide Web in terms of up-to-date stock information at your fingertips. You can, for example, create your own portfolio by clicking the **My Portfolio** link in the Stocks panel. This link allows you to obtain quotes for many stocks at the same time. Once you create a portfolio, you can use the My Portfolio link to display it as often as you want.

Saving Information Displayed in Netscape

Many different types of Web pages are accessible on the World Wide Web. Because these pages can help you accumulate information about areas of interest, you may wish to save the information you discover for future reference. The different types of Web pages and the different ways you may want to use them require different ways of saving. Netscape can save an entire Web page, individual pictures, or selected pieces of a Web page.

Saving a Web Page

The steps on the next page save the Asian Art Web page on a floppy disk in drive A.

More About

Saving a Web Page

Saving a Web page saves only the page text, not any images or pictures on the page. You must save pictures separately.

Steps To Save a Web Page

1 Insert a formatted floppy disk into drive A. Click the Location field arrow and click scsite.com/nn6/asianart.htm. (If the URL is not in the list, double-click the Location field in the Navigation toolbar, type scsite.com/nn6/asianart.htm **and then press the ENTER key.)**

The Asian Art Web page displays.

2 Click File on the menu bar and then point to Save Page As.

The File menu displays as shown in Figure 1-48. The Save Page As command saves the Web page in the content area to a disk file.

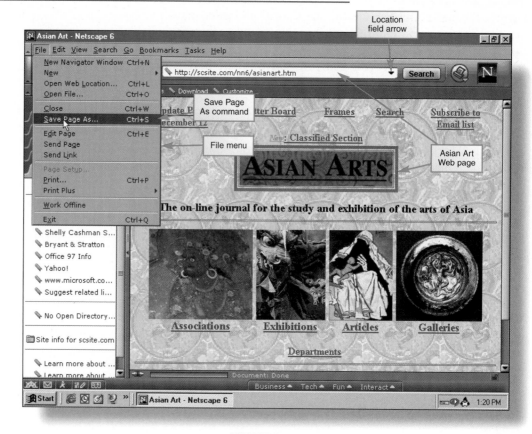

FIGURE 1-48

3 Click Save Page As. When the Save File dialog box displays, point to the Save in box arrow.

The Save File dialog box displays (Figure 1-49). The Save in box contains the Desktop entry, the list contains a list of the icons on the desktop, and the File name text box contains the Web page title (asianart).

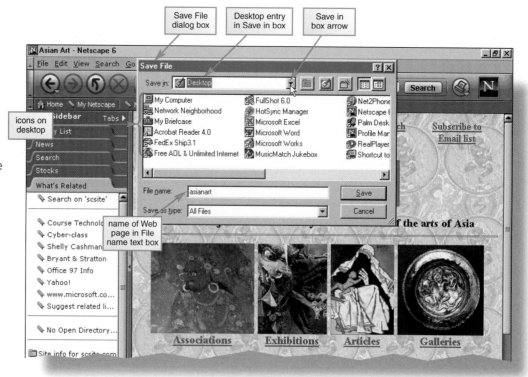

FIGURE 1-49

4 Click the Save in box arrow, click 3½ Floppy (A:) in the Save in list, and then point to the Save button.

The 3½ Floppy [A:] drive name displays in the Save in box (Figure 1-50).

5 Click the Save button.

The Save File dialog box closes and a Saving File dialog box displays listing the URL of the Web page being saved, the file name, and a progress bar. When the save process is complete, the Saving File dialog box disappears.

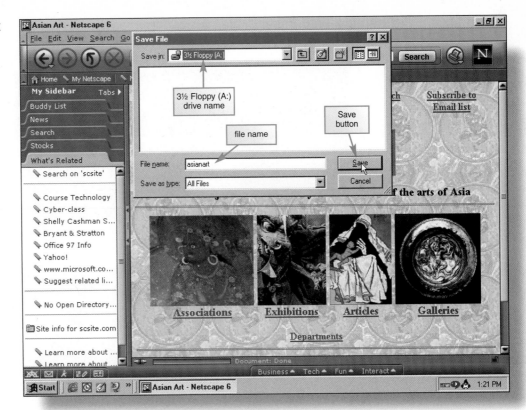

FIGURE 1-50

Other Ways

1. Press CTRL+S
2. Press ALT+F, type S

Netscape saves the Web page with an extension of htm, which means it is stored in a format that a browser can interpret. You can view the Web page you saved to drive A by double-clicking the URL in the Location field, typing : (a colon) and then pressing the ENTER key. When Netscape displays the list of files on the floppy disk in drive A, click asianart.htm. When the Web page displays, the graphics will be missing, but the text will display. To display the graphics, you have to save the pictures on the Web page one at a time to drive A, and then modify the Asian Art Web page's HTML so that the references to the graphics point to drive A.

Saving a Picture on a Web Page

A second method of saving information is to save a picture located on a Web page. In the following steps, the Galleries picture located on the Asian Arts Web page is saved on the floppy disk in drive A using the **Joint Photographic Experts Group (JPEG)** format. The file format JPEG is a method of encoding pictures on a computer. When you save a picture as a JPEG file, Netscape can display it. Perform the steps on the next page to save the Galleries picture on a floppy disk in drive A in the JPEG format using the file name galleries.jpg.

Steps: **To Save a Picture on a Web Page**

1 **Right-click the Galleries picture and then point to Save Image As on the pop-up menu.**

A pop-up menu displays with a list of commands that pertain to manipulating pictures (Figure 1-51).

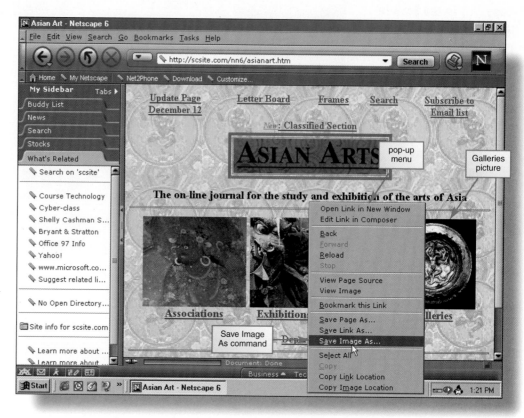

FIGURE 1-51

2 **Click Save Image As. When the Save File dialog box displays, type** galleries.jpg **in the File name text box. If necessary, click the Save in box arrow and then click 3½ Floppy (A:) in the Save in list. Point to the Save button.**

The Save File dialog box displays as shown in Figure 1-52.

3 **Click the Save button.**

Netscape saves the picture on the floppy disk in drive A using the file name, galleries.jpg.

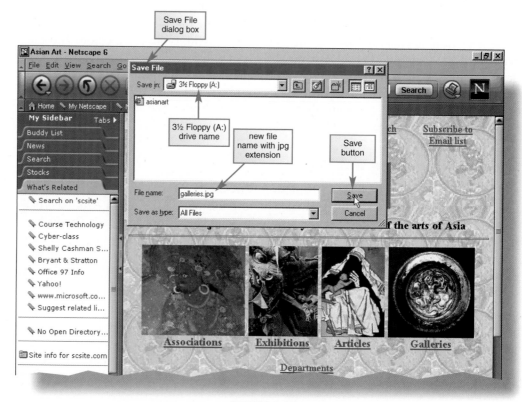

FIGURE 1-52

The picture now is stored as a file on your floppy disk and can be displayed using a browser, image viewers such as Paint, or a word processor.

Copying and Pasting Using the Clipboard

A third method of saving information, called the **copy and paste method**, allows you to copy an entire Web page, or portions thereof, and insert the information in any Windows document. The **Clipboard**, which is a storage area in main memory, temporarily holds the information being copied. The portion of the Web page you select is **copied** from the Web page to the Clipboard and then **pasted** from the Clipboard into the document. Information you copy to the Clipboard remains there until you add more information or clear it.

The following pages demonstrate how to copy text from a Web page to Word Pad. **WordPad** is a word processing program that comes with Windows.

Starting WordPad

Before copying information from the Web page in Netscape to the Clipboard, follow these steps to start WordPad.

More *About*

Copying and Pasting

You cannot copy images and pictures on a Web page to the Clipboard by dragging. To copy an image to another Windows application, right-click the image and use the Save Image As command on the pop-up menu.

Steps **To Start WordPad**

1 **Click the Start button on the taskbar, point to Programs on the Start menu, point to Accessories on the Programs submenu, and then point to WordPad on the Accessories submenu.**

The Start menu, Programs submenu, and Accessories submenu display (Figure 1-53). The highlighted WordPad command displays on the Accessories submenu.

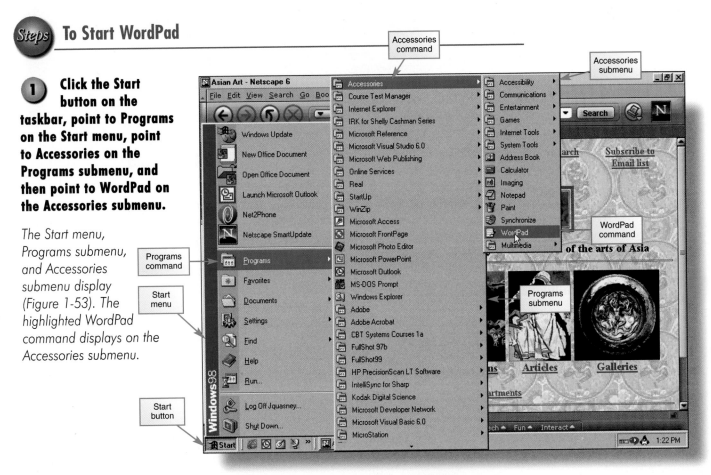

FIGURE 1-53

2 **Click WordPad. If WordPad is maximized, click the Restore button on the title bar.**

Windows starts WordPad, opens the active Document - WordPad window on top of the inactive Asian Arts - Netscape 6 window, and displays the Document - WordPad button on the taskbar (Figure 1-54). An empty WordPad document, into which the text can be pasted, displays in the Document - WordPad window. An insertion point and the I-beam mouse pointer display in the empty WordPad document.

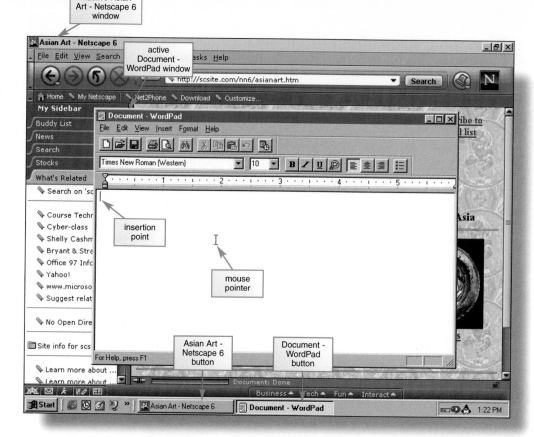

FIGURE 1-54

Activating a Minimized Netscape Window and Displaying the Exhibitions Web Page

After starting WordPad and before copying text from a Web page to the Clipboard, activate the minimized Asian Art - Netscape 6 window and then display the Exhibitions Web page as shown in the following steps.

 To Activate a Minimized Netscape Window

1 **Point to the Asian Art - Netscape 6 button on the taskbar (Figure 1-55).**

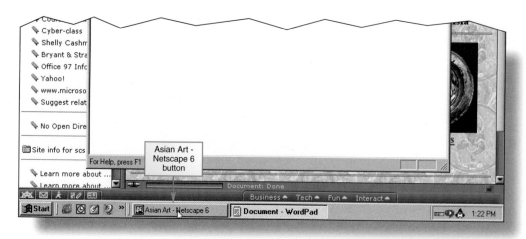

FIGURE 1-55

2 **Click the Asian Art - Netscape 6 button and then point to the Exhibitions picture link.**

The Asian Art - Netscape 6 window displays on top of the Document - WordPad window on the desktop (Figure 1-56). Although no longer visible, the window still is open, as evidenced by the button on the taskbar. The content area in Netscape contains the Asian Art Web page.

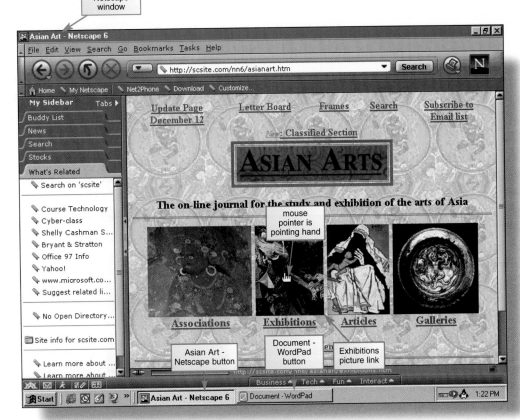

Asian Art - Netscape window

Asian Art - Netscape button

Document - WordPad button

Exhibitions picture link

mouse pointer is pointing hand

FIGURE 1-56

3 **Click the Exhibitions picture link.**

The Exhibitions Web page displays in the Exhibitions - Netscape 6 window (Figure 1-57). The title bar and button name change.

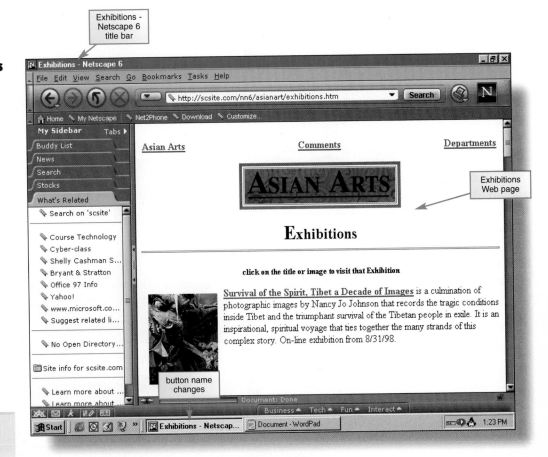

Exhibitions - Netscape 6 title bar

Exhibitions Web page

button name changes

FIGURE 1-57

Other **Ways**

1. Press ALT+TAB, hold down ALT and press TAB to select

Copying Text from a Web Page and Pasting It into a WordPad Document

The following steps show how to copy the text about the Splendors of Imperial China to the Clipboard, switch to WordPad, and paste the text on the Clipboard into the WordPad document.

Steps To Copy and Paste Text from a Web Page into a WordPad Document

1 Scroll through the Exhibitions Web page to display The Splendors of Imperial China: Treasures from the National Palace Museum, Taipei link, and then position the mouse pointer (I-beam) at the beginning of the text that follows the text link.

The text description of The Splendors of Imperial China: Treasures from the National Palace Museum, Taipei displays (Figure 1-58).

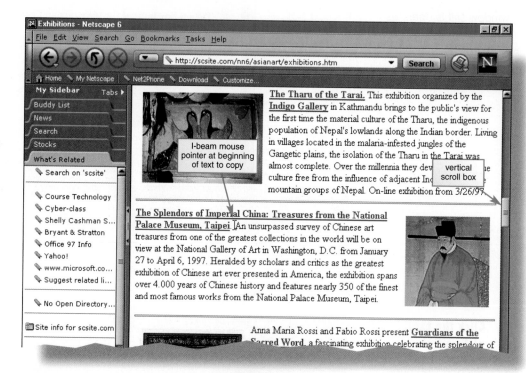

FIGURE 1-58

2 Drag through the last word in the paragraph to select the text that follows the link, right-click the selected text, and then point to the Copy command on the pop-up menu.

Netscape highlights the selected text and displays a pop-up menu (Figure 1-59).

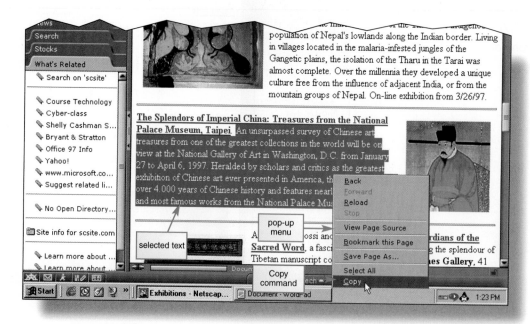

FIGURE 1-59

3 Click Copy.

Netscape copies the selected text to the Clipboard.

4 Click the Document - WordPad button on the taskbar, right-click the empty text area in the Document - WordPad window, and then point to Paste on the pop-up menu.

Netscape displays the Document - WordPad window and a pop-up menu (Figure 1-60).

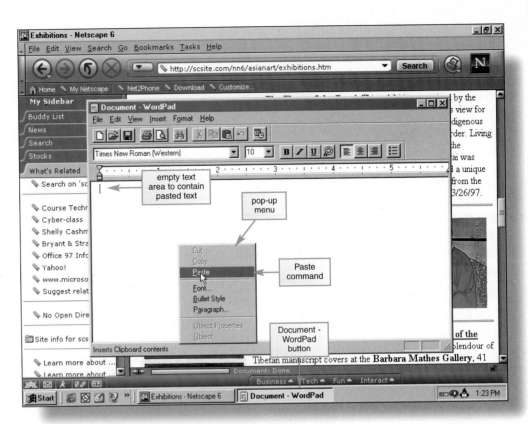

FIGURE 1-60

5 Click Paste.

Netscape pastes the contents of the Clipboard into the Document - WordPad window (Figure 1-61).

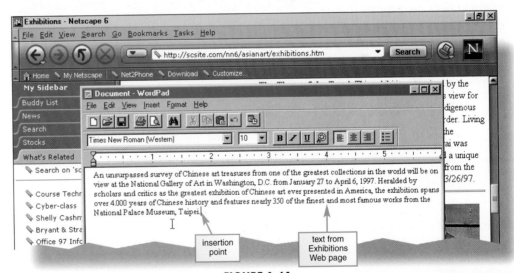

FIGURE 1-61

The text portion of the copy and paste operation is complete. The WordPad document contains a paragraph of text retrieved from a Web page.

Saving the WordPad Document and Quitting WordPad

When you are finished with the WordPad document, you can save it on a floppy disk for later use and then quit WordPad. Perform the steps on the next page to save the WordPad document using Splendors of Imperial China as the file name and then quit WordPad.

Other Ways

1. Select text, on Edit menu click Copy, select paste area, on Edit menu click Paste

2. Select text, press CTRL+C, select paste area, press CTRL+V

3. Select text, press ALT+E, type C, select paste area, press ALT+E, type P

To Save the WordPad Document and Quit WordPad

1 **With WordPad active, click the Save button on the toolbar. When the Save As dialog box displays, type** Splendors of Imperial China **in the File name text box. If necessary, click the Save in box arrow and click 3½ Floppy (A:) in the Save in list. Point to the Save button in the Save As dialog box.**

The Save As dialog box displays as shown in Figure 1-62.

2 **Click the Save button.**

The Save As dialog box closes and Netscape saves the Splendors of Imperial China document on the floppy disk in drive A.

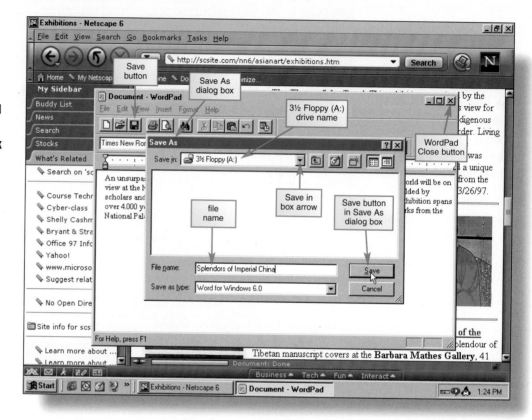

FIGURE 1-62

 3 **Click the Close button on the right side of the Document - WordPad title bar.**

The WordPad window closes and the Netscape window is visible on the desktop.

Other Ways

1. On File menu click Exit
2. Right-click WordPad button on taskbar, click Close
3. Double-click Control-menu icon
4. Press ALT+F, type X

More About

WordPad

WordPad can save a file as a Microsoft Word document, RTF or Rich Text Format, or as a plain text file.

Computer users commonly search for and save text and pictures found on the World Wide Web to a disk for future use.

Printing a Web Page in Netscape

As you visit Web sites, you may want to print some of the pages you view. A printed version of a Web page is called a **hard copy** or **printout**.

You might want a printout for several reasons. First, to present the Web page to someone who does not have access to a computer, it must be in printed form. A printout, for example, can be handed out in a management meeting about relevant information on a Web page. In addition, Web pages often are kept for reference by persons other than those who prepare them. In some cases, Web pages are printed and kept in binders for use by others.

Netscape's printing capability allows you to print both the text and picture portions of a Web page. Perform the following steps to print the Exhibitions Web page.

 To Print a Web Page

1 **With Netscape active and the Exhibitions Web page in the content area, point to the Print button on the Navigation toolbar (Figure 1-63).**

FIGURE 1-63

2 **Click the Print button.**

3 **When the Print dialog box displays, point to the OK button.**

The Print dialog box displays (Figure 1-64).

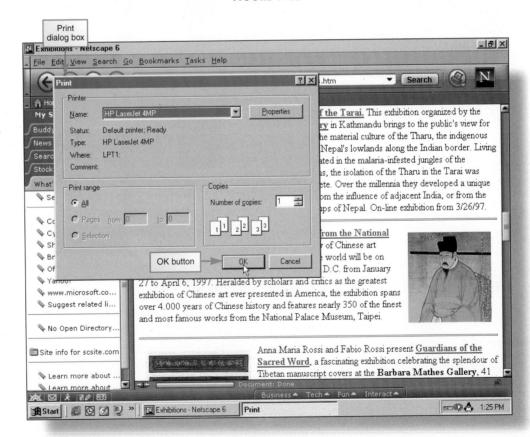

FIGURE 1-64

4 **Click the OK button. When the printer stops, retrieve the printout.**

The Exhibitions Web page prints (Figure 1-65).

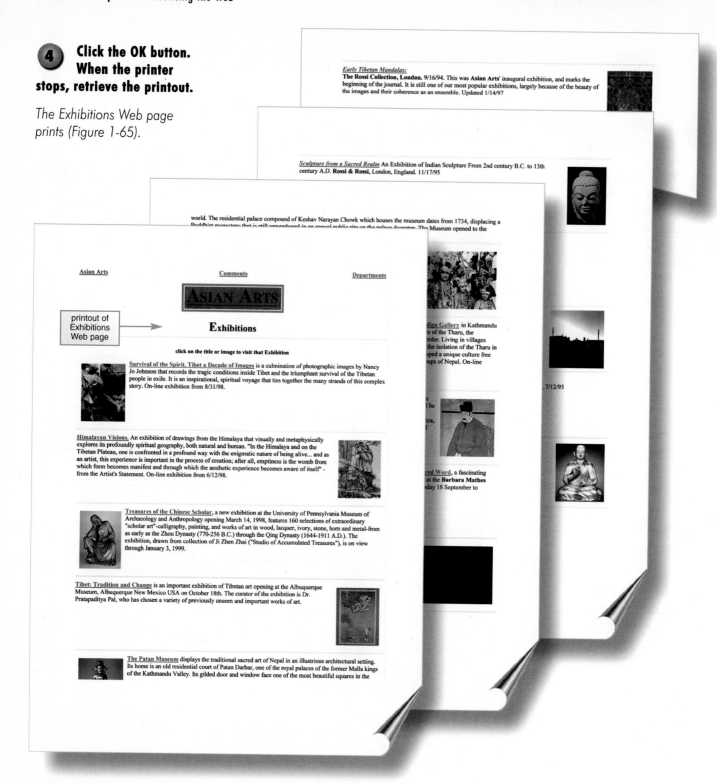

FIGURE 1-65

Other Ways

1. Press CTRL+P
2. Press ALT+F, type P

The Print dialog box in Figure 1-64 on the previous page offers several different options. You can print the entire document or selected pages of the document. The document can be printed to a disk file or on paper. Multiple copies can be produced. Printer properties can be changed, and the printing request can be canceled, returning you to the Netscape window. To cancel the print request, click the Cancel button in the Print dialog box.

My Netscape

My Netscape is a customizable page that provides you with instant access to up-to-the-minute news, stock quotes, sports scores, world events, use of a calculator, and much more. It is similar to the Netscape home page in that it serves as a portal to other Web sites. The difference is that you can customize the My Netscape page to fit your needs. Netscape allows you to move, add, or remove channels and tools from the My Netscape page. A **channel** is a page that contains a set of links that pertain to a specific category, such as news, weather, sports, and travel. A **tool** is an application that carries out a function, such as searching the Web, an address book, calendar, and calculator.

The following steps show how to display and customize the My Netscape page. These steps assume you are signed in to Netscape. If you are not signed in, the Sign Out link (Figure 1-67) displays as a Sign In link. You must be signed in for these steps to work. If you do not have a user-id and password, see your instructor.

Steps To Display and Customize the My Netscape Page

1. **Point to the My Netscape button on the Personal toolbar (Figure 1-66).**

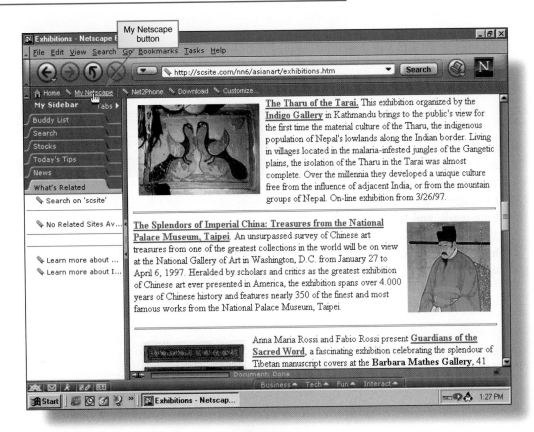

FIGURE 1-66

2 Click the My Netscape button. If necessary, click the My Sidebar handle to hide My Sidebar.

Netscape displays the My Netscape page. If this is the first time you are viewing the page, then it displays a default set of channels and tools in three columns (Figure 1-67).

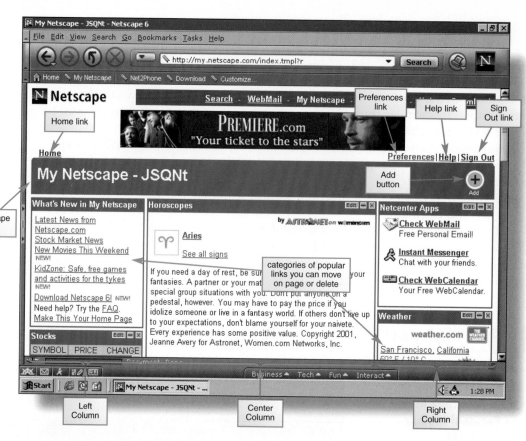

FIGURE 1-67

3 Click the Add button on the right side of the page. When the Add Channels page displays, click the Travel check box under Channels to remove the check mark, and then click What's Cool under Channels to add it. Point to the Save button.

Netscape displays the Add Channels page (Figure 1-68). This page allows you to add channels and tools to the My Netscape page.

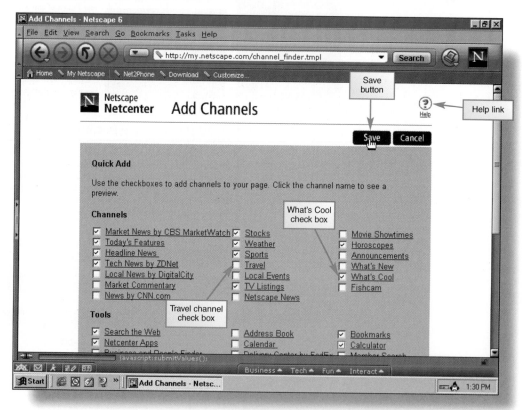

FIGURE 1-68

4 Click the Save button. When the My Netscape page redisplays, scroll down to the bottom of the page to view the addition of the What's Cool channel.

Netscape redisplays the My Netscape page with the new channel (Figure 1-69).

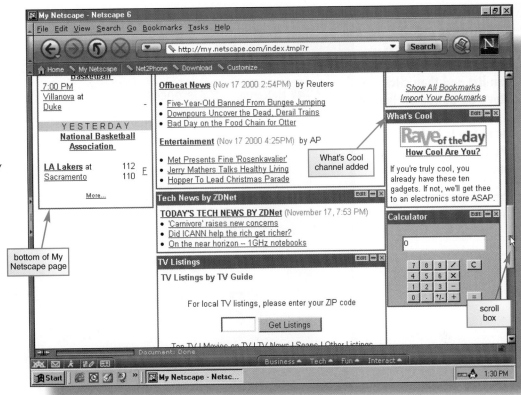

FIGURE 1-69

5 Scroll up to the top of the My Netscape page and point to the Preferences link (Figure 1-70).

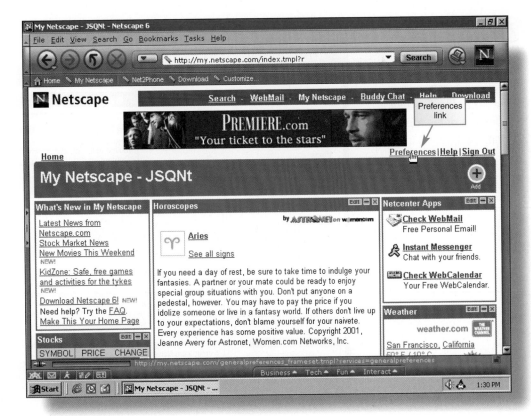

FIGURE 1-70

6 **Click Preferences. When the Preferences page displays, click Calculator in the Right Column list and then click the Move Up button on the right until the Calculator tool is at the top of the list. Point to the Save button.**

The Preferences page displays as shown in Figure 1-71.

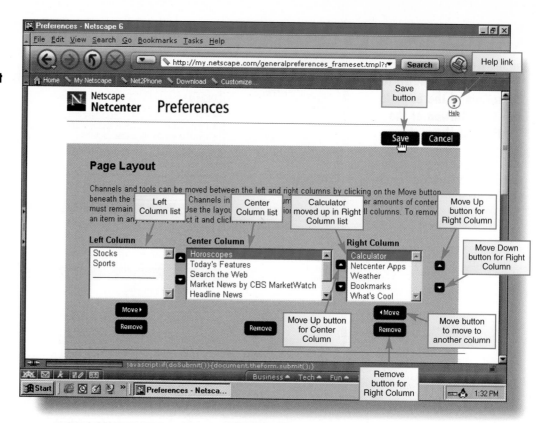

FIGURE 1-71

7 **Click the Save button.**

The customized My Netscape page displays as shown in Figure 1-72. The Calculator tool displays at the top of the column.

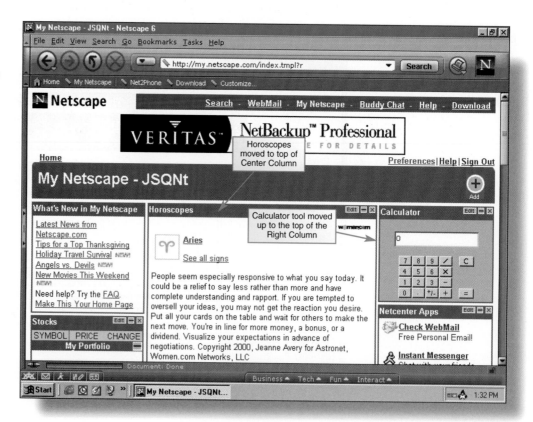

FIGURE 1-72

The My Netscape page is divided into three columns. You can add, move, and remove channels and tools from the three columns to create a personalized portal. If you need help in customizing your personal My Netscape page, Help links are provided on the My Netscape page (Figure 1-67 on page NN 1.52), the Add Channels page (Figure 1-68 on page NN 1.52), and the Preferences page (Figure 1-71).

Netscape Help

Netscape is a program with many features and options. Although you quickly will master some of these features and options, it is not necessary for you to remember everything about each of them. Reference materials and other forms of assistance are available from within **Netscape's Help facility**. You can display these materials and learn how to use the multitude of features available with Netscape. To illustrate how to use Netscape Help, assume you want to learn more about the browsing the Web. The following steps show how to obtain the desired information using Help.

To Obtain Netscape Help

1 **Click Help on the menu bar. Point to the Help Contents command.**

The Help menu displays (Figure 1-73). Several commands are available to provide helpful information about Netscape.

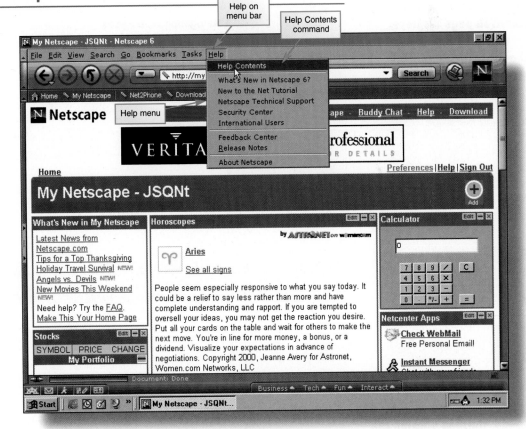

FIGURE 1-73

2 **Click Help Contents. When the Help: Contents window opens, point to the Browsing the Web link.**

The Help: Contents windows displays as shown in Figure 1-74.

Browsing the Web link

other Help links

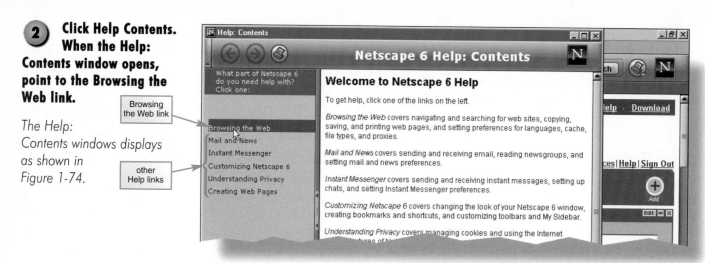

FIGURE 1-74

3 **Click Browsing the Web. When the Netscape 6 Help: Browsing the Web page displays, point to the Visiting Bookmarked Pages link.**

Netscape displays a page of links to information on using Netscape (Figure 1-75).

links to other categories of Help

link to help on visiting bookmarked pages

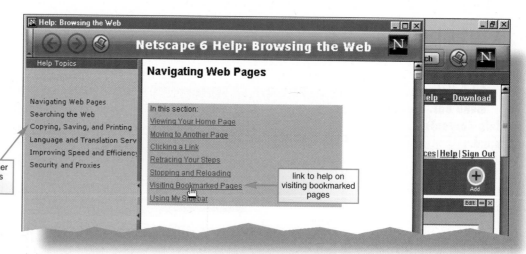

FIGURE 1-75

4 **Click the Visiting Bookmarked Pages link.**

Information about the topic, Visiting Bookmarked Pages, displays (Figure 1-76).

5 **When you are finished viewing the information, click the Close button on the right side of the title bar to close the Help Contents window.**

help on visiting bookmarked pages

Close button

My Sidebar handle

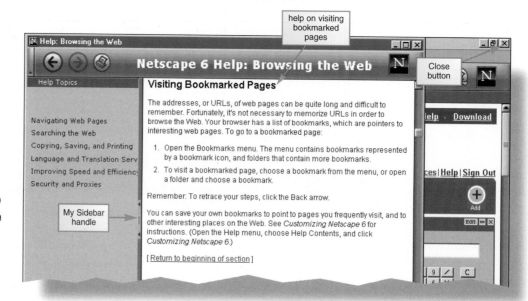

FIGURE 1-76

The Help menu contains several other commands (see Figure 1-73 on page NN 1.55), which are summarized in Table 1-2.

Table 1-2 Commands on the Help Menu

MENU COMMAND	FUNCTION
Help Contents	Displays Help, with links to contents and index entries.
What's New in Netscape 6?	Describes the features of Netscape 6.
New to the Net Tutorial	Learn more about the Internet and your browser.
Netscape Technical Support	Phone numbers to call for technical support.
Security Center	Information about security on the Web.
International Users	Displays information for international users.
Feedback Center	Send an e-mail to Netscape to notify them of a problem or to suggest improvements.
Release Notes	Includes system requirements.
About Netscape	Displays version, copyright, and license information about Netscape.

 uitting Netscape

After you have browsed the World Wide Web and learned how to manage Web pages, Project 1 is complete. To quit Netscape and return control to Windows, perform the following steps.

Steps To Quit Netscape

1 **Point to the Close button in the upper-right corner of the title bar (Figure 1-77).**

2 **Click the Close button.**

The My Netscape window closes and the Windows desktop displays.

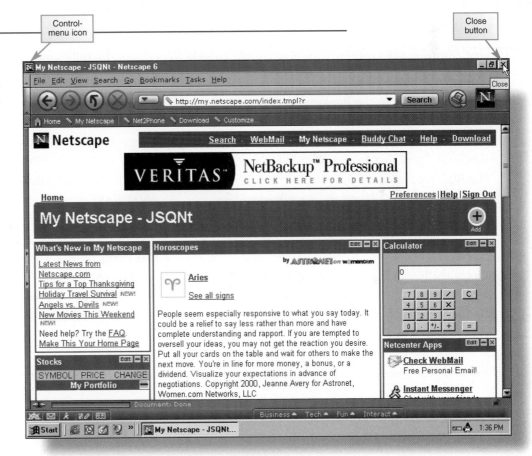

FIGURE 1-77

If you have only one Netscape window open, you can click the Close button on its title bar or click Close on the File menu to quit Netscape. Alternatively, if you have more than one Netscape window open and you want to quit Netscape (close all windows), then use the Exit command on the File menu.

Other Ways

1. Double-click Control-menu icon
2. On File menu click Exit
3. Press CTRL+Q
4. Press ALT+F, type Q

CASE PERSPECTIVE SUMMARY

The Fine Arts Department Head and the students are pleased with the topics you plan to cover in the half-day course. Emphasis on the Asian Art Web site for the Fine Arts majors, the use of My Sidebar, and Netscape's home page will maintain interest in the class. Learning how to save Web pages and copy and paste text and graphics will help the students when they start doing research on the Web.

Project Summary

In this project, you learned about the Internet, the World Wide Web, URLs, and how to display Web pages using Netscape Navigator. You then learned how to follow links, use the Back and Forward buttons, the history list, and how to create and use bookmarks. You learned how to use My Sidebar and the Netscape's home page portal. Using the techniques presented, the steps for saving and printing images and Web pages were illustrated. Finally, you learned how to use Netscape's online Help facility.

What You Should Know

Having completed the project, you now should be able to perform the following tasks:

- Activate a Minimized Netscape Window (*NN 1.44*)
- Add a Bookmark to the Bookmarks Menu (*NN 1.28*)
- Browse the Web by Entering a URL (*NN 1.15*)
- Copy and Paste Text from a Web Page into a WordPad Document (*NN 1.46*)
- Display a Web Page Using the Back Button List (*NN 1.24*)
- Display and Customize the My Netscape Page (*NN 1.51*)
- Display the Home Page Using the Home Button (*NN 1.29*)
- Obtain Netscape Help (*NN 1.55*)
- Print a Web Page (*NN 1.49*)
- Quit Netscape (*NN 1.57*)
- Reload a Web Page (*NN 1.20*)

- Remove a Bookmark from the Bookmark List (*NN 1.31*)
- Retrieve a Web Page Using a Bookmark (*NN 1.30*)
- Save a Picture on a Web Page (*NN 1.42*)
- Save a Web Page (*NN 1.40*)
- Save the WordPad Document and Quit WordPad (*NN 1.48*)
- Start Netscape (*NN 1.10*)
- Start WordPad (*NN 1.43*)
- Use Links on the What's Related Panel in My Sidebar (*NN 1.36*)
- Use the Back and Forward Buttons to Revisit Web Pages (*NN 1.22*)
- Use the History List to Redisplay Web Pages (*NN 1.25*)
- Use the Stocks Tab on My Sidebar (*NN 1.38*)

Test Your Knowledge

1 True/False

Instructions: Circle T if the statement is true or F if the statement is false.

T   F   1. The Internet has high-speed data lines that connect major computer systems located around the world, which form the last mile.

T   F   2. The collection of links throughout the Internet creates an interconnected network called the World Wide Web, which also is referred to as the Web, or WWW.

T   F   3. A Uniform Resource Locator or URL (pronounced you are ell) is important because it is the unique address of each Web page on the World Wide Web.

T   F   4. A protocol is a set of rules.

T   F   5. A typical URL (Uniform Resource Locator) is composed of a range name and file name.

T   F   6. The domain name is the Internet address of the computer on the Internet where the Web page is located.

T   F   7. Double-click the Control-menu icon or click the Close button on the title bar to quit Netscape.

T   F   8. A bookmark consists of the title of the Web page and the URL of that page.

T   F   9. The Link field displays the URL for the page currently shown in the content area.

T   F   10. Most Web sites require you to enter http:// to begin a URL.

2 Multiple Choice

Instructions: Circle the correct answer.

1. _____ describes the rules used to transmit Web pages electronically over the Internet.
   a. HyperText transport protocol (HTTP)
   b. Communications (com)
   c. World Wide Web (WWW)
   d. Netscape (net)

2. The starting page for most Web sites is called a _____.
   a. browser
   b. URL
   c. root directory
   d. home page

3. Each computer on the Internet has a unique address called a(n) _____.
   a. home address
   b. mail address
   c. Internet Protocol address
   d. World Wide Web address

4. Web page authors use a special formatting language called _____ to create Web pages.
   a. applets
   b. hyperText markup language (HTML)
   c. Practical Extraction and Reporting Language (PERL)
   d. Java

(continued)

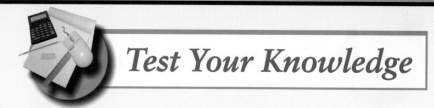

Test Your Knowledge

Multiple Choice (*continued*)

5. You can identify a link because the _____.
   a. link is in reverse video
   b. computer beeps when the mouse pointer is moved over the link
   c. color of the link changes when the mouse pointer is moved over it
   d. mouse pointer changes to a pointing hand when moved over the link

6. When you click the _____, it shows or hides the toolbar.
   a. handle
   b. Toolbar On/Off button
   c. Reload button
   d. Show/Hide button

7. The _____ command on the Bookmarks menu allows you to move bookmarks between folders or delete unwanted bookmarks or folders.
   a. Move Bookmarks
   b. Manage Bookmarks
   c. Move/Delete Bookmarks
   d. Edit Bookmarks

8. A _____ is a Web page designed to offer a variety of Web-related services from one, convenient location.
   a. window
   b. dialog box
   c. front page
   d. portal

9. To save a picture on a Web page, right-click the _____.
   a. picture name
   b. corresponding text link
   c. Location field
   d. picture

10. You show or hide My Sidebar by clicking its _____.
    a. handle
    b. My Sidebar button
    c. Show/Hide button
    d. bottom border

3 Understanding the Netscape Window

Instructions: In Figure 1-78, arrows point to major components of the Netscape window. Identify the various parts of the window in the spaces provided.

Test Your Knowledge

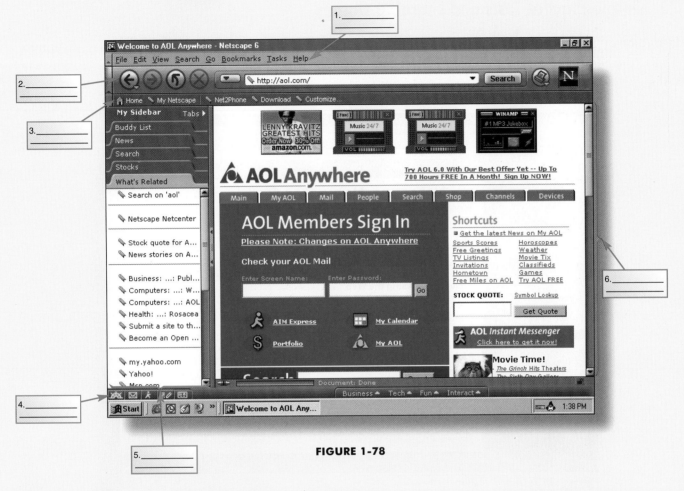

1. _____

2. _____

3. _____

6. _____

4. _____

5. _____

FIGURE 1-78

4 Understanding Toolbar Components

Instructions:

In Figure 1-79, arrows point to several items on Netscape toolbars and My Sidebar. In the spaces provided, identify the item.

3. _____   4. _____   5. _____   6. _____   7. _____   9. _____   10. _____

2. _____

8. _____

1. _____

FIGURE 1-79

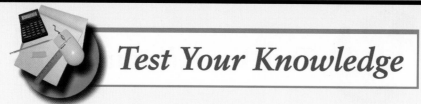

Test Your Knowledge

5 Online Practice Tests and Learning Games

Instructions: Start Netscape. Double-click the Location field and enter the URL scsite.com/nn6/practice.htm to display the Netscape Navigator 6 Practice Tests and Learning Games page (Figure 1-80). Complete the following tasks.

FIGURE 1-80

1. Practice Test: Click Practice Test under Project 1. Answer each question, enter your first and last name at the bottom of the page, and then click the Grade Test button. When the system displays the graded practice test, click Print on the File menu to print a hard copy. Submit the printout to your instructor.

2. Who Wants to be a Computer Genius: Click Computer Genius under Project 1. Read the instructions, enter your first and last name at the bottom of the page, and then click the Play button. Submit your score to your instructor.

3. Wheel of Terms: Click Wheel of Terms under Project 1. Read the instructions and then enter your first name, last name, and your school name. Click View High Scores to see other student scores. Close the High Scores window. Click the Play button. Submit your score to your instructor.

4. Crossword Puzzle Challenge: Click Crossword Puzzle Challenge under Project 1. Read the instructions and then enter your first and last name. Click the Submit button. Solve the crossword puzzle. When you are finished, click the Submit button. When the crossword puzzle redisplays, click the Print button. Submit the printout to your instructor.

In the Lab

1 Browsing the World Wide Web Using URLs and Links

Instructions: Start Netscape and perform the following tasks:

1. Double-click the URL in the Location field on the Navigation toolbar, type `fbi.gov` and then press the ENTER key to display the FBI's home page (Figure 1-81). Print the Web page.

2. Using links on the FBI home page, display the Web page that contains the list of the 10 most wanted fugitives. Print the Web page.

3. Double-click the URL in the Location field on the Navigation toolbar, type `cbs.com` and then press the ENTER key to display the CBS home page. Using links on the CBS home page, display the Web page that lists the latest news. Print the Web page.

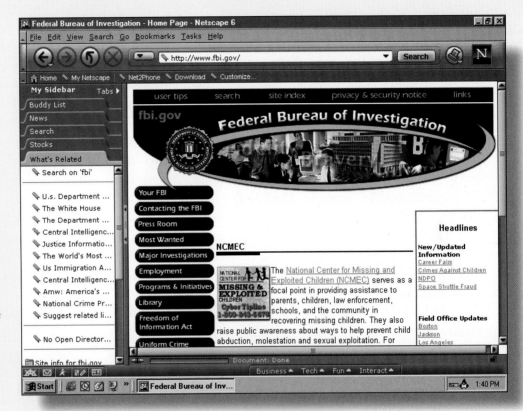

FIGURE 1-81

4. Bookmark the CBS home page by using the Add Current Page command on the Bookmarks menu.

5. Double-click the URL in the Location field, type `usatoday.com` and then press the ENTER key to display the USA TODAY home page.

6. Using a link on the USA TODAY home page, display Technology news (Tech). Print the page.

7. Use the Go menu on the menu bar to redisplay the FBI home page. If the FBI home page is not on the Go menu, type `fbi.gov` in the Location field on the Navigation toolbar. Click the What's Related tab on My Sidebar (left side of Figure 1-81). Use the links on the What's Related panel and the navigation techniques presented in this project to visit two different Web sites. Print each page.

8. Use the Bookmarks menu to display the CBS home page you bookmarked earlier in Step 4. Using links on the CBS home page, find the Web page that contains David Letterman's Top Ten Archive list. Select any year and display the Top Ten list for the date closest to your birthday. Print the Top Ten list for that day. Use the Manage Bookmarks command on the Bookmarks menu to delete the CBS home page bookmark.

In the Lab

2 Using Toolbars and the Netscape Home Page to Visit Popular Web Sites

Instructions Part 1: Start Netscape and perform the following tasks:

1. If the Netscape home page (Figure 1-82) does not display, double-click the URL in the Location field, type `netscape.com` and then press the ENTER key. Click the My Sidebar handle to close My Sidebar.

2. On the Netscape home page, click the Autos link under Departments. When the Autos page displays, click the Used Cars link. When the Used Cars Web page displays, scroll down and click the Kelley Blue Book link. If you experience difficulty displaying the Kelley Blue Book page, type `kbb.com` in the Location field and then press the ENTER key. When the Kelley Blue Book page displays, click USED CAR VALUES. Click the Trade In link. Display and print the Blue Book values for the following cars: (1) 1999 Cadillac Deville, Sedan 4D, 60,000 miles, Excellent condition, use your zip code, and the default options; and (2) 2000 Dodge Avenger, ES Coupe 2D, 33,000 miles, Good condition, use your zip code, and the default options.

3. Click the Home button on the Personal toolbar. If the Netscape home page does not display, use the Back button or enter `netscape.com` in the Location field. On the Netscape home page, click Local under Departments. When the Local page displays, click Dining. When the Dining page displays, click a city near where you live. Scroll down, click a favorite cuisine, and then print the initial list of restaurants.

4. Bookmark the page with the list of restaurants by using the Add Current Page command on the Bookmarks menu. Click the Home button on the Personal toolbar. Display the Bookmarks menu with the list of your bookmarked restaurants.

5. Use the Bookmarks menu to display the page with the list of restaurants you bookmarked. Click the Visitor's Guide tab (or link) and print the page.

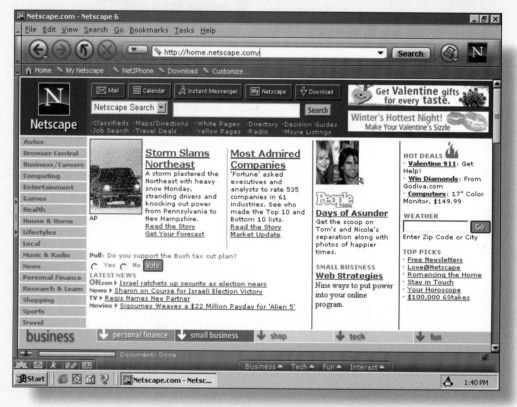

FIGURE 1-82

In the Lab

Instructions Part 2: With Netscape Navigator active, perform the following tasks:

1. Visit Web sites from three different categories listed on the Bookmarks menu. Print each page.
2. Visit one Web site from each of the following: Business, Tech, Fun, and Interact on the Task toolbar at the bottom of the screen. Print each page.
3. Click the My Sidebar handle to display it. Click the News CNN.com tab on My Sidebar. Click one of the Top Stories and print the page.

Instructions Part 3: With Netscape active, click the Home button on the Personal toolbar. Click Tasks on the menu bar. Point to Tools and click History. Click the column name Title at the top of the screen to sort the History list in ascending sequence by Web page name. Double-click a Web page name to display it. After the page displays, click the History button on the taskbar to switch to the History window. Repeat two more times, displaying a Web page in the History list and returning to the History window. When you are finished, click the Close button on the right side of the History window's title bar.

3 Saving a Web Page on a Floppy Disk

Instructions: Start Netscape and perform the following tasks:

1. Double-click the URL in the Location field, type dbc.com and then press the ENTER key to display the Data Broadcasting Corporation Web page (Figure 1-83).

2. Type the Motorola stock symbol mot in the Fast Quote text box and then click the Go button to retrieve the current Motorola stock price. When the Motorola page displays, click Fundamentals to display an expanded view of the Motorola stock. Save the Web page on a floppy disk in drive A using the Save Page As command on the File menu. Use the stock symbol (mot) as the file name.

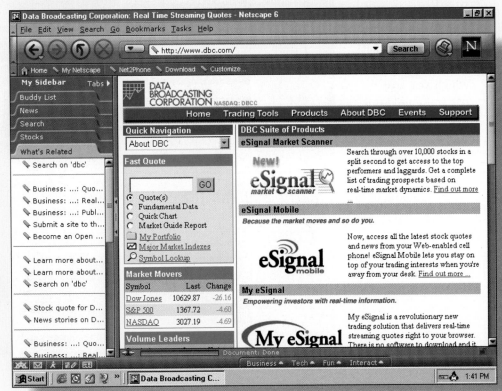

FIGURE 1-83

(continued)

In the Lab

Saving a Web Page on a Floppy Disk *(continued)*

3. Repeat Step 2 for the following stock symbols: medi (Medimunne), pfe (Pfizer), pep (Pepsi), and PAYX (Paychex).
4. Double-click the Location field on the Navigation toolbar, type : (a colon) and then press the ENTER key. Click the filename, mot, to display the Motorola Web page you saved to drive A in Step 2. Print the page.
5. Repeat Step 4 for the Web pages saved to the floppy disk in Step 3.

4 Displaying and Printing the Current US Weather Map

Instructions: Start Netscape and perform the following tasks:

1. Double-click the Location field, type weather.com and then press the ENTER key to display the weather.com home page.
2. Click the Current U.S. Weather map picture to enlarge it. Click the picture a second time to enlarge it again. Click the My Sidebar handle to hide My Sidebar so there is more room to display the Current U.S. Weather map picture. Scroll down and to the right so the picture displays similar to Figure 1-84.
3. Print the enlarged Current U.S. Weather map.
4. Scroll through the Current U.S. Weather map and find the link that pertains to the part of the country in which you live. Click the link and then print the page.
5. Enter your zip code in the Any City or US Zip box and click the Go button. Print the page.

FIGURE 1-84

In the Lab

5 Copying and Pasting Text

Instructions Part 1: Start Netscape and perform the following tasks:

1. Double-click the Location field, type historychannel.com and then press the ENTER key to display the History Channel home page (Figure 1-85).

2. Click the link that contains the full story associated with The Day in History picture (Figure 1-85).

3. Copy the story title and text to the Clipboard. Start Microsoft WordPad. Paste the text on the Clipboard into the WordPad document.

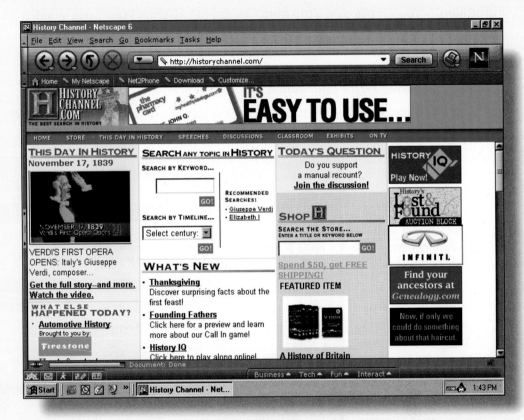

FIGURE 1-85

4. Save the WordPad document on a floppy disk using the file name This Day in History.

5. Print the WordPad document.

6. Click the Close button to close the This Day in History - WordPad window.

Instructions Part 2: Display the History Channel home page by using the Back button on the Navigation toolbar or by typing historychannel.com in the Location field and pressing the ENTER key. Perform the following tasks:

1. When the History Channel's home page displays, use the vertical scroll bar to locate the What Happened on Your Birthday text boxes. Use the Month and Day boxes to select your birth month and birthdate and then click the GO button to learn what happened on your birthday.

2. Copy and paste the stories from the Web page into a blank WordPad document, save the document on a floppy disk using the file name, my birthday. Print the WordPad document.

3. Close the WordPad window and quit Netscape Navigator.

In the Lab

6 Planning a Trip on the Web

Instructions: You are planning a trip from Chicago to Las Vegas exactly one month from today. You plan to stay in Las Vegas seven days, including travel days. You want to use Expedia.com to summarize flights, hotels, car rentals, areas of interest, and directions from your hotel to the Hoover Dam museum in Boulder City, Nevada.

Part 1: *Summarizing Flight Information*

1. Start Netscape. Double-click the Location field, type `expedia.com` and then press the ENTER key to display the Expedia.com home page (Figure 1-86).

2. Type `Chicago` in the Departing from box; type `Las Vegas` in the Going to box; select 2 in the Adults box; select the date and time (i.e., July 7 noon) in the When are you leaving? boxes; and seven days from the date of departure, including the date of departure (i.e., July 13 noon) in the When are you returning? boxes. Click the Search button.

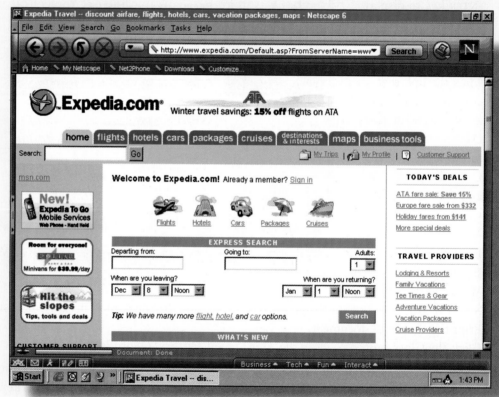

FIGURE 1-86

3. When the Roundtrip search page displays, select Chicago, IL (ORD-O'Hare) in the From list. Scroll down and carefully check the remaining entries. If necessary, in Step 3, select Economy/Coach in the Class box, click the Only direct flights check box, and select Search All Airlines in the Airline box. Click the Search by best available fares link. Scroll through the flight information and then print it.

Part 2: *Summarizing Hotel Information*

1. With the Expedia.com page displaying, click the hotels tab at the top of the page.

In the Lab

2. Click the Las Vegas option button or type Las Vegas in the Search in and around box. Enter the same dates and number of adults as described in Step 2 of Part 1. Click the Search button.

3. When the Search results page displays, scroll through the page and find hotel Bellagio. If it is not on the page displayed, then request the next group of hotels by clicking the next numeric range near the top of the page. Print the page that includes hotel Bellagio.

Part 3: Summarizing Car Rental Information

1. With the Expedia.com page displaying, click the cars tab at the top of the page.

2. Type McCarran Airport in the Pick-up location box; enter the same pick up dates you used in Step 2 of Part 1; select Midsize in the Car class box; leave the Pick-up time, Drop-off time, and Rental car company boxes at their default. Click the Search button. Print the page.

Part 4: Summarizing Areas of Interest

1. With the Expedia.com page displaying, click the destinations & interests tab. Click the Destination Guides link on the left side of the page. Scroll down through the list of cities and states and then click Las Vegas.

2. When the Las Vegas page displays, click Highlights. Print the page.

Part 5: Maps and Directions

1. With the Expedia.com page displaying, click the maps tab. Click the Get Driving Directions link.

2. When the Get Driving Directions page displays, type Bellagio Hotel, Las Vegas in the Place name box in Step 1. Type Hoover dam in the Place name box in Step 2. If necessary, in Step 3 select Quickest in the Route. Type box and Miles in the Units box. Click the Get driving directions link.

3. When the Get Driving Directions page redisplays with messages regarding multiple matches, select Bellagio Hotel/Casino, Las Vegas, Nevada in the Place name box in Step 1. Scroll down and click the Get driving directions link. Print the map and directions.

7 Comparing Prices Online

Instructions: You are interested in purchasing a Palm handheld device, an HP ink jet printer, and a Kodak digital camera. A friend suggested you look on the Web for the lowest prices even though you are not yet ready to purchase online. You decide to use the Web to compare prices and obtain company phone numbers so you can contact the company with the best price and make the purchases using the telephone. Perform the following tasks:

1. Start Netscape. Double-click the Location field on the Navigation toolbar, type computershopper.com and then press the ENTER key to display the ZD Net COMPUTER SHOPPER.COM page (Figure 1-87 on the next page).

2. Click the Handhelds link. When the next page displays, click the Palm (or 3Com/Palm) link under Brands. Print the Search Results page. Scroll down and click Palm VII (or another Palm) to display the list of merchants. Click the company info link of the line item that has the lowest price to obtain the telephone number. Print the page.

(continued)

In the Lab

Comparing Prices Online *(continued)*

FIGURE 1-87

3. Use the Back button or type `computershopper.com` in the Location field to display the ZD Net COMPUTER SHOPPER.COM home page. Click the Digital Cameras link on the left side of the page. When the next page displays, click the Kodak (or another brand) link under Brands. Print the Search Results page. Scroll down and click a digital camera model to display the list of merchants. Click the company info link of the line item that has the lowest price to obtain the telephone number. Print the page.

4. Use the Back button or type `computershopper.com` in the Location field to display the ZD Net COMPUTER SHOPPER.COM home page. Click the Printers link on the left side of the page. When the next page displays, click the Hewlett-Packard (or another brand) link under Brands. Print the Search Results page. Scroll down and click an ink jet model to display the list of merchants. Click the company info link of the line item that has the lowest price to obtain the telephone number. Print the page.

In the Lab

8 Job Hunting on the Web

Instructions: You are job hunting, and your area of expertise is e-commerce.

Part 1: *Finding a Job*

1. Start Netscape. Type `computerjobs.com` in the Location field and press the ENTER key.
2. When the computerjobs.com home page displays (Figure 1-88), click the e-commerce/Internet link or type `e-commerce` in the keyword search text box and then press the ENTER key. When the first page of the e-commerce listings displays, print it.
3. Type `monster.com` in the Location field and press the ENTER key.
4. When the monster.com home page displays, click Search Jobs near the top of the screen. Type `e-commerce` in the Keyword Search box and then press the ENTER key. When the first page of the e-commerce listings displays, print it.
5. Type `careerpath.com` in the Location field and press the ENTER key.
6. When the CareerPath.com home page displays, click Find a job. When the Career Builder page displays, click the quick search link, type `e-commerce` in the Keywords box, and then click the Go button. When the first page of the e-commerce listings displays, print it.

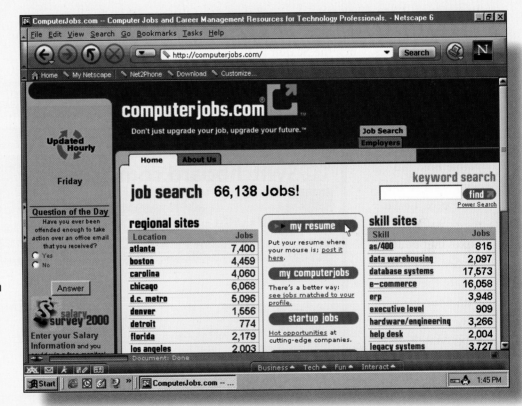

FIGURE 1-88

Part 2: *Posting a Resume*

1. Select one of the three Web sites visited in Part 1 of this exercise. Post your resume by clicking the appropriate link on the home page. You will have to register to post your resume.
2. When you are finished, print the resume or the page on which the resume displays.

In the Lab

9 Finding a Person on the Web

Instructions: You want to use the Web to obtain information on a person and a business.

Part 1: *Finding a Person*

1. Start Netscape. Type `switchboard.com` in the Location field and press the ENTER key.
2. When the CBS Switchboard.com home page displays (Figure 1-89), click the Find a Person link.
3. When the Find a Person page displays, type the last name of the President of the United States in the Last Name box. Type `Washington` in the City box and `DC` in the State box. Click the Search button.
4. When the Find a Person page displays, find the President of the United States. The president lives at 1600 Pennsylvania Ave. Click the name and then print the page that displays.
5. Click the Find a Person link at the top of the page. Type your last name and the state where you live in the appropriate boxes. Click the Search button. Print the page.
6. Click the Find a Person link at the top of the page. Type your last name in the Last Name box and your state in the State box. Leave the remaining boxes empty. Click the Search button. Locate the page with your name on it by using the Next Matches link after the last name, if necessary. Print the page with your name on it. If you can't find your name, print the page on which your name should have displayed.

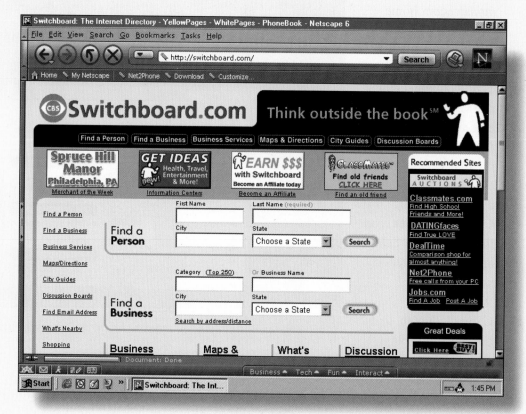

FIGURE 1-89

Part 2: *Finding a Business*

1. With a page from the CBS Switchboard.com Web site displaying, click the Find a Business link.
2. Locate antique dealers near your hometown. You must enter a city and state. Print the page with the list of antique shops.

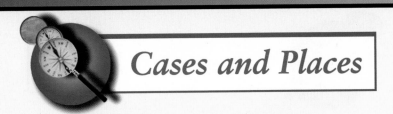

Cases and Places

The difficulty of these case studies varies:
▶ are the least difficult; ▶▶ are more difficult; and ▶▶▶ are the most difficult.

1 ▶ Visit the Shelly Cashman Guide to World Wide Web Sites at scsite.com/nn6/websites.htm. Click a category of Web sites of your choice. Visit and print the initial page of each site in the selected category.

2 ▶ Your old car broke down and you are in the market for a new one. Type the URL carpoint.com to display the Microsoft Network CarPoint home page. Select your favorite make and model and then click the Go button to search for a new car. Check the availability and prices for two additional models of the same make. Print three pages with some results.

3 ▶▶ Your aunt would like to invest in the stock market. She has asked you to find fundamental stock information about Microsoft Corporation (MSFT), Cisco (CSCO), Sun Microsystems (SUNW), IBM (IBM), and Yahoo! (YHOO). Use the Yahoo! Web site (quote.yahoo.com) to obtain today's stock price, dividend rate, daily volume, 52-week high, 52-week low, and the P/E (price earnings ratio). To display this information, enter the stock symbol. When the stock price displays, click the Detailed link above the date and time to display the desired information. Print the detailed results for each stock. In addition, when the detailed information displays for Intel, scroll down and click the first topic under Recent News. Print the page.

4 ▶▶ Your cousin from Los Angeles is planning a vacation to Boston, Massachusetts. He wants to leave exactly one month from today and plans to stay seven days, including the travel days. Check flight availability and price with United Airlines (unitedairlines.com), Continental Airlines (flycontinental. com), Southwest Airlines (southwest.com) and American Airlines (aa.com). For each Web site, print the flights and round-trip ticket prices. Write a brief report that summarizes the information you find.

5 ▶▶ Visit the World Wide Web Consortium Web site at w3.org. Click the About W3C link and print the page. Return to the World Wide Web Consortium's home page, review the links and click one that interests you. Write a one-page, double-spaced summary report about the World Wide Web.

6 ▶▶▶ You have decided to purchase a computer online. You plan to spend between $1,400 and $1,500 for a computer system with monitor and printer. Visit three online computer stores, such as Compaq (compaq.com), Dell (dell.com), and Gateway (gateway.com). On each site, find a computer system that sells for the amount you plan to spend. For each site, print the page that indicates the system and price. Compare the three computer systems. Which one is the best buy? Why?

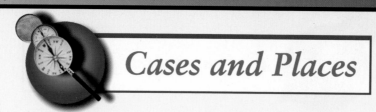

Cases and Places

7 ▶▶▶ Visit five daily newspaper Web sites, such as the New York Times (nytimes.com), Chicago Tribune (chicagotribune.com), Los Angeles Times (latimes.com), Miami Herald (miamiherald.com), and a local newspaper's Web site. Print at least one page from each newspaper site. Compare the latest headline news. Navigate through each site. How are the newspaper sites similar and dissimilar? Which newspaper has the best Web site? Why?

Netscape Navigator 6

Netscape Navigator 6

PROJECT

2

Web Search Tools and Research Techniques

You will have mastered the material in this project when you can:

- Describe the seven types of Web pages
- Use Netscape's Internet Keyword system to display Web pages
- Search the Web using Netscape Search
- Search the Web using the Netscape Search subject directory
- Search the Web using the Google search engine
- Search the Web using multiple search engines
- Search the Web using the AltaVista Simple search engine, Power search engine, and Images search engine
- Search the Yahoo! Yellow Pages
- Find directions and create a map using Yahoo!'s Map tool
- List the criteria for evaluating a Web resource
- Describe how to create a working bibliography
- Cite Web sources in a research paper

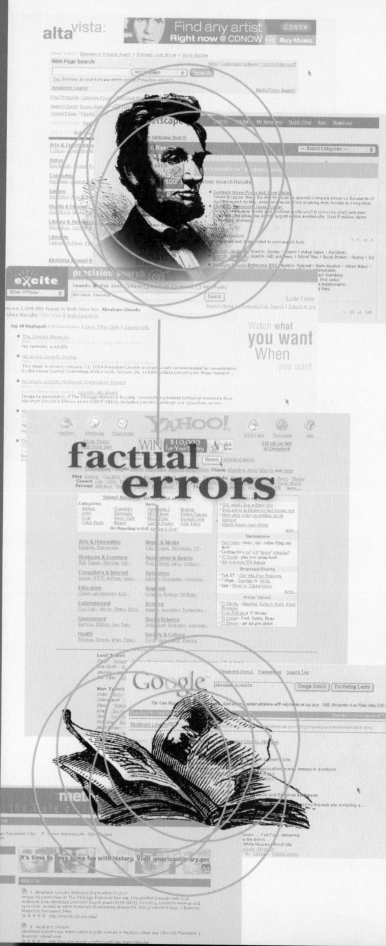

Searching the Web

Where Do You Start?

You have been assigned a research project that will account for a large percentage of your grade. After choosing Abraham Lincoln as your topic, you begin your research. Shunning traditional printed reference materials in favor of Web resources, you begin your search for information. Where do you start? An initial inquiry for information on Abraham Lincoln returns several hundreds of thousands of pages. After mentally slogging through hundreds of likely looking Web sites, you compile the needed information and compose your report. Smugly, you await your grade, knowing that your information was gleaned from the largest, most current source available. Imagine your shock when you receive an F, entirely due to factual errors.

This would be a difficult way to learn a simple lesson: virtually anyone can post information on the Web and few controls exist. Simply because information is on the Web does not guarantee its accuracy. This is not to say that all information on the Web is faulty, or that all printed sources are beyond reproach; however, printed materials typically have been through an editorial process conducted by professionals. The same cannot always be said of Web sources. Search engines were developed to address some of these problems. By indexing the enormous

keywords matches, hits concept-based navigation

amount — by some estimates, more than 22 million pages and growing every day — search engines can help you both narrow your search and cull the information you need. Some search engines, such as Netscape Search and Yahoo!, provide editor-reviewed or editor-compiled links, which have a higher degree of accuracy.

Search engines are to the World Wide Web what a card catalog is to a library. They allow the user quickly to search and locate specific topics on the Web, much as a library card catalog guides patrons to the correct location of printed information. Most search engines share a common method of locating information: the *keyword*. A user types a word or phrase, such as aviation or global warming, and the search engine scans the sites on the Web to find matches, or *hits*.

While many search engines exist and are readily available to Web users, several are well known and widely used. Yahoo! is praised as being the fastest and most current because it is updated daily. Another favorite search engine, AltaVista, arguably is the largest Web index, and can perform detailed searches for any type of information.

One search engine differs in its approach to finding information on the Web. Excite uses concept-based navigation on the Web. This unique approach, though slower and more likely to return irrelevant information, can perform more abstract searches. Rather than using Civil War as a keyword, for example, you could type, What caused the Civil War?

This project presents techniques for searching the vast amount of materials that are available on the Web. In addition to using the popular Yahoo! and AltaVista search engines, you will learn how to use Google, and the traditional Internet services such as FTP and gopher to perform the online research required for your classroom assignments and distance learning courses.

Samuel Johnson, the English author, said "Knowledge is of two kinds: we know a subject ourselves, or we know where we can find information upon it." Although he died in 1784, his words are just as true today, especially when applied to search engines.

Netscape Navigator 6

Web Search Tools and Research Techniques

CASE PERSPECTIVE

You just attended the first day of class in an introductory English research course. Your instructor informed the class that 75 percent of the bibliography of the final research paper must be Web-based. You have no idea how to do research on the Web.

Finding information on a specific topic is difficult at times because the Web is very large and changes every day. To resolve this problem, companies have developed search engines and subject directories to help Web users find information. While these two search tools make it easy to find information on the Web, they do not address the issue as to whether the information is correct. You must learn how to use evaluation criteria and published style guides to ensure the materials you obtain from the Web are accurate.

Your instructor also indicated that to pass the class, you must show proficiency in searching the Web by taking an online final examination that covers four search engines — Netscape Search, Google, AltaVista, and Yahoo! Your objective is to learn how to use these search engines.

Introduction

Research is an important tool for success in an academic career. Writing papers, preparing speeches, and doing homework assignments are all activities that rely heavily on research. When researching, you are trying to find information to support an idea or position, to prove a point, or to learn about a topic or concept. Traditionally, research was accomplished using books, papers, periodicals, and other materials found in libraries. The World Wide Web provides a new and useful resource for supplementing the traditional print materials found in the library. Recent estimates place the number of Web pages at over 500 billion, up from just a few million pages in 1994.

While the Web is a valuable resource, you should not rely solely on the Web for research information. The Web changes quite frequently, which means Web pages may become unavailable. In addition, the information found on Web pages is not always up-to-date, accurate, or verifiable.

This project demonstrates successful techniques for finding information on the Web and then evaluating the information for its usefulness as a source.

Types of Web Pages

Web pages are organized by content into seven categories: advocacy, business/marketing, informational, news, personal, portal, and other. The next several sections describe the types of Web pages.

Advocacy Web Pages

An **advocacy Web page** contains content that describes a cause, opinion, or idea. The purpose of an advocacy Web page is to convince the reader of the validity of an opinion or idea. These Web pages usually present an unbalanced view that is skewed to support their cause. The American Medical Association, American Association of Retired Persons, the Democratic Party, the Republican Party, and the Greenpeace organization are examples of sponsors of advocacy Web pages. The domain name in the URL of advocacy Web pages usually ends with the .org extension. Figure 2-1 shows the Web page for the Sierra Club, an environmentalist advocacy group.

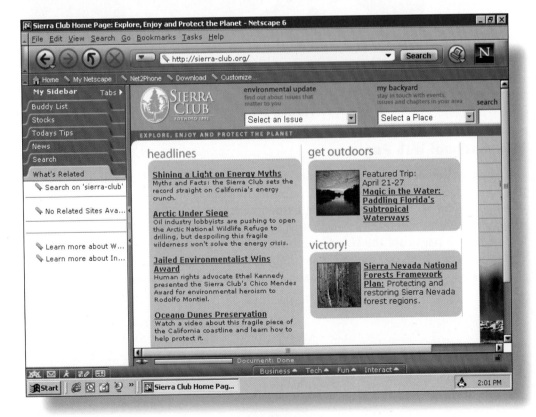

FIGURE 2-1

More About

Web Research Materials

Reference materials, such as dictionaries, thesauruses, and collections of quotations, as well as entire literary works are available on the Web. Search for the word, ameliorate, using the Merriam-Webster dictionary Web site (www.m-w.com), and then find a synonym for the word, exciting.

More About

Advocacy Web Pages

Other advocacy Web pages include Southern Carolina Democratic Party (www.scdp.org), Maine Democratic Party (www.mainedems.org), Kentucky Republican Party (www.rpk.org), and California Republican Party (www.cagop.org),

Business/Marketing Web Pages

A **business/marketing Web page** contains content that tries to promote or sell products or services. The domain name in URLs of business/marketing Web pages usually ends with the .com extension. Nearly every business maintains a business/marketing Web page. For example, AT&T, Dell, Walt Disney Company, and CDNOW are examples of business/marketing Web pages. Figure 2-2 shows the Walt Disney Company home page, an example of a business/marketing Web page.

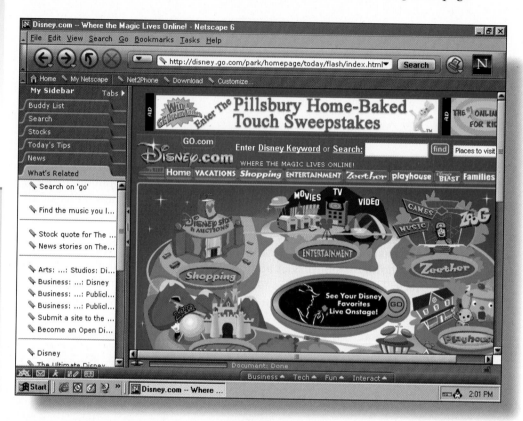

FIGURE 2-2

Informational Web Pages

An **informational Web page** contains factual information, such as public transportation schedules, library holdings, published research findings, or quarterly fiscal results for a corporation. The domain name in URLs of informational Web pages usually end with the .gov or .com extension. Some organizations that maintain informational Web pages are the U.S. Government (U.S. census data, tax codes, congressional budget, and so on) and airlines (flight information and schedules). Figure 2-3 shows an informational Web page of the United States Senate (senate.gov).

FIGURE 2-3

News Web Pages

A **news Web page** contains newsworthy material, such as stories and articles that contain information about current events, life, money, sports, and the weather. Many magazines and newspapers sponsor Web sites that provide summaries of printed articles, as well as articles not included in the printed versions. Newspapers and television and radio stations are some of the media that maintain news Web pages. The domain name in URLs of news Web pages usually end with the .com extension. Figure 2-4 shows a sample news Web page of the Chicago Tribune newspaper (chicago.tribune.com).

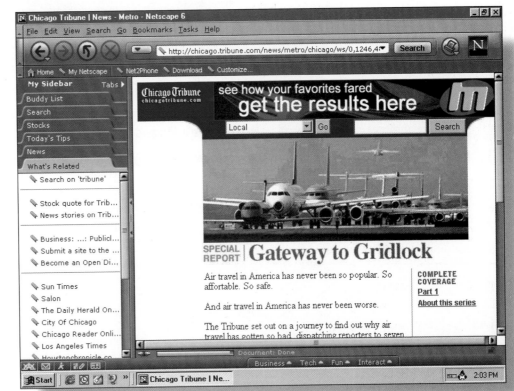

FIGURE 2-4

Personal Web Pages

A **personal Web page** is maintained by an individual and normally is not associated with any organization. People publish personal Web pages for a variety of reasons, and the pages can contain content on just about anything imaginable. The domain name in URLs of personal Web pages may end with the .com, .gov, or .edu extension, depending on where the individual is maintaining his or her site. Figure 2-5 shows a sample personal Web page.

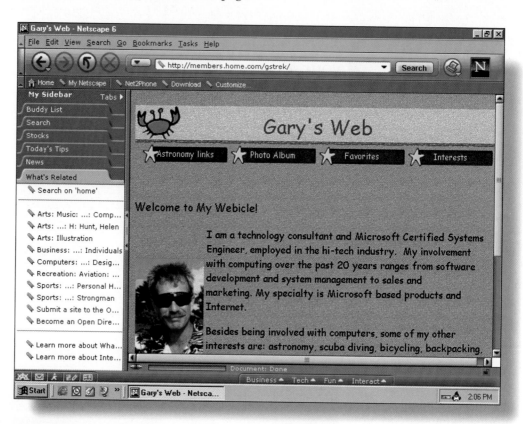

FIGURE 2-5

Table 2-1	Major Portals and Their URLs
PORTAL	**URL**
AltaVista	altavista.com
America Online	aol.com
Dogpile	dogpile.com
euroseek.com	euroseek.com
Excite	excite.com
GO.com	go.com
Google!	google.com
HotBot	hotbot.com
looksmart	looksmart.com
Lycos	lycos.com
Microsoft Network	msn.com
Netscape Netcenter	netscape.com
Netscape Search	search.netscape.com
Yahoo!	yahoo.com

Portal Web Pages

A **portal Web page** (Figure 2-6) is designed to offer a variety of Internet services from a single convenient location. Web pages offer the following free services: search engine and subject directory for searching the Web; local, national, and worldwide news; sports and weather; free personal Web pages; reference tools, such as yellow pages, stock quotes, and maps; shopping malls and auctions; e-mail; instant messaging; message boards; calendars; address books; and chat rooms. Table 2-1 lists some of the major portals and their URLs.

Other Resources

A number of other resources where you will find useful information are available on the Internet. File transfer protocol (FTP) and gopher sites, newsgroups, and for-profit database services all contain information and files that you can use for research purposes.

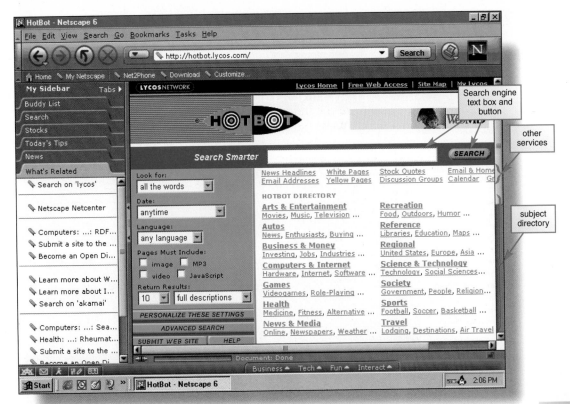

FIGURE 2-6

Papers, documents, manuals, and complete ready-to-execute programs are available using FTP. **File transfer protocol** (**FTP**) allows you to download and upload files over the Internet.

Gopher started out as a document retrieval system to assist people in getting help for computing problems. It since has become a menu-driven method of retrieving files. Many government agencies have organized gopher sites to provide information and distribute documents and forms.

Newsgroups are online discussion groups. Individuals can send messages to a newsgroup, receive replies, and read what others have to say about a topic. Discussion on current events, ongoing research, and other topics that have not yet found their way into print often occur in newsgroup discussions. Newsgroups are discussed in Project 3.

A number of **database services**, such as Lexis/Nexis (Figure 2-7 on the next page), have been developed. These services, for a small fee, allow you to perform searches for information. Some schools subscribe to these database services and make the searching services available to faculty, staff, and students. Ask a librarian how to access these database services.

More About

Gopher

In the past, federal, state, and local government agencies used Gopher extensively as a means for making information, copies of forms and documents, and other government services available. You can experiment with a gopher by searching the National Archives and Records Administration Web site (www.gopher.gov).

More About

Finding Current Information

Newsgroups provide a forum for finding current information on a topic. Many experts and professionals read the threads in newsgroups pertaining to their areas of expertise and are willing to answer questions and supply information. For more information about accessing newsgroups, see Project 3 of this book.

FIGURE 2-7

Summary of Type of Web Resources

Determining the exact category into which a Web resource falls is sometimes difficult because of the overlap of information on the page. You will find advertising on news Web pages. Personal Web pages may be advocating some cause or opinion. A business/marketing Web page may contain factual information that is verifiable from other sources. In spite of this overlapping, identifying the general category in which the Web page falls can help you evaluate the usefulness of the Web page as a source of information for a research paper.

Netscape's Search Tools

The World Wide Web includes billions of Web pages, and bibliographic control does not exist. To find information for a term paper, learn more about a topic of interest, or display the home page of a governmental agency, you must know either the URL of the Web page with the information you are after or you must use a search tool. **Search tools** are software programs that help you find Web pages containing the desired information.

The three basic types of search tools are:

- Internet Keyword system
- Subject directory
- Search engine

Search Engines

Search engines can provide access to more than just Web pages. Some search engines allow you to search a newsgroup, periodical or newspaper, business directory, and personal directory.

The first type of search tool, an Internet Keyword system, is part of your browser. An **Internet Keyword system** allows you to enter a name or word in the Location field to display a corresponding Web page. The second type of search tool, called a **subject directory**, groups related Web pages by subject (Figure 2-8). A third type of search tool, called a **search engine**, retrieves and displays a list of links to Web pages based upon a query. A **query** is the **keyword** or **search term** (a word, set of words, or phrase) you enter in the Search text box (Figure 2-8) to tell the search engine the topic on which you want information. The search engine uses the keyword to search an index of Web pages in its database.

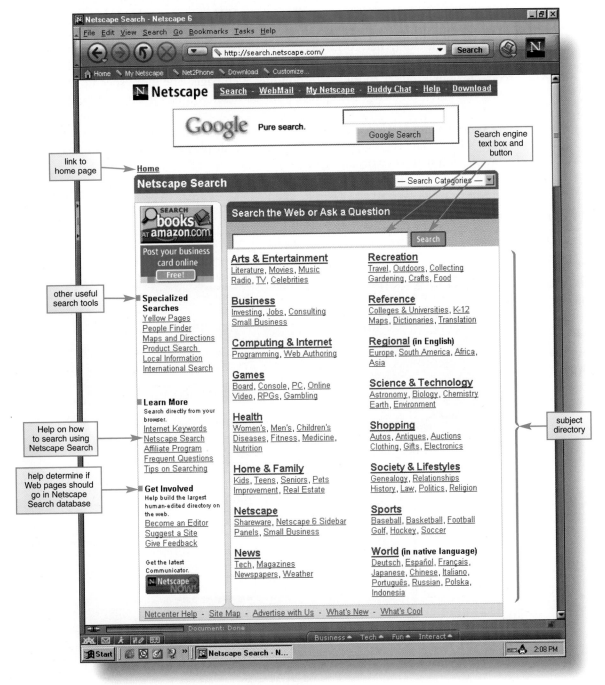

FIGURE 2-8

All the major portal Web sites listed in Table 2-1 on page NN 2.8 have both a search engine and a subject directory as shown by the **Netscape Search Web page** (search.netscape.com) shown in Figure 2-8 on the previous page. Most portals also include specialized search tools that display maps and directions (Maps and Directions), provide information about businesses (Yellow Pages), and help find people (People Finder).

Using the Netscape Internet Keyword System to Display Web Pages

If you type a specific product, trademark, company name, or institution name in the Location field where you normally enter a URL and press the ENTER key, Netscape will display a corresponding Web page. Any Location field entry that does not end with a .com, .net, .org, .de, or .jp is passed to the Internet Keyword system. The Internet Keyword system matches your keyword to a URL and immediately redirects your browser to the corresponding Web page. The more specific the keyword you enter, the better the chance your browser will be directed to the desired site.

Assume you want information on Purdue University, but do not know the university's URL. The following steps show how to display the university's home page using the Internet Keyword system.

To Use the Internet Keyword System to Display a Web Page

1 If Netscape is not active, double-click the Netscape icon on the desktop. When the Netscape home page displays, double-click the Location field and type purdue university as the entry (Figure 2-9).

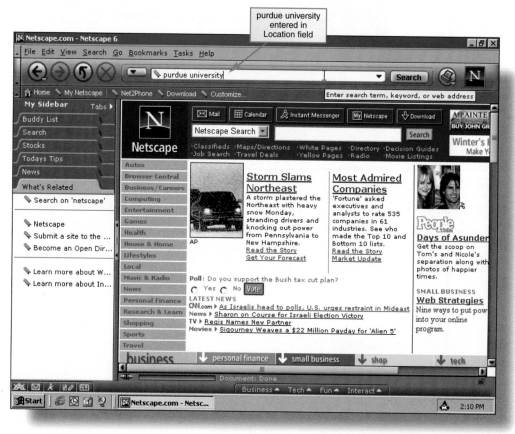

FIGURE 2-9

② Press the ENTER key.

Because the entry does not have a www. or .com or .org, your browser sends the keyword, purdue university, to the Internet Keyword system. The Internet Keyword system matches purdue university to its database of keywords and URLs and redirects your browser to the Purdue University home page (Figure 2-10).

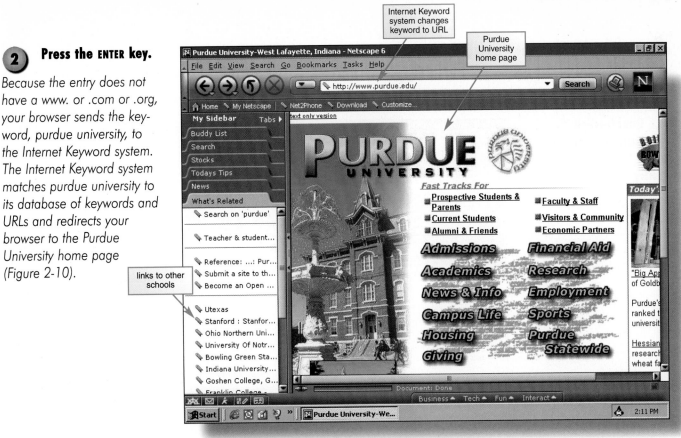

FIGURE 2-10

Because there is only one Purdue University home page, the Internet Keyword system redirects your browser to the correct Web page. Thus, this system works well with company names, organization names, association names, and specific products and services.

More often than not, however, the topic on which you want information is much more general. If you enter a general keyword, such as concerts, home gardening, or construction jobs, the Internet Keyword system passes the keyword to Netscape Search, which returns a Web page with several related links from which you can choose. **Netscape Search** is Netscape's primary search tool.

As an example, assume you need information on the topic, DNA profiling, for your term paper. The following steps illustrate how the Internet Keyword system passes the general topic DNA Profiling to Netscape Search, which displays a page of links from which you can choose.

More About

Directory and Keyword Search Engines

Today, most search engines provide both a directory and the capability of performing keyword searches.

Steps **To Use the Internet Keyword System to Display a List of Related Web Pages**

1 **Double-click the Location field and type** dna profiling **as the entry (Figure 2-11).**

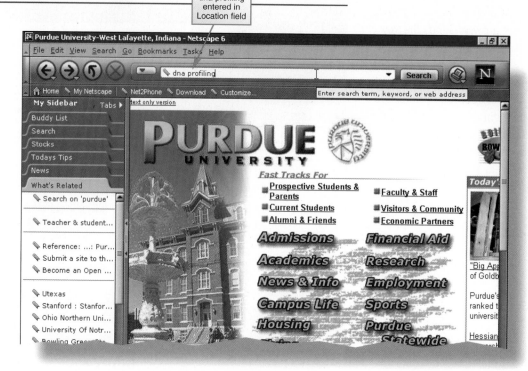

dna profiling entered in Location field

FIGURE 2-11

2 **Press the ENTER key. When the Search Results page displays, scroll down to view the Reviewed Web Sites section, and then point to the first link.**

Because the keyword, dna profiling, has no specific Web page, the Internet Keyword system passes the entry to Netscape Search, which displays a page of related links (Figure 2-12), rather than a specific Web page. The Search panel in My Sidebar displays with a list of links because the Internet Keyword system passed the keyword to Netscape Search.

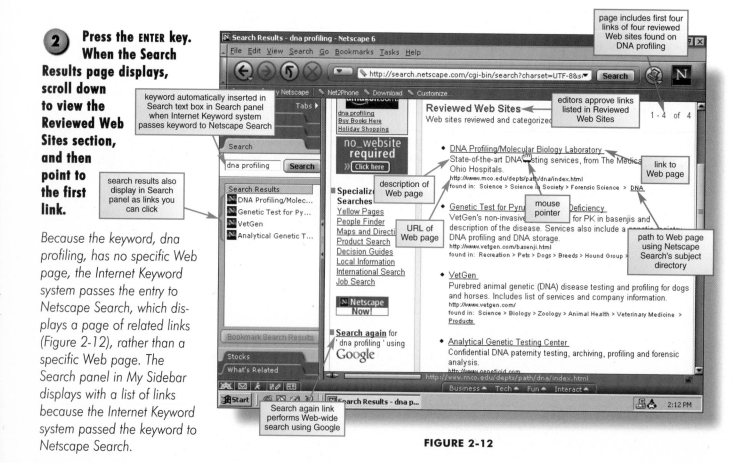

page includes first four links of four reviewed Web sites found on DNA profiling

keyword automatically inserted in Search text box in Search panel when Internet Keyword system passes keyword to Netscape Search

editors approve links listed in Reviewed Web Sites

search results also display in Search panel as links you can click

description of Web page

mouse pointer

link to Web page

URL of Web page

path to Web page using Netscape Search's subject directory

Search again link performs Web-wide search using Google

FIGURE 2-12

3 **Click the first link.**

A page with information on DNA profiling similar to the one in Figure 2-13 displays.

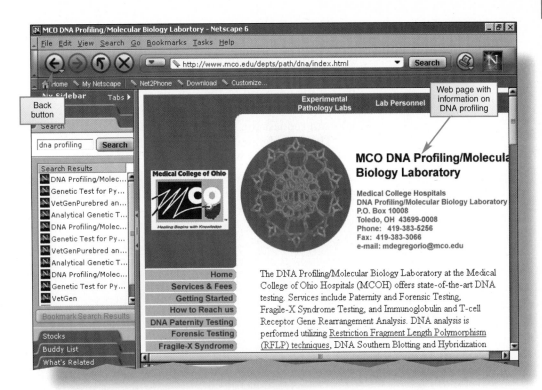

FIGURE 2-13

4 **After reviewing the contents of the page, click the Back button on the Navigation toolbar. When the Search results page displays again, scroll down and click the Search Again link to complete a Web-wide search using the Google search engine. When the Google Results page displays, scroll down to display the first few links.**

A page with 10 additional links displays. These 10 links are the first of hundreds of links to pages concerning DNA profiling found by the Google search engine. The number of pages found is indicated immediately below and to the right of the title of the page (Figure 2-14).

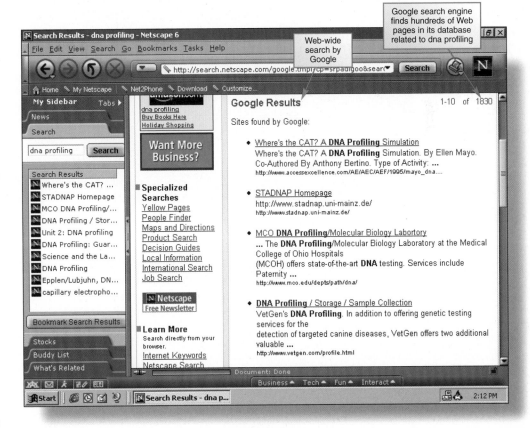

FIGURE 2-14

The steps show the three levels of searching available with Netscape, Internet Keyword system, Netscape Search, and the Google search engine. If the Internet Keyword system cannot find a specific Web page that corresponds to the keyword, then it passes it to Netscape Search. If Netscape Search fails to find Web pages, it passes the keyword to the Google search engine. As illustrated in Step 4 on the previous page, if you prefer to continue the search after Netscape Search displays results, you can request the Google search engine to do a Web-wide search.

Through the use of the Internet Keyword system, you are only a few clicks away from thousands of Web resources. Table 2-2 shows topics and corresponding examples that improve considerably the chances that the Internet Keyword system will return specific Web pages or links that yield the desired information.

Table 2-2	Examples of Using Netscape's Internet Keyword System		
CATEGORY	*TOPIC*	*GENERAL FORM*	*EXAMPLE*
General Information	Buy a car	[city] car	chicago car
	Find a job in a particular city	[city] careers	pittsburgh careers
	Shop for an item	Shop [item]	shop shoes
	Locate a company	[company name]	cisco
	Explore colleges	[college name]	stanford
	Search for a home	[city] real estate	omaha real estate
	Check out a city, state, or zip code area	[city] or [state] or zip [zip code]	Atlanta or Indiana or zip 60612
Local Information	Concerts	[city] concerts	philedelphia concerts
	Dine	[city] dining	miami dining
	Directions	[city] driving directions	los angeles directions
	Movies	[city] movies	detriot movies
	Shop	[city] shopping	new york shopping
News	Latest news	[city] news	
	Latest sports news	[city] sports	buffalo sports
	Latest weather	[city] weather	houston weather
	Stock quote	quote [ticker symbol]	quote ibm

Using the Choose Keyword Button

You can click the **Choose keyword** button on the left side of the Location field to select a phrase to speed up your Internet Keyword search, rather than typing the phrase in the Location field as described in Table 2-2. The following steps show how to use the Choose keyword button to display job market information for the Boston area.

 **To Use the Choose Keyword Button to Speed Up a Search**

1 **Click the Choose keyword button on the left side of the Location field and then point to Get a job in the list (Figure 2-15).**

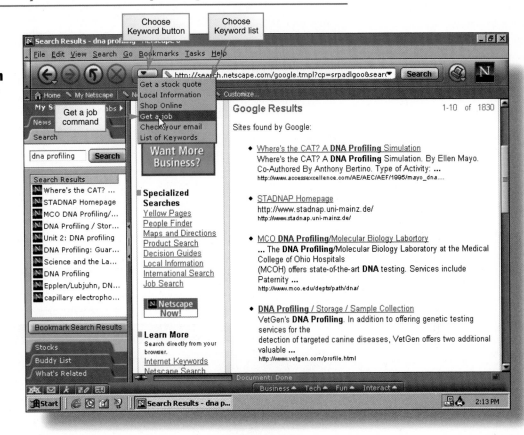

FIGURE 2-15

2 **Click Get a job.**

Netscape displays Your city careers in the Location field (Figure 2-16). Netscape highlights Your city in the Location field so that the characters you type replace Your city.

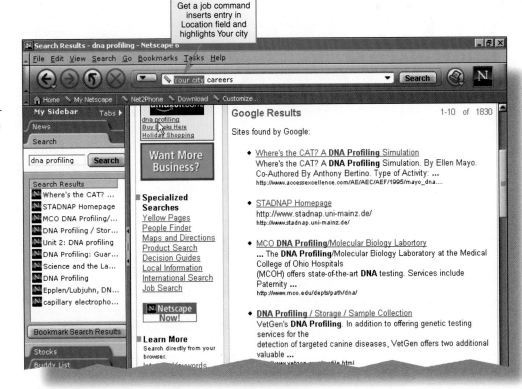

FIGURE 2-16

3 **With Your city highlighted in the Location field, type** boston **as the city name as shown in Figure 2-17.**

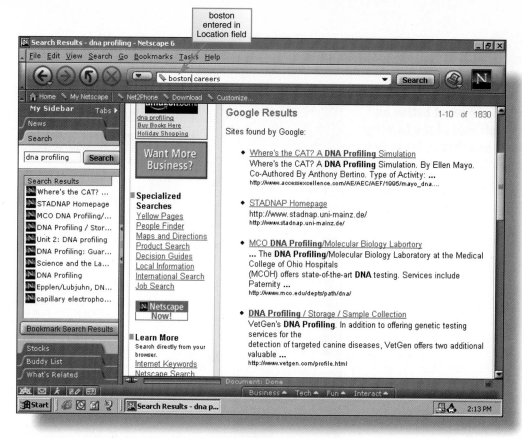

FIGURE 2-17

4 **Press the ENTER key.**

Netscape displays the Boston - Jobs and Careers page (Figure 2-18).

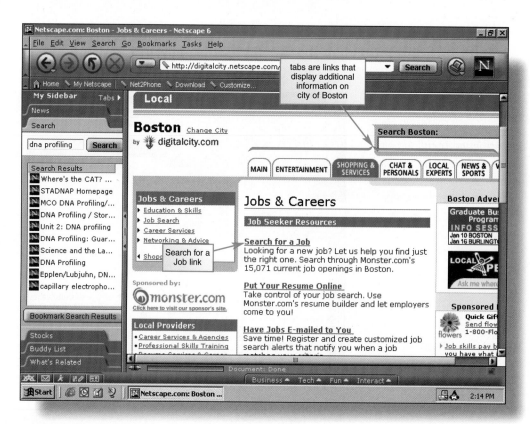

FIGURE 2-18

From the page shown in Figure 2-18, you can click links that will display information on jobs in the Boston area.

Other commands in the Choose keyword list (see Figure 2-15 on page NN 2.17) that can speed up your search for information include obtaining stock quotes, local information, shopping online, checking your e-mail, and additional information on keywords.

Using Netscape Search to Find Web Pages

Netscape's search engine, Netscape Search, includes a database of over 2 million Web sites organized into nearly 300,000 categories and reviewed by 25,000 subject experts. Netscape uses human beings to create its database of Web sites, rather than software programs. Netscape Search places the best matches at the top so you do not have to wade through unrelated links to find what you are seeking.

In an earlier set of steps, the keyword, dna profiling, was passed to Netscape Search by the Internet Keyword system because it was too general. If the keyword is general in nature, you can save time by bypassing the Internet Keyword system and send the keyword directly to Netscape Search. You bypass the Internet Keyword system by clicking the Search button to the right of the Location field, rather than pressing the ENTER key.

The following steps show how to use the Search button to access Netscape Search to locate Web pages on the topic, physical fitness.

More **About**

Netscape Search

Netscape Search is not case-sensitive. That is, the keywords Physical Fitness, physical fitness, or PHYSICAL FITNESS all return the same links. In this book, all keywords are entered in lowercase.

Steps **To Use Netscape Search to Find Web Pages**

1. **Double-click the Location field and type** physical fitness **as the entry. Point to the Search button to the right of the Location field.**

   Netscape displays a ScreenTip when you point to the Search button (Figure 2-19).

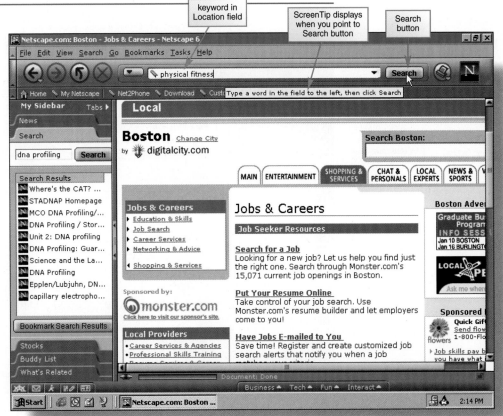

FIGURE 2-19

2 **Click the Search button. When the Search Results page displays, scroll down to display the first few links under the Reviewed Web Sites category. Read the descriptions of each link. Point to the first link under Reviewed Web Sites.**

Netscape Search displays a list of links to Web pages that have been reviewed by editors. Netscape Search refreshes the Search panel in My Sidebar with the keyword entered and the same list of links shown on the Search Results page (Figure 2-20).

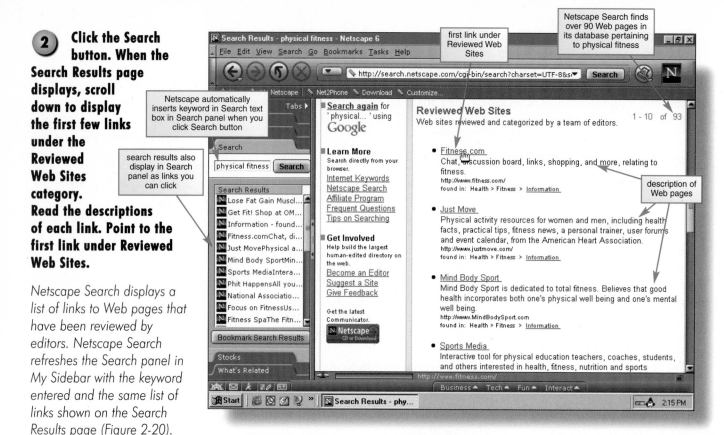

FIGURE 2-20

3 **Click the first link under Reviewed Web Sites.**

A Web page that discusses physical fitness displays (Figure 2-21). The list of physical fitness links found in the previous search continue to display on the Search panel in My Sidebar. This allows you to display other Web pages without using the Back button to redisplay the search results.

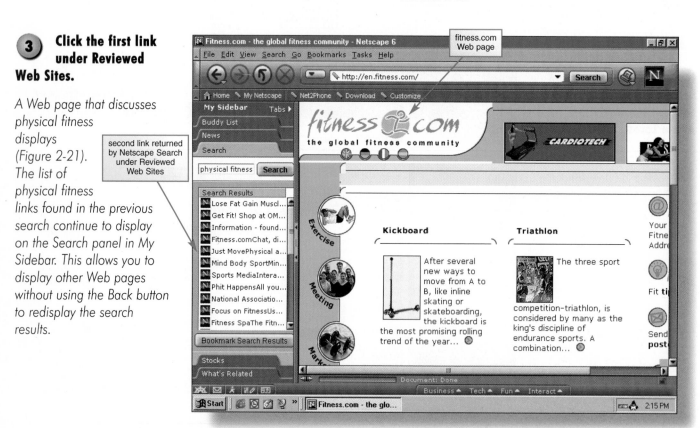

FIGURE 2-21

4 **In the Search panel in My Sidebar, click the link immediately below the link you clicked in Step 3.**

A second Web page on physical fitness displays (Figure 2-22).

5 **Click the Back button on the Navigation toolbar until the results of the Netscape Search redisplay.**

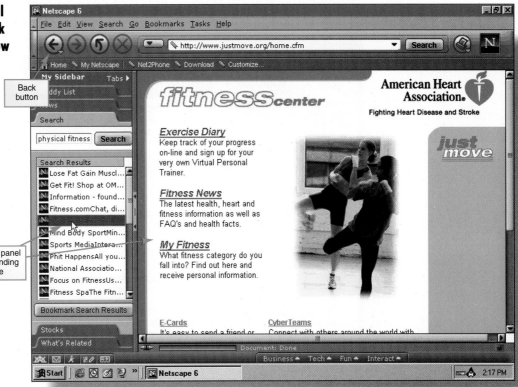

FIGURE 2-22

After clicking a link on the results page returned by Netscape Search (see Figure 2-20), you can use the Back button to redisplay the page of links to visit other Web sites. An alternative, however, is to use the Search panel on My Sidebar. As you visit sites, the Search panel maintains the physical fitness links until you request a new search by using one of the Search buttons.

In the previous set of steps, the keyword was entered in the Location field. You also can access Netscape Search by entering the keyword in the Search text box in the Search panel in My Sidebar. Another way to access Netscape Search is to click the **Search the Web command** on the Search menu or delete the entry entirely in the Location field and click the Search button. When the Netscape Search page displays (see Figure 2-8 on page NN 2.11), enter the keyword in the Search the Web or Ask a Question text box and then click the Search button.

It is important to note that after typing a keyword in the Location field, you have two search tools available, depending on your next action. If you press the ENTER key, Netscape passes the keyword to the Internet Keyword system. If, instead of pressing the ENTER key, you click the Search button, then Netscape passes the keyword to Netscape's search engine, Netscape Search.

The Order of the Results Returned by Netscape Search

Regardless of whether you use the Location field, Search panel on My Sidebar, or the Search the Web command on the Search menu to initiate a search, Netscape Search returns the results (Figure 2-23 on the next page) in the following sequence:

PARTNER SEARCH RESULTS: Sites that match your keyword and have partnered with Netscape.

Other **Ways**

1. Enter keyword in Search text box on Search panel in My Sidebar, click Search button

2. On Search menu click Search the Web, type keyword in Search text box, click Search button

3. Delete entry in Location field, click Search button

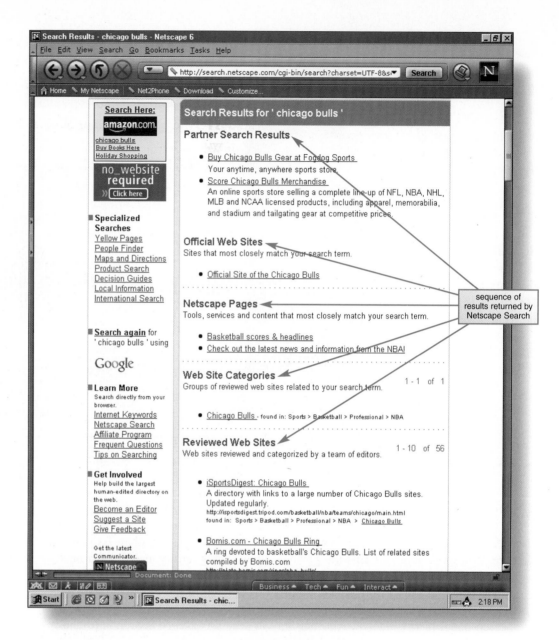

FIGURE 2-23

OFFICIAL WEB SITES: Sites that most closely match your keyword.

NETSCAPE PAGES: Tools, services, and premium content within Netscape Search that most closely match your keyword. This section will display only if the keyword pertains to commerce, such as concerts or airline flights.

WEB SITE CATEGORIES: Links to Web pages with multiple links to sites related to your keyword. This section will display only if Netscape Search has links to Web pages with multiple links for your keyword.

REVIEWED WEB SITES: Hand-selected Web sites that have been reviewed and categorized by a team of editors. This section will display only if the editors at Netscape have reviewed Web sites for your keyword.

UNREVIEWED WEB SITES: Web sites that contain the keyword in the domain name.

If no results are found in a particular section, that section will not appear. If no results are found within any of the sections, Netscape Search passes the keyword to the Google search engine, which returns a list of non-reviewed Web sites.

Netscape Search and Complex Keywords

For Netscape Search to be effective, it is best to enter in the Location field as many words that exactly qualify the subject in which you are interested. The more precise you can be, the better the results. When you enter a keyword made up of multiple words, such as physical fitness in the previous example, Netscape Search automatically enters the Boolean operator **and** between the words, so that only links to pages containing both words are returned. Links to pages that mention physical, but not fitness, and vice versa, are returned only if no pages are found that contain both words.

For Netscape Search to return links to pages containing either physical or fitness, use the Boolean operator **or**. For example, if you enter

    physical or fitness

in the Location field, then Netscape Search will return links to pages that contain either or both words.

A third Boolean operator, **and not**, indicates that the pages found cannot contain the word that follows the term and not. For example, to find pages that contain the word physical but not the word fitness, enter

    physical and not fitness

in the Location field.

You can combine Boolean operators in a keyword. For example, if you enter

    physical and fitness or exercise and not diet

in the Location field, then Netscape Search returns links to pages with the combined words, physical fitness, or the word, exercise, but only if the pages do not contain the word, diet.

You can prefix the words in a keyword with - (minus sign) and **+** (plus sign) to force the exclusion or inclusion of that word. The minus sign means the same as the Boolean operator and not. The plus sign means the same as Boolean operator and. For example, if you enter the keyword

    +physical +fitness -diet

in the Location field, then Netscape Search will return the same links as if you entered

    physical and fitness and not diet

in the Location field.

Parentheses are used to group Boolean operators together to simplify complicated keywords. For example, to find documents that contain the word physical and either the word fitness or the word exercise, enter the keyword

    physical and (fitness or exercise)

in the Location field. In this case, Netscape Search will return links to pages that include physical and fitness or physical and exercise. On the other hand, if you enter the keyword

    physical and fitness or exercise

without parentheses, then Netscape Search will return links to pages that include the two words physical and fitness or the word exercise. It is recommended that when you create a complex keyword containing more than one Boolean operator, you use parentheses to ensure the search tool interprets the keyword correctly.

More About

Complex Keywords

When Netscape Search turns a complex keyword over to the Google search engine, the list of links on the Search panel in My Sidebar from the previous search remain unchanged. That is, the Google search engine does not update.

If the order of the words you are searching for matters, then surround the phrase with quotation marks. This search technique is called **phrase searching**. Phase searching can greatly reduce the number of sites that are matched by Netscape Search. For example, if you enter

```
"physical fitness"
```

(with the quotation marks) in the Location field, then Netscape Search returns links only to pages containing the term, physical fitness.

Netscape Search allows the use of the asterisk (*) at the end of words. The asterisk (*), which is referred to as the **wildcard character**, is a substitute for any combination of characters. For example, if you enter the keyword

```
phy*
```

in the Location field, Netscape Search will return links to pages containing physical, physics, physiology, and so on. The wildcard character is particularly useful if you are unsure of the keyword's correct spelling, when you are trying to match a word that may or may not be plural, or might use one of several verb tenses. For example, if you wanted to find sites that pertained to swimming, enter

```
swim*
```

in the Location field, and Netscape Search will return links to pages with the words swim, swims, swimmer, swimming, and swimsuit. Netscape Search does not support arbitrary wildcards, so searches on *ming or sw*ing will not work.

You can mix and match the above search methods to create very complex searches. For example, if you enter

```
physical fitness +swim* -jogging
```

Netscape Search will return links for sites pertaining to physical fitness and alternative forms of swim, but will exclude all links to pages that mention jogging.

Entering a Complex Keyword Using Netscape Search

The following steps show how to enter the complex keyword

```
physical fitness +jogging +tennis -swim* -calisthenics
```

This search will find links to pages that include the terms, physical fitness and jogging and tennis. Further, it will exclude links to pages with variants of the word swim or the term calisthenics.

 To Enter a Complex Keyword Using Netscape Search

1 **Double-click the Location field and type** physical fitness +jogging +tennis -swim* -calisthenics **as the entry. Point to the Search button to the right of the Location field.**

The complex keyword displays in the Location field as shown in Figure 2-24.

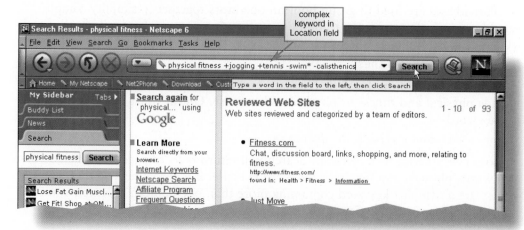

FIGURE 2-24

2 Click the Search button. When the **Google Results page** displays, scroll down to display the first few links and their descriptions.

The first 10 links to Web pages found by the Google search engine display (Figure 2-25).

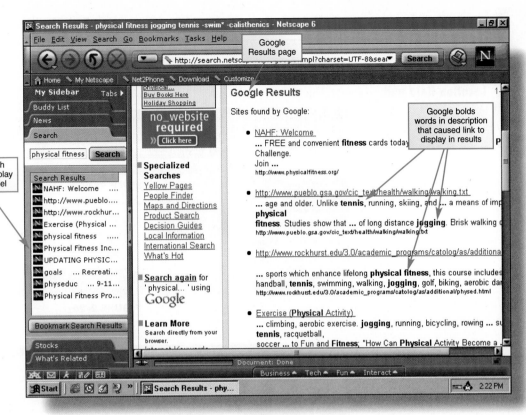

FIGURE 2-25

Complex keywords submitted to Netscape Search are passed to the Web-wide Google search engine as shown in Figure 2-25. The Google search engine bolds the words in the description of each link that match the words in the complex keyword.

Searching for Keywords in Web Page Titles Using Netscape Search

A **title search** is a Netscape Search feature that restricts searches to the titles of Web pages. To conduct a title search, append the word, title, followed by a colon to the front of the keyword. For example, if you enter

`title:physical fitness`

in the Location field and click the Search button, then Netscape Search will return links to pages with physical fitness in the title of the Web page. This search method is shown in the steps on the next page.

Steps **To Search for Keywords in Web Page Titles Using Netscape Search**

1 **Double-click the Location field and type** `title:physical fitness` **as the entry. Point to the Search button (Figure 2-26).**

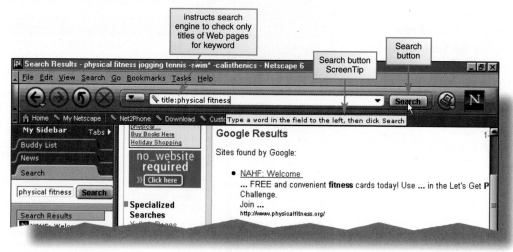

FIGURE 2-26

2 **Click the Search button. When the Google Results page displays, scroll down to display the first few links and their descriptions.**

Google displays a list of links to Web pages with the keywords, physical or fitness in their title (Figure 2-27).

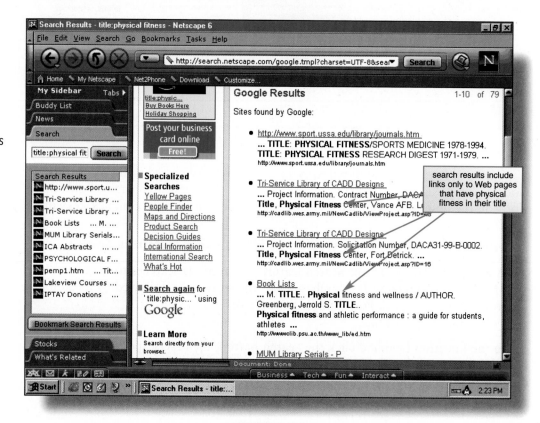

FIGURE 2-27

Netscape Search passes the complex keyword over to the Google search engine, which means it could not find any matching Web pages in its own database. The Google search engine returns a list of links to Web pages that include physical fitness in their title. Table 2-3 summarizes the Netscape Search operators and special characters you can use in a keyword to qualify the subject for which you are searching.

Table 2-3 Netscape Search Operators and Special Characters

CATEGORY OF OPERATOR	OPERATOR	KEYWORD EXAMPLES	DESCRIPTION
Boolean	and (+)	art and music smoking health hazards fish +pollutants +runoff	Requires both words to be in the page. No operator between words or the plus sign (+) are shortcuts for the Boolean operator and.
	or	mental illness or insane canine or dog or puppy flight attendant or stewardess or steward	Requires only one of the two words to be in the page.
	and not (-)	auto* and not SUV and not convertible computers −programming shakespeare− hamlet −(romeo +juliet)	Excludes page with the word following and not. The minus sign (-) is a shortcut for the Boolean operator and not.
Parentheses	( )	physics and (relativity or einstein)	Parentheses group portions of Boolean operators together.
Phrase Searching	" "	"harry potter" "19th century literature"	Requires the exact phrase within quotation marks to be in the page.
Wildcard	*	writ* clou*	The asterisk (*) at the end of words substitutes for any combination of characters.
Title	title:	title:new york title:(indiana or hoosier state)	The word title: or t: instructs Netscape Search to search titles of Web pages.

Finding Text on a Web Page

Netscape includes the **Find in this Page command** on the Search menu to search for text in the active Web page. Initially, the steps below use Netscape Search to display links to Web pages on the topic, "sun exposure" and complexion. The steps next display the first Web page under Sites found by Google, and then find the first and second occurrence of the word, complexion, on the active Web page.

 Steps To Find Text on a Web Page

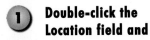 Double-click the Location field and type "sun exposure" and complexion **as the entry. Click the Search button to the right of the Location field. When the Google Results page displays, point to the first link under Sites found by Google.**

Netscape Search displays a list of links to Web pages found by Google that discuss sun exposure and complexion (Figure 2-28).

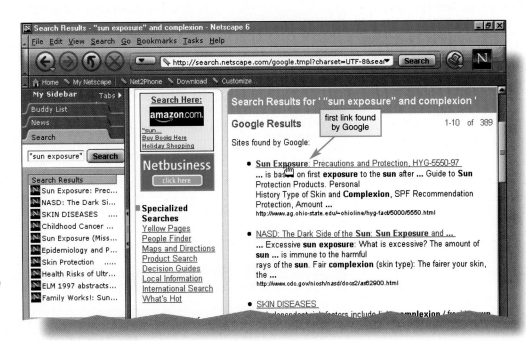

FIGURE 2-28

2 Click the first link under the Google Results. Click Search on the menu bar and point to the Find in This Page command.

Netscape displays the Web page that corresponds to the first link under Google Results, and the Search menu displays (Figure 2-29).

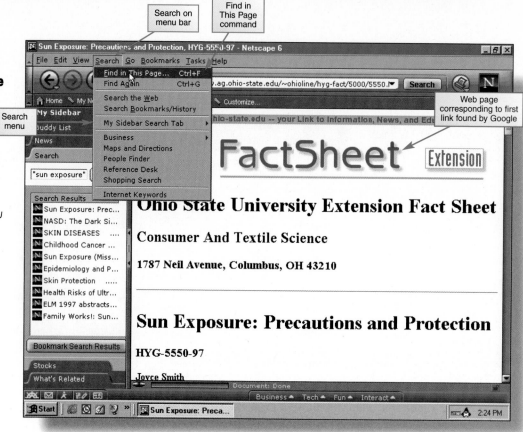

FIGURE 2-29

3 Click Find in This Page. When the Find in This Page dialog box displays, type complexion in the Find text text box. Point to the Find button.

The Find in This Page dialog box displays as shown in Figure 2-30.

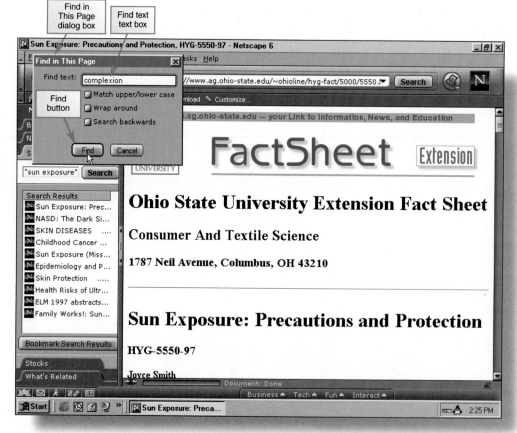

FIGURE 2-30

4 **Click the Find button.**

Netscape highlights the first occurrence of the word complexion (Figure 2-31). In this example, the text, complexion, is found within the plural word, complexions.

5 **Click the Find button a second time.**

Netscape highlights the second occurrence of the word, complexion.

6 **Click the Cancel button in the Find in This Page dialog box. Click the Back button to return to the Netscape Search page to redisplay the Google results for the keyword "sun exposure" and complexion (see Figure 2-28 on page NN 2.27).**

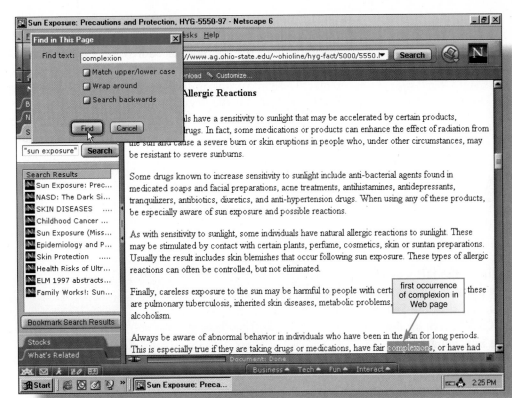

FIGURE 2-31

Other Ways

1. Press CTRL+F
2. Press ALT+S, type F

The Find in This Page dialog box shown in Figure 2-31 includes three options. If you click the **Match upper/lower case check box**, then the search will be case-sensitive. If you click the **Wrap around check box**, then when Netscape reaches the bottom of the document, it will continue to search for the text at the top of the document. If you click the **Search backwards check box**, then Netscape will conduct the search from bottom to top, rather than from top to bottom.

If you close the Find in This Page dialog box, Netscape will remember the text for which you last searched. You then can use the **Find Again command** on the Search menu (see Figure 2-29) to search for the text you previously entered in the Find text text box.

Using Multiple Search Engines to Search the Web

If the results returned by Netscape Search or Google do not contain adequate information, you can have Netscape use up to 15 additional search engines at the same time. Each search engine has its own database. Thus, each will return a different set of links to Web pages for the keyword you enter.

The Search panel must be in the **advanced mode** for Netscape to use multiple search engines. The alternative to advanced mode is basic mode. When the Search panel is in **basic mode**, Netscape uses Netscape Search to search its database; if it fails, it then passes the keyword to Google to do a Web-wide search.

More About

Web Search Engines

Fierce competition exists among search engines. Each search engine claims to have the largest index of Web resources. This competition is healthy and ensures that there are large, up-to-date indexes of Web resources.

To place the Search panel in the advanced mode, click the **Advanced command** on the **My Sidebar Search Tab submenu**. You display the My Sidebar Search Tab submenu by pointing to the **My Sidebar Search Tab command** on the Search menu. Once the Search panel is in advanced mode, you can select additional search engines on the panel. To search using multiple search engines, you must enter the keyword in the Search text box in the Search panel in My Sidebar.

The following steps illustrate how to use multiple search engines to list links to pages with information on the topic, "sun and exposure" and complexion.

Steps **To Use Multiple Search Engines to Search the Web**

1 **If My Sidebar is hidden, click its handle on the left side of the window to display it. If necessary, click the Search tab. Click Search on the menu bar, point to My Sidebar Search Tab, and then point to Advanced on the My Sidebar Search Tab submenu.**

The Search panel in My Sidebar, the Search menu, and the My Sidebar Search Tab submenu display (Figure 2-32).

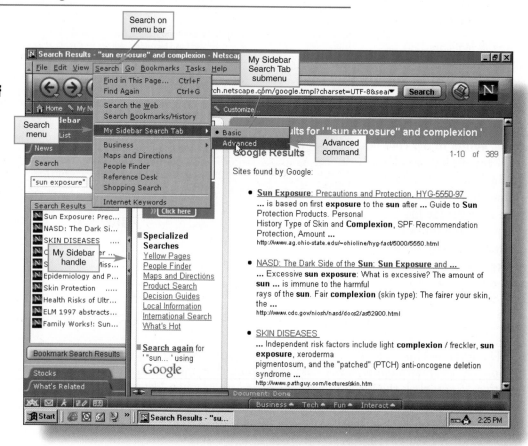

FIGURE 2-32

② Click Advanced.

The Search panel in My Sidebar lists several search engines (Figure 2-33). The list of search engines on your computer may be different.

in advanced mode, search panel displays list of search engines with check boxes

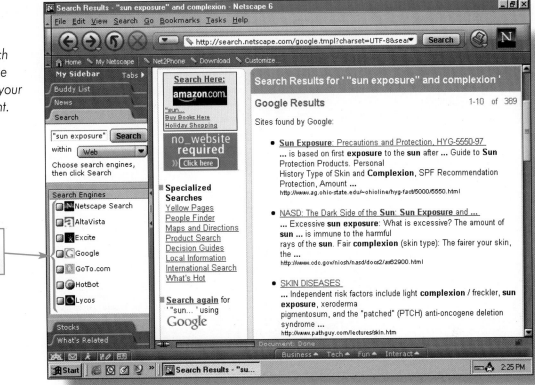

FIGURE 2-33

③ In the Search panel, click the check box to the left of Netscape Search, AltaVista, Excite, Google, and HotBot.

The Search panel displays as shown in Figure 2-34.

five of seven search engines selected

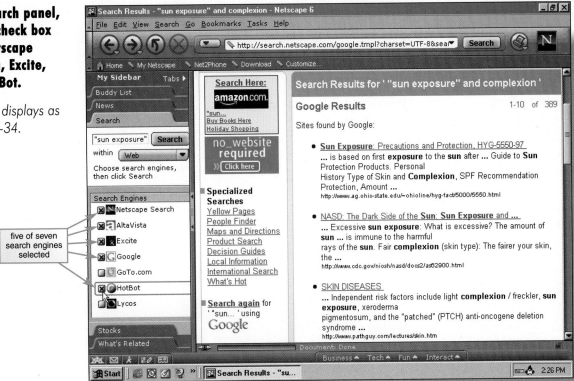

FIGURE 2-34

4 If necessary, click Web in the within list, and then point to the Search button in the Search panel.

The Search panel displays as shown in Figure 2-35.

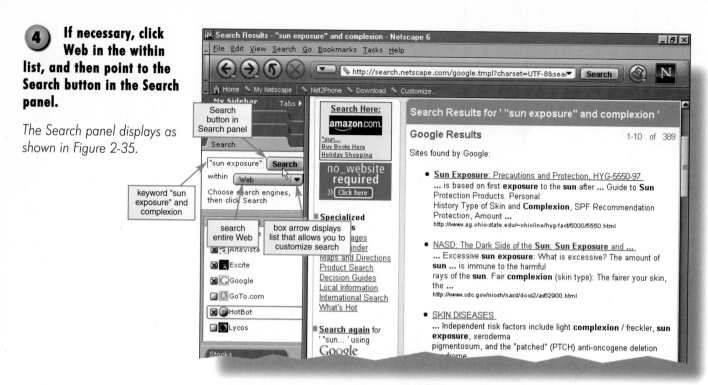

FIGURE 2-35

5 Click the Search button. When the Search Results page displays, click the My Sidebar handle to hide My Sidebar so that the Search Results page displays in its entirety. Drag the split bar between the two frames so it appears as shown in Figure 2-36. Click the first item in the top frame.

Netscape displays the Search Results page with two frames. The top frame lists links to Web pages with information on sun exposure and complexion returned by each search engine in page rank order. The lower frame displays a summary of the item selected in the top frame.

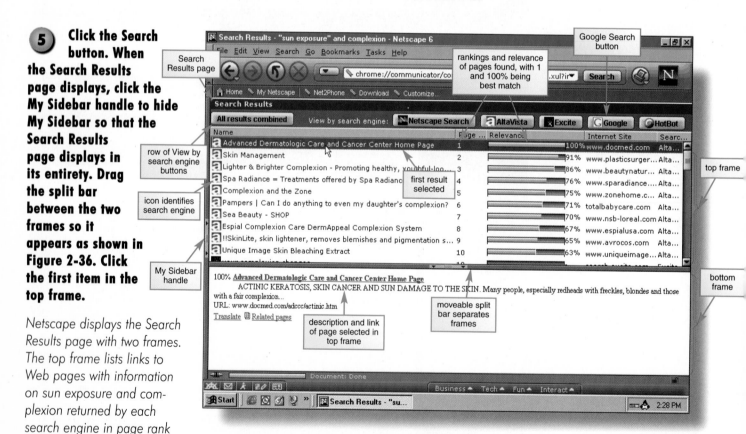

FIGURE 2-36

6 **Click several of the Web page titles in the top frame. Use the arrow keys to scroll down through the list in the top frame. Click the Google Search button in the View by search engine area.**

Netscape displays a list of links to Web pages returned by the Google search engine with information on sun exposure and complexion (Figure 2-37).

7 **Click the Home button on the Personal toolbar to display the home page. If necessary, click the My Sidebar handle to hide My Sidebar.**

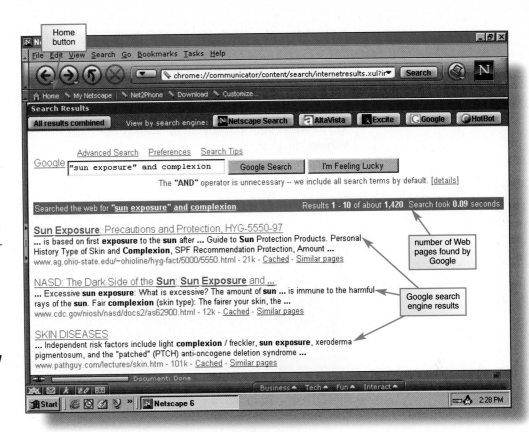

FIGURE 2-37

An icon precedes each row in the top frame. The icon identifies the search engine that found the Web page (see Figure 2-36). If you click a Web page title in the top frame, the link and a short description of the corresponding Web page display in the lower frame.

You can bookmark all of the links displayed in the top frame of the Search Results page by clicking the **Bookmark Search Results button** that displays at the bottom of the Search panel in My Sidebar after completing a search (see Figure 2-32 on page NN 2.30). You then can display the list at anytime by clicking Bookmarks on the menu bar and pointing to Search: "sun exposure" and complexion.

You can click several buttons and items on the Search Results page (see Figure 2-36) to change the view. Each of the five buttons on the right in the View by search engine area display a subset of the results. You also can click the column headings (Name, Page Ranking, Relevance, Internet Site, Search Engine) to sort the results by that column. You can change the size of the two frames by dragging the split bar up or down. You also can click the small rectangle in the middle of the split bar to hide or display the lower frame.

One other control that can speed the search is the **within list** below the Search text box on the Search panel in My Sidebar (see Figure 2-35). When you click the within button arrow, a list of categories displays (Music – Artist, Shareware, Shopping, Tech News, and Web). All the categories, with the exception of Web, limit the search to a subset of the Web.

Searching the Web Using the Netscape Subject Directory

Netscape Search includes a subject directory that allows you to start with general categories and become increasingly more specific as you close in on the topic for which you are searching. Because the Netscape Search directory uses a series of menus to organize links to Web pages, you can perform searches without entering keywords. The following steps display the Netscape Search page, which includes the subject directory.

Steps ## To Display the Netscape Search Directory

1 **Type** search. netscape.com **in the Location field (Figure 2-38).**

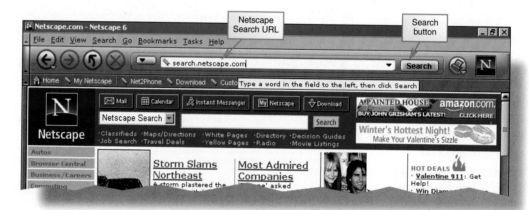

FIGURE 2-38

2 **Press the ENTER key.**

The Netscape Search page displays as shown in Figure 2-39.

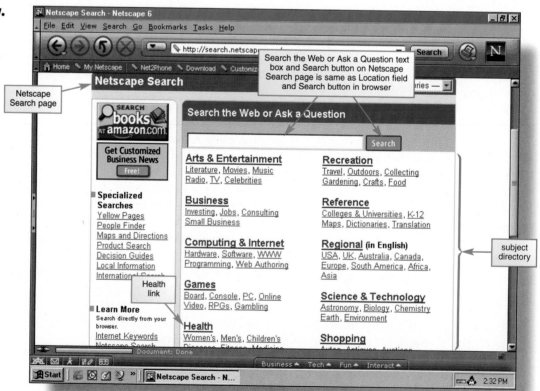

FIGURE 2-39

The **Search the Web or Ask a Question text box** and the Search button below the Netscape Search page title allow you to perform a keyword search in the same fashion as the Location field in the Navigation toolbar or the Search text box in the Search panel in My Sidebar. The links on the left side of the Web page allow you to display telephone directories, online maps, and more. The links below the Search the Web or Ask a Question text box comprise the top-level Netscape search directory.

Web pages in the subject directory are organized into the broad subject categories. You must decide into which category the search topic falls and then select the corresponding link. When you select a general link, another page of links displays with more specific topics from which to choose. You continue following the links until you find the information you are seeking or until you get to a point where you prefer to use a keyword to search the remainder of the subject directory.

Assume you want information on carbohydrates and dieting, which is a health-related topic. Because health is a major category, it is appropriate to start the search with it. The following steps show how to navigate through the subject directory to retrieve information about carbohydrates and nutrition.

Steps To Search the Web Using the Netscape Search Subject Directory

1 Click the Health link on the Netscape Search page. When the Health page displays, scroll down and point to the Nutrition link.

The Health page displays as shown in Figure 2-40. Scrolling through the Health page reveals links to virtually every health category imaginable. The number in parentheses to the right of the Nutrition link indicates Netscape Search has hundreds of links to pages related specifically to nutrition in the subject directory.

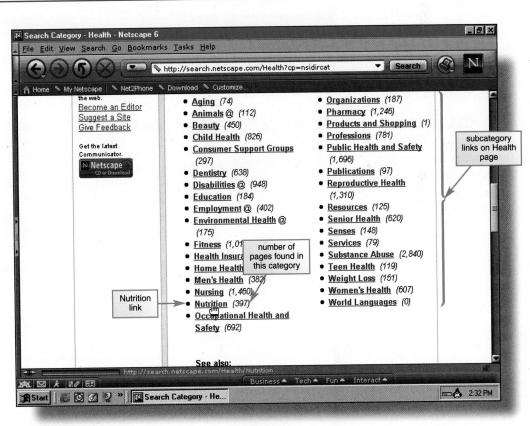

FIGURE 2-40

2 **Click the Nutrition link. When the Nutrition page displays, scroll down and point to the Dietary Options link.**

The Nutrition page displays (Figure 2-41). Each time you click a link to display the next subcategory of links, the Search only in Nutrition option button below the Search the Web or Ask a Question text box changes to allow you to search the remainder of the directory.

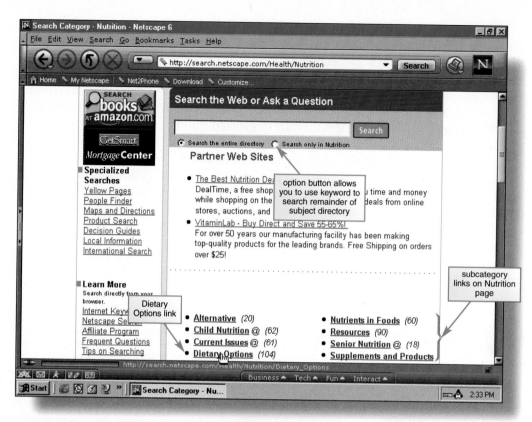

FIGURE 2-41

3 **Click the Dietary Options link. When the Dietary Options page displays, scroll down and point to the Low Carbohydrate link.**

The Dietary Options page displays (Figure 2-42).

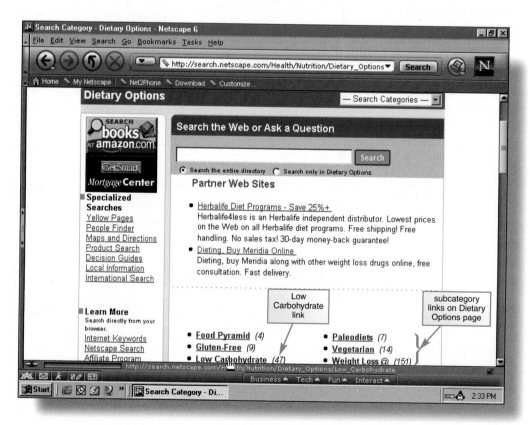

FIGURE 2-42

4 **Click the Low Carbohydrate link. Scroll down and view the links and corresponding explanations.**

Netscape Search displays many links to pages that discuss low carbohydrates, but not necessarily nutrition (Figure 2-43).

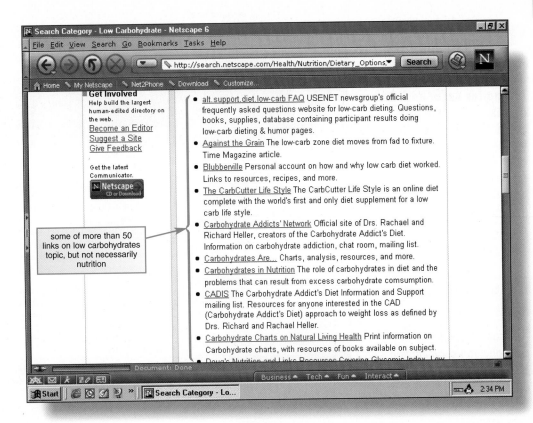

FIGURE 2-43

5 **Scroll to the top of the Low Carbohydrate page and type** carbohydrates and nutrition **in the Search the Web or Ask a Question text box. Click the Search only in Low Carbohydrate option button below the text box. Point to the Search button.**

The Low Carbohydrate page displays as shown in Figure 2-44.

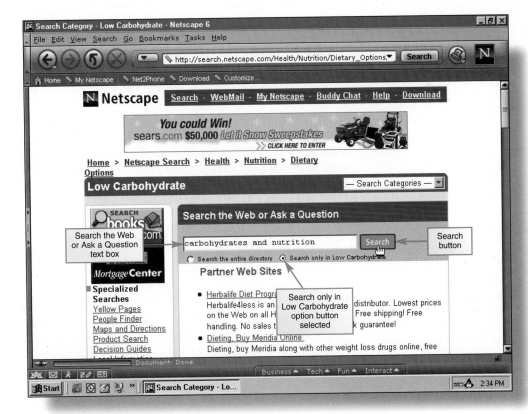

FIGURE 2-44

6 **Click the Search button. When the Netscape Search results page displays, read the summaries under each link and then click the link titled Carbohydrates in Nutrition.**

A Web page titled, Carbohydrates in Nutrition, displays (Figure 2-45).

7 **Click Bookmarks on the menu bar, and then click Add Current Page.**

Netscape bookmarks the Carbohydrates in Nutrition page. This bookmark will be used later in this project.

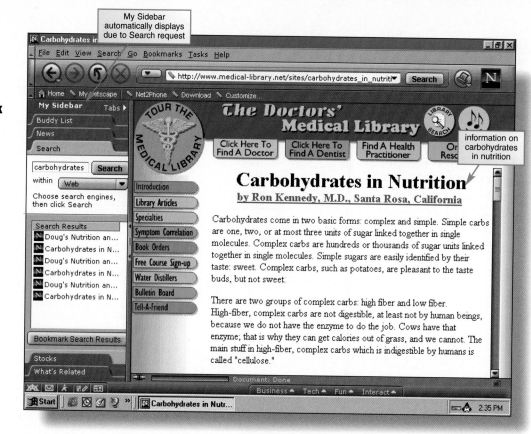

FIGURE 2-45

The Web page in Figure 2-45 contains information about high-fiber and low-fiber carbohydrates. If this page does not contain the desired information, you can try the links on the page or use the Back button and try another link on the Search Results page.

By completing the previous steps, you learned to search the World Wide Web using Netscape's subject directory. Selecting from a list of categories offers you an alternative to creating sophisticated keywords and using a search engine. You may need to spend considerable time, however, traveling through several levels of menus in the search directory, only to discover that no information on the topic is available.

Using the Google Search Engine

The **Google search engine** has over one billion Web pages indexed in its database. This is the same search engine to which Netscape Search passes your keyword for a Web-wide search if it is unsuccessful in finding links in its subject directory.

If you prefer, you can bypass Netscape Search and use Google directly by visiting google.com. Google uses the same search operators and special characters listed in Table 2-3 on page NN 2.27, except it does not support the Boolean operator, or. Google ignores common words and characters in a keyword, such as where, how, and single digits and letters. Also, like Netscape Search, Google searches are not case-sensitive. Thus, Jefferson davis, Jefferson Davis, and jEFFerson dAVIs will return the same results.

The following steps show how to use Google to locate Web pages on the topic, college study guide.

Steps **To Search the Web Using Google**

1 Double-click the Location field, type `google.com` as the entry, and then press the ENTER key. When the Google page displays, type "`college study guide`" in the Search text box. Point to the Google Search button.

The Google page displays as shown in Figure 2-46.

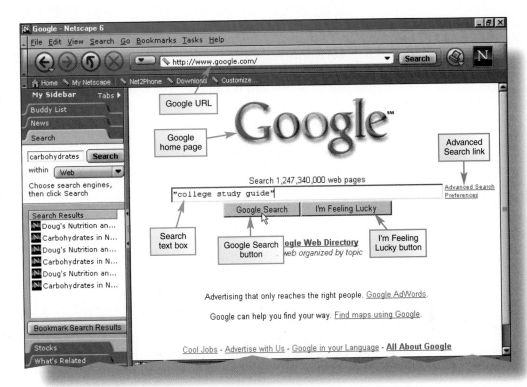

FIGURE 2-46

2 Click the Google Search button. When Google displays the results of the search, scroll through the list of links and read the descriptions of the Web pages.

Google displays the first 10 of 175 links to Web pages that contain the phrase, college study guide (Figure 2-47). Because Netscape also uses Google for Web-wide searches, it automatically shows My Sidebar with the Search panel active. The links in the Search panel correspond to the links on the Google results page.

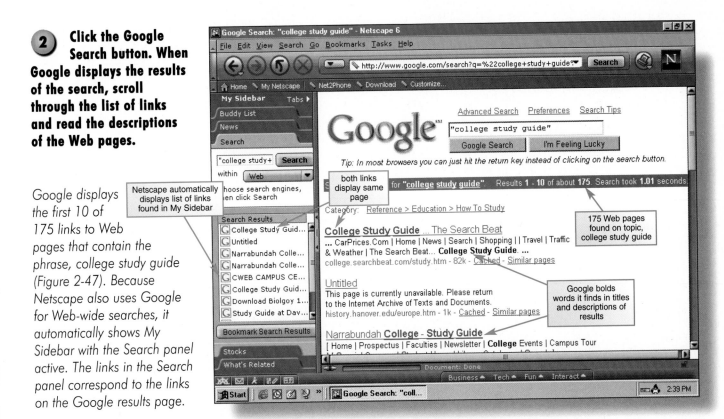

FIGURE 2-47

Google finds pages that are both important and relevant to the keyword. In deciding whether it should include a page in its results, Google checks what the pages that link to the page under consideration have to say about it. Google also gives preference to pages in which the words in a keyword are near each other.

In reviewing the results in Figure 2-47 on the previous page, it is easy to find keywords in the description of a page, because Google bolds them. It also displays the byte size and the URL of the page. Two links, Cached and Similar Pages, are in each description. If you click Cached, Google displays the page as it was when it examined and added it to the database. If you click Similar Pages, Google displays a list of pages that are similar to the page.

Whereas the Google search button displays the search results, the **I'm Feeling Lucky button** (see Figure 2-46 on the previous page) automatically displays the highest ranking page or first page Google lists on the results page.

Google Advanced Search

Google has an advanced search that allows you to narrow your search until you find what you are seeking. The advanced search allows you to control your search without using Boolean operators. It also allows you to restrict your search to a given Web site, exclude pages from a Web site, restrict your search to a given language, find all pages that link to a given Web page, and find all pages that are related to a given Web page.

The following steps show how to search for the phrase, florida vacations; exclude all pages that contain the word, disney; exclude any .com site; include only pages written in English; and filter out any adult sites.

Steps To Search the Web Using the Google Advanced Search

1 Type google.com in the Location field and press the ENTER key. Click the Advanced Search link to the right of the Google search text box (see Figure 2-46 on page NN 2.39). When the Advanced Search page displays, click the My Sidebar handle to hide it. Type florida vacations in the Find results with the exact phrase text box. Press the TAB key and then type disney in the Find results without the words text box. Select English in the Return pages written in list. Select Don't in the return results from the site or domain list, and then type .com in the corresponding text box. Click the Filter using SafeSearch option button. Point to the Google Search button.

The Google Advanced Search page displays as shown in Figure 2-48.

2 Click the Google Search button. When the results of the search display, scroll down to the bottom of the page.

The results of the advanced search display as shown in Figure 2-49.

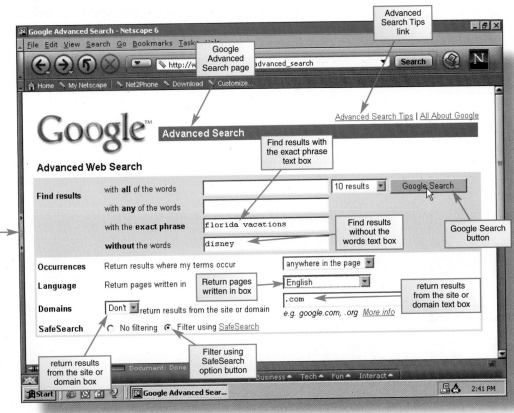

FIGURE 2-48

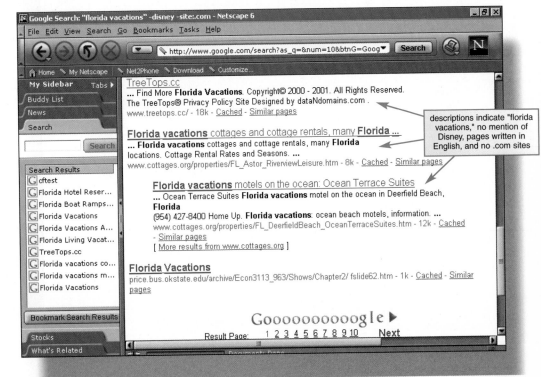

FIGURE 2-49

Google converts the Advanced Search entries to a keyword search as shown in the Search text box in Figure 2-49 on the previous page. If the results are less than adequate, you can modify the keyword in the Search text box and have Google search the Web again. If you use the Back button to return to the Google Advanced Search page to change the search, you must start over again because the entries selected no longer display.

Using the AltaVista Search Engine

AltaVista (Figure 2-50) is one of the most widely used search engines. It has an index of over 350 million Web pages. Each day, its **robot programs**, also called **spiders**, visit over 10 million sites, capturing URLs and corresponding text to update its index. The robot programs also check for **dead links**, which are URLs that no longer work. No human judgment is involved in selecting Web pages to index. Because no editorial decisions are made regarding content, the AltaVista search engine may return a higher number of links that do not directly apply to your keyword, but its sheer size makes it one of the most popular and most frequently used search engines on the Web.

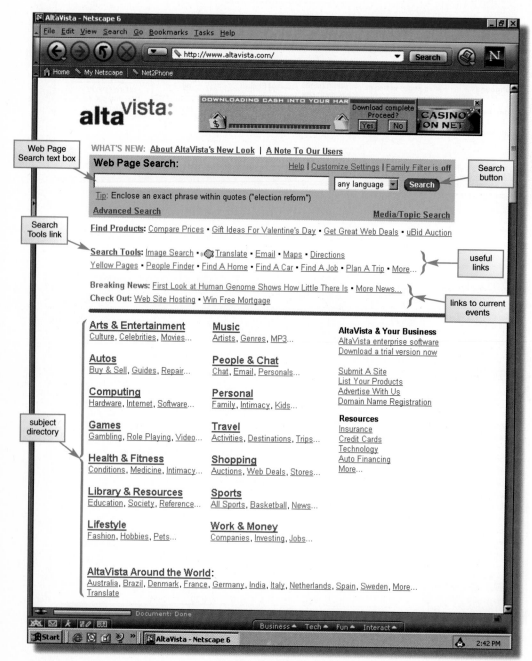

FIGURE 2-50

Figure 2-50 shows that AltaVista is much more than a search engine. Its home page includes a subject directory, free e-mail, free Internet access, a message system, and a language translator. Like Netscape Search, a team of editors, rather than a robot, compiles the subject directory. The left side of Figure 2-50 also shows that there are multiple levels of search engines and that you can specify search categories, such as Web pages (the default), images, maps, people, and much more. The following sections illustrate the search capabilities of AltaVista.

AltaVista Simple Search

You initiate a **Simple search** with AltaVista by entering a keyword in the **Web Page Search** text box (see Figure 2-50). The following steps show how to complete a simple search for the keyword, mark twain.

 To Search the Web Using the AltaVista Simple Search

1 **If necessary, click the My Sidebar handle to hide My Sidebar. Double-click the Location field, type** altavista.com **and then press the ENTER key. Type** mark twain **in the Web Page Search text box, and then point to the Search button.**

The AltaVista home page displays as shown in Figure 2-51.

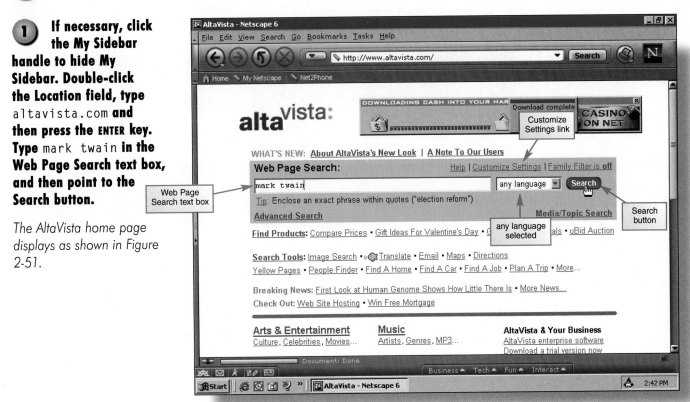

FIGURE 2-51

2 **Click the Search button. When AltaVista returns the results of the Web-wide search, scroll down and review the suggested links on the first page, and then scroll up to the top of the page. If necessary, click the My Sidebar handle to hide My Sidebar. Point to the Mark Twain Online link to the right of See reviewed sites in.**

The results display as shown in Figure 2-52. AltaVista found thousands of Web pages with mark twain in their description.

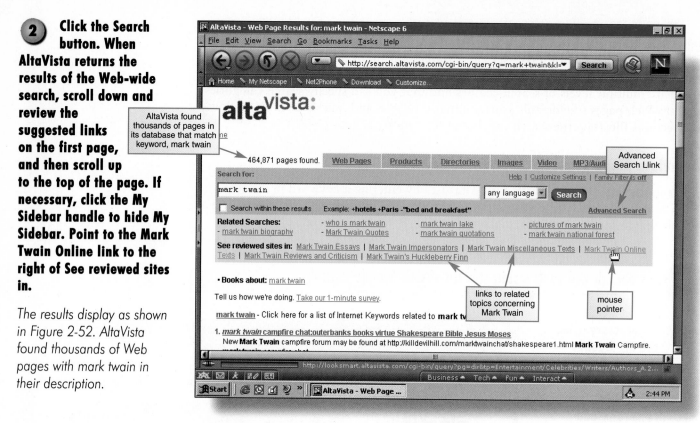

FIGURE 2-52

3 **Click the Mark Twain Online link. When the results display, scroll down through the links.**

AltaVista displays the links and corresponding descriptions of the top 10 sites of the editor-selected sites found (Figure 2-53).

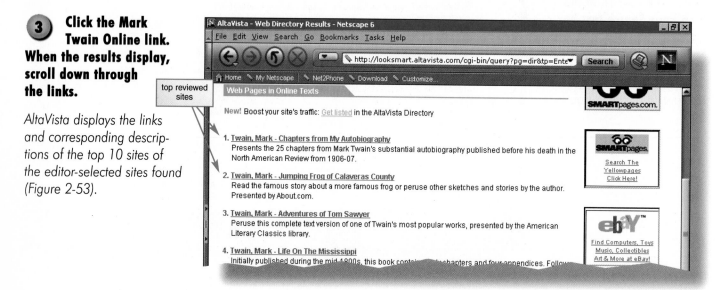

FIGURE 2-53

The initial Web-wide search found several thousand Web pages (see Figure 2-52) for the keyword, mark twain. AltaVista sequences the results to show first the pages containing both words, then both words closest together, and then nearest the top of the page. By clicking the link, Mark Twain Online, next to See reviewed sites in, you instruct AltaVista to display only links in its subject directory database. Recall that the subject directory is organized by editors, not software programs, and thus is more valuable.

You can instruct AltaVista to search any one of 25 languages or search all 25 available languages. The default is any language as shown in Figure 2-51 on page NN 2.43. You also can customize the search to display additional Web page information by clicking the **Customize Settings link** shown in Figure 2-51. The Customize Settings link allows you to instruct AltaVista to display additional page characteristics, such as last date modified, Web page size in bytes, and Web page language.

Table 2-4 summarizes the Boolean operators and other special characters you can use in keywords to customize a Simple search in AltaVista.

Table 2-4 AltaVista Simple Search Operators and Special Characters		
OPERATOR/SPECIAL CHARACTER	KEYWORD EXAMPLES	DESCRIPTION
No operator	police detective	If you use no operator, then the search will be for either police or detective. Pages with both words rank higher.
Case Sensitivity	Mark Twain (case-sensitive) mark twain (not case-sensitive)	If you use capital letters in a keyword, then the search will be case-sensitive.
""	"Romeo and Juliet"	Quotation marks make the keyword a required phrase.
+	+ picasso art	Word that follows plus sign must be found in page.
-	+picasso —art	Word that follows minus sign cannot be found in page.
*	+pica*	The asterisk (*) at the end of words substitutes for any combination of characters.
title:	title: mark twain	Keyword must be in page title.

You can improve your AltaVista search by following these suggestions, many of which apply to other search engines as well:

▶ Include in your keyword additional words that are likely to appear on pages that discuss the material for which you are searching.
▶ Include alternative words. For example, instead of cat, use: cat kitten feline tomcat.
▶ Use quotation marks to create phrases, so that AltaVista finds the exact sequence of words.
▶ Use the asterisk (*) to find plurals of words.
▶ Use lowercase keywords.
▶ Use a hyphen alternative. For example, use: email e-mail.
▶ Limit the search by language.

AltaVista Power Search

AltaVista recommends that beginners use the Power search as a way to fine-tune a search. The **Power search page** makes it easy for you to limit the results in many ways. You approach the subject area by filling out an online form primarily composed of lists (Figure 2-54 on the next page). The Power Search page is divided into sections titled Search By, Date, Language, Location, and Show Me. At the top of the page, you enter the keyword, similar to the way you enter a keyword for a Simple search. You then make selections in the sections of the form. Table 2-5 on page NN 2.47 explains the sections and the selections you can make.

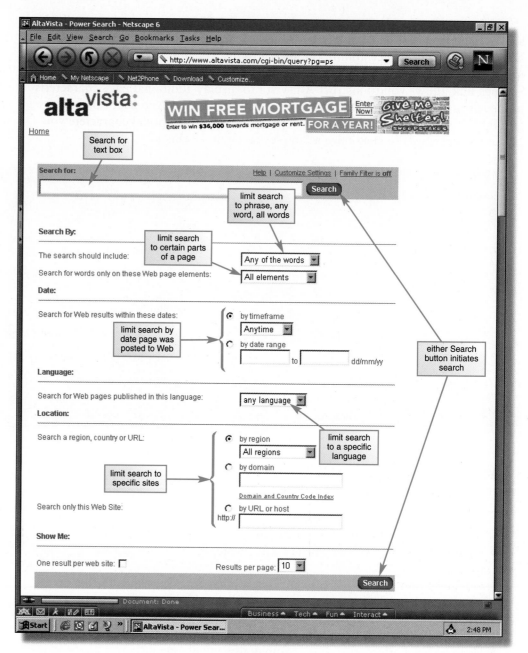

FIGURE 2-54

Each box on the Power search page has a default value. Therefore, you can skip one, several, or all the boxes. If you leave the default values in the boxes, then the Power search becomes a Simple search. Power search provides two Search buttons: one at the top of the page, the other at the bottom. Clicking either button initiates the search.

The following steps use the AltaVista Power search to find links for the exact phrase, stephen king, in the titles of English language Web pages posted in the past year.

Table 2-5 AltaVista Power Search Sections and Entries

POWER SEARCH FORM SECTION	TITLE OF ENTRY	CHOICES
Search By	The search should include	1. **All the words** (find only pages with all the words)
		2. **Any** (find pages with any of the words)
		3. **Exact** (find pages with all the words in the order given)
		4. **Boolean** (use the specified operators and, or, and not, near)
	Search for words only on these Web page elements	1. **All elements** (searches all parts of pages)
		2. **Page text** (searches only text on pages)
		3. **Title of the page** (searches only title of pages)
		4. **Links to URL** (searches links on pages)
Date	Search for Web results within these dates	1. **By timeframe** (searches pages within timeframe)
		2. **By date range** (searches pages within date range)
Language	Search for Web pages published in this language	1. **Any language** (searches all 25 languages supported by AltaVista)
		2. **Pick a language** (searches only the language selected)
Location	Search a region, country, or URL	1. **By region** (search only this region)
		2. **By domain** (search only this domain)
	Search only this Web site	1. **By URL or host** (search only this URL)
Show Me	One result per Web site	1. **Check box selected** (search returns one page per Web site)
		2. **Check box unselected** (search returns as many pages as possible per Web site)
	Results per page	1. **Select number** (determines how many links will display per page)

 ## To Search the Web Using the AltaVista Power Search

1 **Double-click the Location field, type** altavista.com **and then press the ENTER key. Click the Search Tools link below the Search for text box (see Figure 2-50 on page NN 2.42). When the AltaVista Tools page displays, click the Power Search link below the Tools category, and then type** stephen king **in the Search for text box. Select Exact phrase in The search should include list. Select Title of the page in the Search for words only on these Web page elements list.**

The top of the Power Search page displays as shown in Figure 2-55.

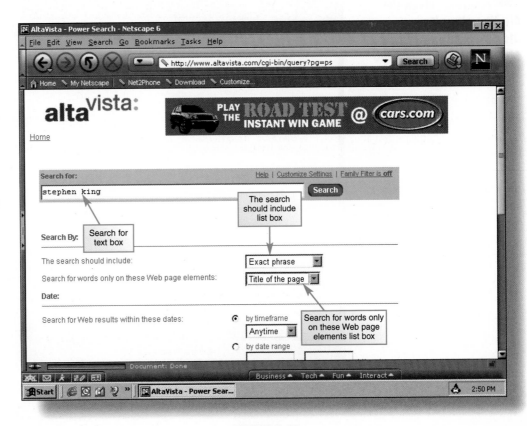

FIGURE 2-55

2 Scroll down and select Year in the by timeframe list in the Date area. Select English in the Search for Web pages published in this language list in the Language area. Point to the Search button at the bottom of the page.

The lower portion of the Power Search page displays as shown in Figure 2-56.

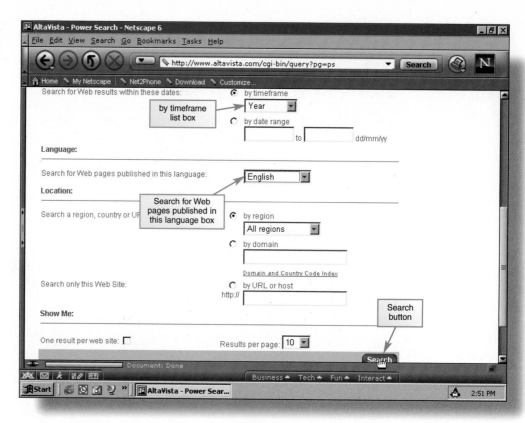

FIGURE 2-56

3 Click the Search button. When the AltaVista Results page displays, close My Sidebar. Scroll down to display the last two links on the page.

The AltaVista search engine returns a list of English-language Web pages posted in the past year with the phrase, stephen king, in their titles (Figure 2-57).

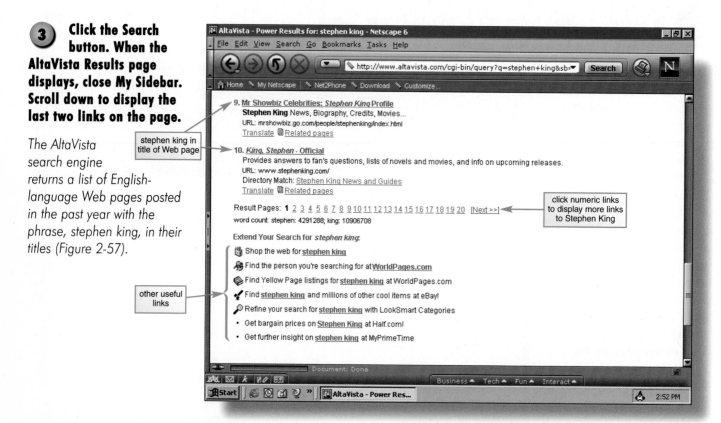

FIGURE 2-57

The Power Search page offers you a convenient way to specify exactly what you want without requiring that you memorize operators and special characters to place in your keyword.

AltaVista Advanced Search

The AltaVista Advanced search is for experienced users. The **Advanced search** gives you the same capabilities of the Power search, plus additional commands that you can use to limit the search. A major difference between the Advanced search and the Power search is that with the Advanced search you primarily use operators, special characters, and commands in your keyword to limit searches, rather than choosing from lists. The Advanced search also allows you to sort the results by any word in the keyword. See In the Lab 6, Part 4 on page NN 2.77 for an example of the use of the AltaVista's Advanced search.

AltaVista Multimedia Search

You can use the AltaVista search engine to find Images (pictures), MP3/Audio, and Video. The following steps show how to display images of the paintings of the famous impressionist artist Claude Monet.

More About

AltaVista Advanced Search

AltaVista offers a tutorial for Advanced Search in AltaVista Help. In Help, click Advanced Search and then click Advanced Search Tutorial.

 To Search the Web Using the AltaVista Multimedia Search for Images

1 **Double-click the Location field, type** altavista.com **and then press the ENTER key. Click Image Search next to the Search Tools link. If necessary, click the My Sidebar handle to hide My Sidebar. When the Image Search page displays, type** claude monet paintings **in the Search for text box. Select None in the Partner Sites list. Point to the Search button.**

The Image Search page displays as shown in Figure 2-58.

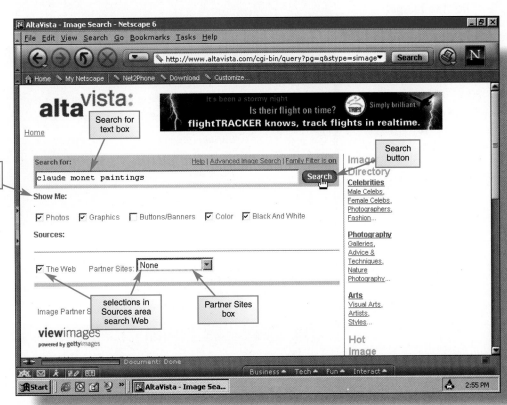

FIGURE 2-58

2 **Click the Search button. When AltaVista returns the results, hide My Sidebar and then scroll down so that the first and second rows of images display. Point to one of the images.**

AltaVista displays a list of images (Figure 2-59). The images are often links to pages that include information, additional images, and possibly a magnified version of the image you click.

mouse pointer pointing at image in column 1, row 2

FIGURE 2-59

3 **Click the image.**

Information about the artist and painting displays (Figure 2-60).

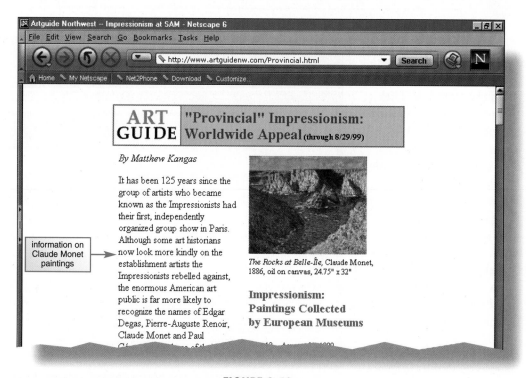

information on Claude Monet paintings

FIGURE 2-60

You can right-click an image and save it to disk. You then can insert the image into a document. Many of the images on the Web are copyrighted. Thus, check the Web site to be sure you can use the image if you decide to save it to disk.

Using the Yahoo! Subject Directory

Yahoo! is one of the most visited portals on the Web. Like Netscape Search, Google, and AltaVista, it allows you to use keywords to search. Also, like Netscape Search, it first returns links from its editor-created directory of links. If it has no links for the keyword in its database, it hands the keyword over to Google to perform a Web-wide search. Yahoo!'s strength, however, is its subject directory (Figure 2-61) made up of a vast collection of subject categories and subcategories constructed by editors. Because you already were introduced to how a subject directory works using Netscape Search, the following sections show how to use the Yellow Pages and Maps search tools in Yahoo!

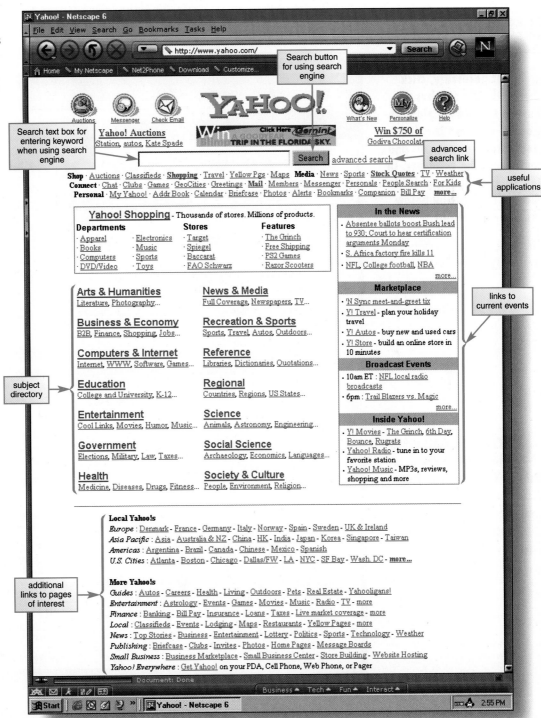

FIGURE 2-61

Yahoo! Yellow Pages

Most portals, such as Netscape, AltaVista, and Yahoo!, offer Yellow Pages. **Yellow Pages** allow you to search the Web for information related to businesses. You use the Yellow Pages search tool in the same fashion you would use the yellow pages in an ordinary telephone book. The following steps use the Yahoo! Yellow Pages to locate pizza restaurants in the Chicago area (zip code 60612), and, more specifically, get directions from O'Hare airport to the California Pizza Restaurant in Chicago.

To Use the Yahoo! Yellow Pages to Locate Businesses

1 If necessary, click the My Sidebar handle to hide My Sidebar. Double-click the Location field, type yahoo.com and then press the ENTER key. In the Shop category, point to the Yellow Pgs link below the Search text box.

The Yahoo! home page displays (Figure 2-62).

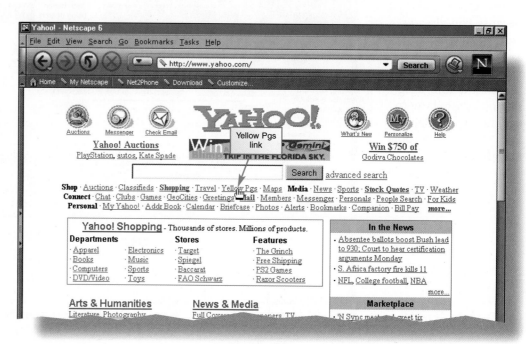

FIGURE 2-62

2 Click the Yellow Pgs link. When the Yahoo! Yellow Pages page displays, scroll down and find the Food and Dining subcategory. Point to the Restaurants link.

The Yahoo! Yellow Pages page displays (Figure 2-63).

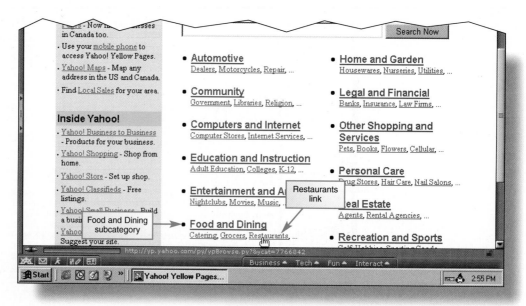

FIGURE 2-63

Using the Yahoo! Subject Directory • NN 2.53

PROJECT 2

3 **Click the Restaurants link. When the Search in a City page displays, type the zip code** 60612 **in the City, State, Zip or just a Zip text box. Point to the Continue button.**

The Search in a City page displays as shown in Figure 2-64.

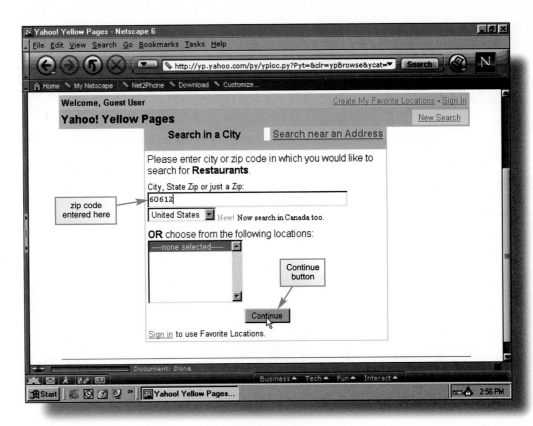

FIGURE 2-64

4 **Click the Continue button. When the Chicago, IL 60612 page displays, scroll down and point to the Pizza link.**

The page displays as shown in Figure 2-65.

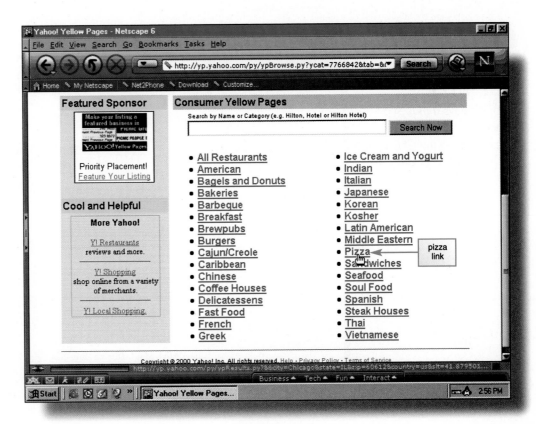

FIGURE 2-65

5 **Click the Pizza link. When the list of pizza restaurants displays, scroll down and point to the California Pizza Kitchen link.**

Yahoo! displays the first 20 of the 100 Chicago-based pizza restaurants contained in its database. Included for each restaurant are the name, address, and phone number. The restaurant name is a link (Figure 2-66). The link gives directions to the restaurant.

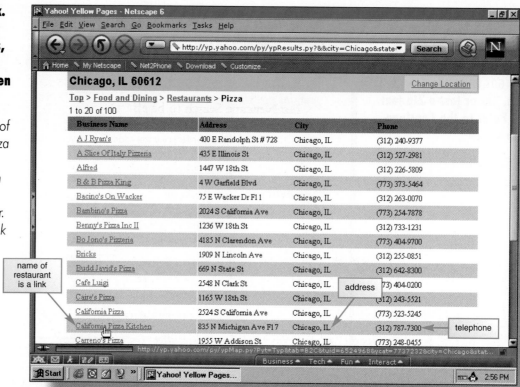

FIGURE 2-66

6 **Click the California Pizza Kitchen link. Scroll down and point to the Driving Directions link.**

Yahoo! displays a map showing the general location of the restaurant in the Chicago area (Figure 2-67).

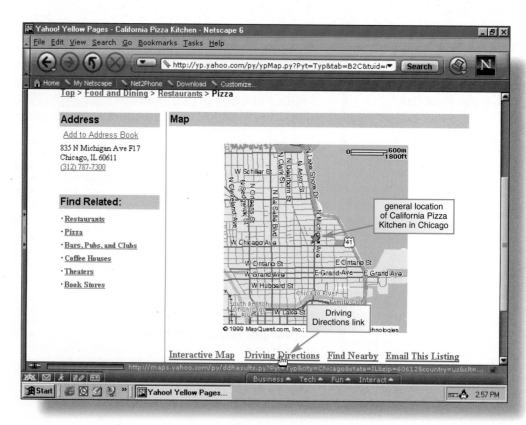

FIGURE 2-67

Using the Yahoo! Subject Directory • NN 2.55

PROJECT 2

7 **Click the Driving Directions link. The next Yahoo! Yellow Pages page that displays allows you to enter a starting address. When it displays, type the code ord for O'Hare Airport in the Street Address, Intersection or Airport Code text box. Point to the Get Directions button.**

The Yellow Pages page that allows you to enter a source destination displays as shown in Figure 2-68.

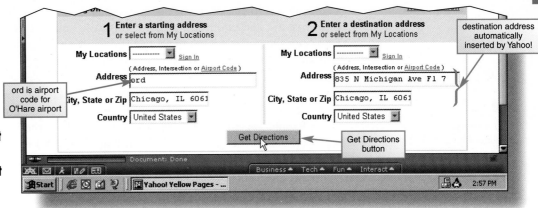

FIGURE 2-68

8 **Click the Get Directions button.**

Yahoo! displays the directions and maps shown in Figure 2-69.

9 **Click File on the menu bar and then click Print. When the Print dialog box displays, click the OK button.**

Netscape prints the map and directions.

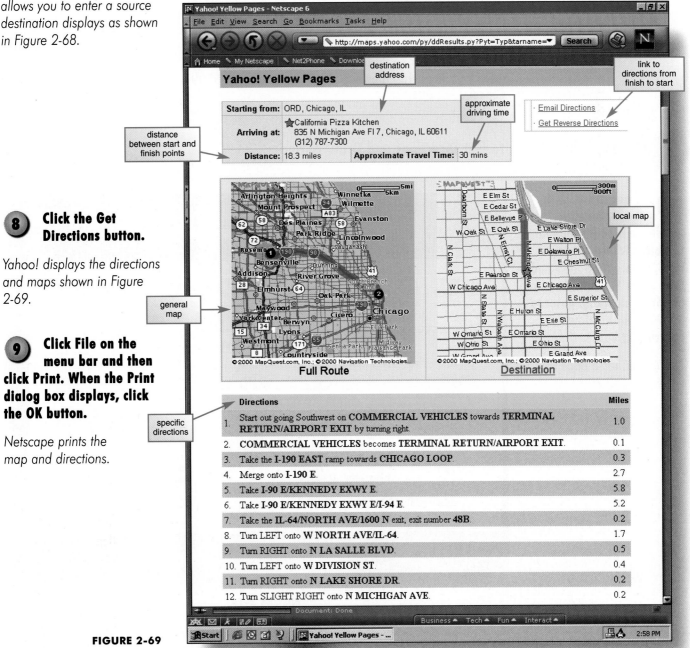

FIGURE 2-69

As shown in the previous set of steps, you can look up the phone number and directions for just about any type of business you can imagine. Once you display the directions and map, you can use the Print command on the File menu to print a hardcopy as described in Step 9 on the previous page.

If you own a business, you can feature it in the Yahoo! Yellow Pages. Also, if you have a Web-enabled mobile phone, you can access the Yahoo! suite of services, which includes Yellow Pages, Driving Directions, and People Search, while you travel. **People Search** is similar to doing a search of the white pages in a telephone directory. See In the Lab 9, Part 3, on page NN 2.80 for an example of performing a People Search.

Yahoo! Maps

Maps is another common search tool that the major portals, such as Netscape, AltaVista, and Yahoo!, offer. The Yahoo! Maps search tool allows you draw a map of a street location and its surroundings. You also can display driving directions from one location to another along with a map of directions. For the latter, you need the address of both locations. The following steps show how to display and print the directions and map that shows how to get from 8201 Calumet Avenue, Munster, IN 46321 to The Museum of Science and Industry, 5700 South Lake Shore Drive, Chicago, IL 60637.

More About

Yahoo!

Two graduate students at Stanford University accumulated lists of their favorite Web sites and started Yahoo!. Yahoo!, which became a corporation in 1996, is a household name among Web users.

Steps **To Use Yahoo! Maps to Get Directions and Draw a Map**

1 If necessary, click the My Sidebar handle to hide My Sidebar. Double-click the Location field, type yahoo.com and then press the ENTER key. In the Shop category, point to the Maps link below the Search text box.

The Yahoo! home page displays (Figure 2-70).

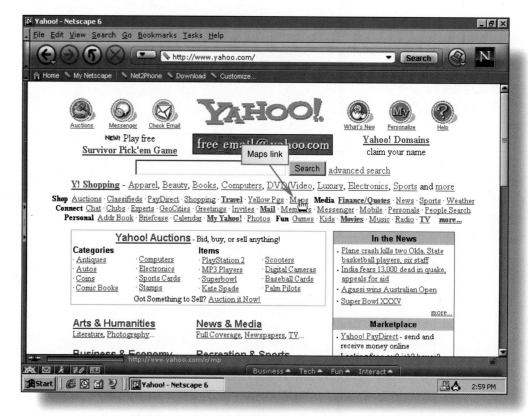

FIGURE 2-70

Using the Yahoo! Subject Directory • NN 2.57

PROJECT 2

2 Click the Maps link. When the Yahoo! Maps page displays, point to the Driving Directions link.

The Yahoo! Maps page displays (Figure 2-71).

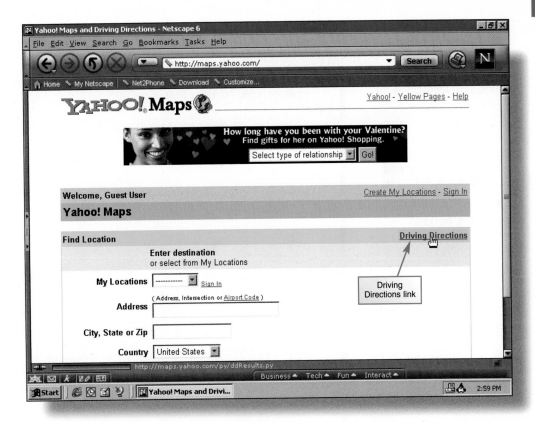

FIGURE 2-71

3 Click the Driving Directions link. When the Yahoo! Maps - Driving Directions page displays, type 8201 Calumet Ave, Munster, IN 46321 **in the appropriate text boxes on the left side of the form. Type** 5700 South Lake Shore Drive, Chicago, IL 60637 **in the appropriate text boxes on the right side of the form. Point to the Get Directions button.**

The Yahoo! Maps - Driving Directions page displays as shown in Figure 2-72.

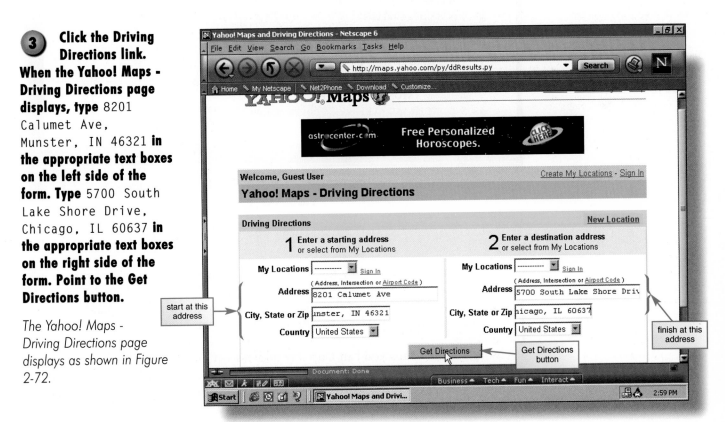

FIGURE 2-72

4 **Click the Get Directions button.**

Yahoo! displays the directions from the start location to the finish location (Figure 2-73).

5 **Click File on the menu bar and then click Print. When the Print dialog box displays, click the OK button.**

Netscape prints the map and directions.

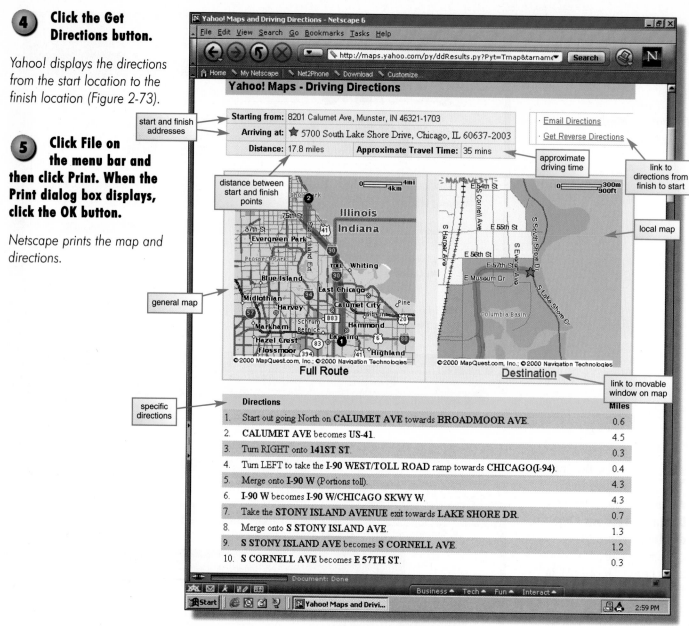

FIGURE 2-73

The Destination link below the local map in Figure 2-73 links you to a page with a movable window through which you view the map. That is, you have North, South, East, and West buttons that allow you to move the window around to see hidden edges of the map. You also can magnify the map by using zoom in and zoom out controls.

With Yahoo! Maps you can map any address within the United States or Canada. All you need to do is enter the street address, city, state, and zip code. For example, you may want to learn more about where you live or some distant place. As shown in the previous steps, it also allows you to display driving directions between any two addresses in the Unites States and Canada. Once you display the driving directions, you can use the browser print capabilities to print them out so you have a hardcopy for your trip.

Translating Web Pages from One Language to Another

Often when you search the entire Web, some of the links returned will be to Web pages written in a foreign language. If you don't understand the language, then the Web page is meaningless. The **Translate command** on the View menu allows you to translate the current Web page displayed to a language of your choice. For example, you can translate Web pages in French, German, Italian, Japanese, Portuguese, and Spanish to English. You also can translate English to French, German, Italian, Japanese, Portuguese, Spanish, Simplified Chinese, and Traditional Chinese. The following steps show how to translate a German Web page (heise.de/ct) to English.

 To Translate a Web Page from One Language to Another

1 **Double-click the Location field,** type heise.de/ct **in the Location field, and then press the ENTER key. When the German-language Web page displays, click View on the menu bar and point to Translate.**

Netscape displays the page written in German (Figure 2-74).

FIGURE 2-74

2 **Click Translate.**
When the Gist-In-Time page displays, the top text box should include the URL of the page that you want to translate. The boxes in Step 2 should indicate a conversion from German to English. Point to the Gist! button.

The Gist-In-Time page displays as shown in Figure 2-75.

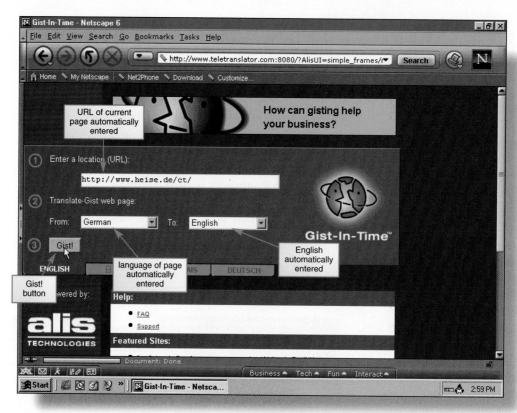

FIGURE 2-75

3 **Click the Gist! button.**

Netscape redisplays the page in English (Figure 2-76).

FIGURE 2-76

Compare the page in Figure 2-76 to the page in Figure 2-74 on page NN 2.59. Translating a page from one language to another is easy. You need only display the page, invoke the Translate command, and click the Gist! button.

Evaluating a Web Source

Once a promising Web page is found, you should evaluate it for its reliability, significance, and content. Remember, anyone can put a page on the Web, and Web pages do not have to be reviewed for accuracy or verified by editors. You have an obligation to ensure the information and other materials you use are accurate, attributable, and verifiable.

Just as there are criteria for evaluating printed materials, there are criteria for evaluating Web pages. These criteria include: authorship, accuracy of information, currency of information, and topic and scope of coverage. Table 2-6 shows the information you should look for within each criterion when evaluating Web resources.

More About

Evaluating Resources

Although a single evaluating tool does not exist, several colleges/universities have Web sites that contain information about evaluating Web sites. These sites include Cornell University (www.library. cornell.edu/okuref/research/ skill26.htm) and Vanguard University of Southern California (www.vanguard. edu/rharris/evalu8it.htm).

Table 2-6 Criteria for Evaluating Web Pages	
CRITERION	**INFORMATION TO EVALUATE**
Authorship	1. Is the name of the organization publishing the page legitimate?
	2. What are the author's credentials?
	3. Is there a link to a page that describes the goals of the organization?
	4. Does the page include a statement of official approval from the parent organization?
	5. Does a copyright notice appear?
	6. What are the author's qualifications?
	7. Are any opinions and biases clearly stated?
	8. Does the page contain advertising? If so, does it concern the content?
	9. Is the information provided as a public service?
Accuracy	1. Has the page been reviewed by professionals in the discipline to which the page refers?
	2. Are any sources used and are they listed on the page?
	3. Is the information covered fact, opinion, or propaganda?
	4. Does the page contain links to other Web sites that verify the information on the page?
	5. Are data and statistics clearly displayed and easy to read?
	6. Is the page grammatically correct?
Currency	1. When was the page written?
	2. When was the page placed on the Web?
	3. When was the page last updated?
	4. Does the page include dates associated with the information?
Topic and Scope	1. What is the purpose of the page?
	2. Does the page declare a topic?
	3. Does the page describe the topic?
	4. Are points clear, well stated, and supported?
	5. Does the page contain links to related sources?

You may wish to create an evaluation worksheet to use as an aid in consistently evaluating the Web pages you find as potential resources. Figure 2-77 on the next page shows a template created from the criteria listed in Table 2-6.

More About

Evaluating a Web Resource

Many Web pages do not meet the necessary criteria for being a research source. You will find that you discard many promising Web pages simply because you cannot find the necessary evaluation criteria.

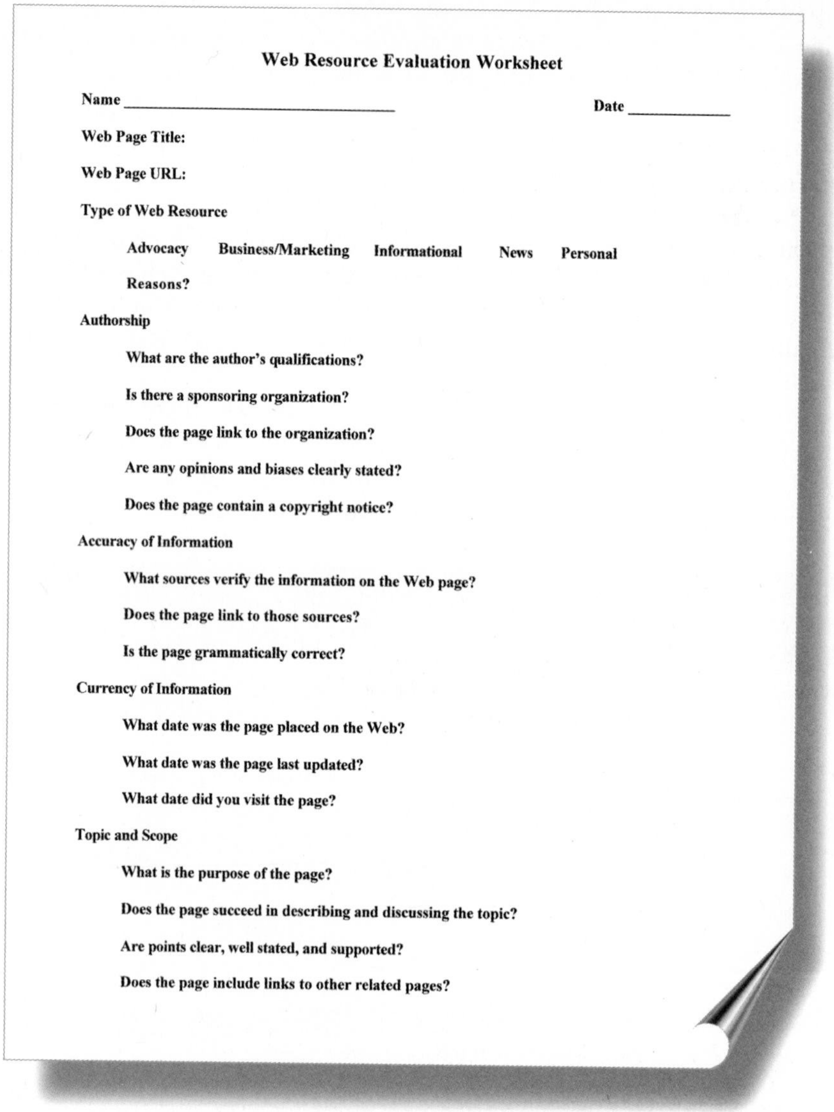

Web Resource Evaluation Worksheet

Name _____   Date _____

Web Page Title:

Web Page URL:

Type of Web Resource

      Advocacy   Business/Marketing   Informational   News   Personal

      Reasons?

Authorship

      What are the author's qualifications?

      Is there a sponsoring organization?

      Does the page link to the organization?

      Are any opinions and biases clearly stated?

      Does the page contain a copyright notice?

Accuracy of Information

      What sources verify the information on the Web page?

      Does the page link to those sources?

      Is the page grammatically correct?

Currency of Information

      What date was the page placed on the Web?

      What date was the page last updated?

      What date did you visit the page?

Topic and Scope

      What is the purpose of the page?

      Does the page succeed in describing and discussing the topic?

      Are points clear, well stated, and supported?

      Does the page include links to other related pages?

FIGURE 2-77

The following steps illustrate how to use the sample worksheet template shown in Figure 2-77 to evaluate the Carbohydrates in Nutrition page displayed and book-marked earlier in this project (Figure 2-45 on page NN 2.38).

Steps ## To Evaluate a Web Resource

1 **Click Bookmarks on the menu bar, and then click Carbohydrates in Nutrition. If Carbohydrates in Nutrition is not on the Bookmarks menu, type** `medical-library.net/ sites/carbohydrates _in_nutrition.html` **in the Location field and press the ENTER key. Scroll to the top of the Carbohydrates in Nutrition page. Write down the Web page title, URL, type of resource, and authorship.**

The top of the Carbohydrates in Nutrition page displays (Figure 2-78).

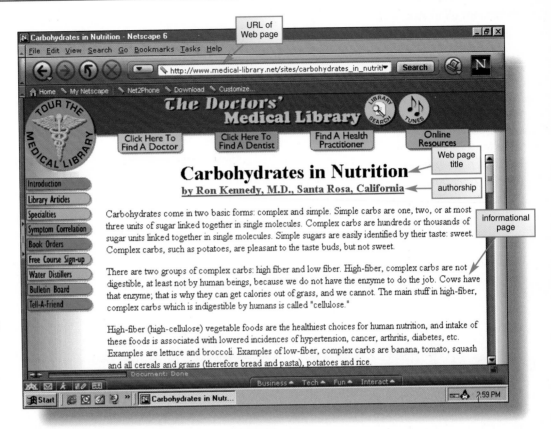

FIGURE 2-78

2 **Slowly scroll through the page and read the article. Display the bottom of the page to check the copyright notice.**

The bottom of the Web page is visible (Figure 2-79). The bottom of the page contains the number of hits, related links, and the copyright notice.

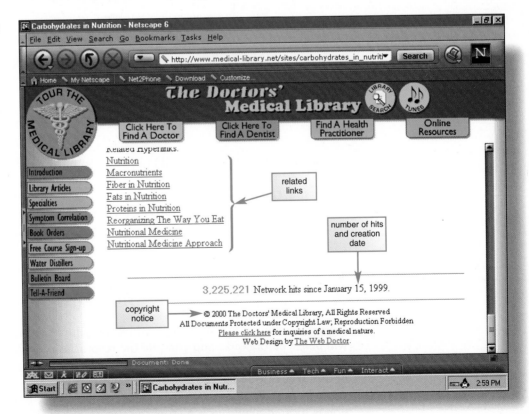

FIGURE 2-79

3 **Fill out the Web Resource Evaluation Worksheet as shown in Figure 2-80.**

The information gathered on the Carbohydrates in Nutrition page is summarized as shown in Figure 2-80. Based on the current worksheet criteria, the Carbohydrates in Nutrition page is an exceptionally strong resource.

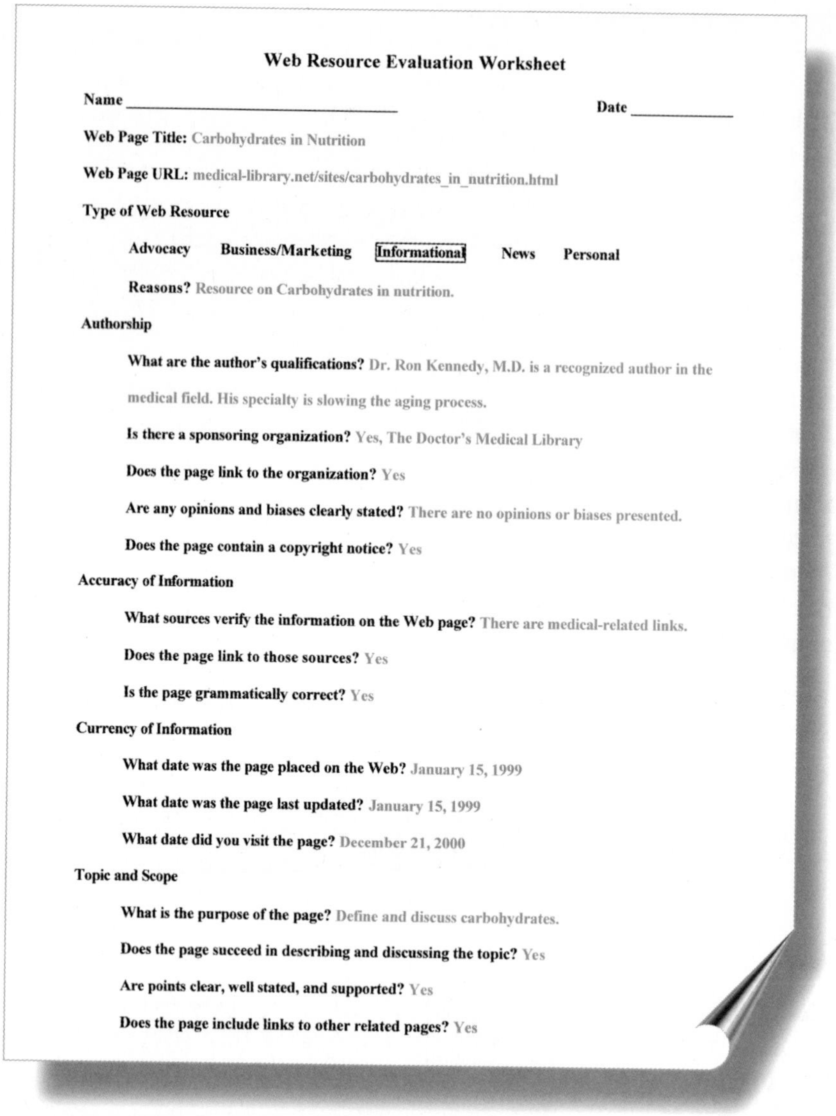

Web Resource Evaluation Worksheet

Name _____   Date _____

Web Page Title: Carbohydrates in Nutrition

Web Page URL: medical-library.net/sites/carbohydrates_in_nutrition.html

Type of Web Resource

Advocacy   Business/Marketing   Informational   News   Personal

Reasons? Resource on Carbohydrates in nutrition.

Authorship

What are the author's qualifications? Dr. Ron Kennedy, M.D. is a recognized author in the medical field. His specialty is slowing the aging process.

Is there a sponsoring organization? Yes, The Doctor's Medical Library

Does the page link to the organization? Yes

Are any opinions and biases clearly stated? There are no opinions or biases presented.

Does the page contain a copyright notice? Yes

Accuracy of Information

What sources verify the information on the Web page? There are medical-related links.

Does the page link to those sources? Yes

Is the page grammatically correct? Yes

Currency of Information

What date was the page placed on the Web? January 15, 1999

What date was the page last updated? January 15, 1999

What date did you visit the page? December 21, 2000

Topic and Scope

What is the purpose of the page? Define and discuss carbohydrates.

Does the page succeed in describing and discussing the topic? Yes

Are points clear, well stated, and supported? Yes

Does the page include links to other related pages? Yes

FIGURE 2-80

Instead of manually recording evaluation information on a printed copy of the worksheet, you can create an electronic version of the worksheet using a word processor. Then, for each Web resource you select, you can open a new copy of the worksheet document, record the entries, and save the document using a document name that reflects the Web resource being evaluated. Use one worksheet document per Web resource.

Creating a Working Bibliography

Once you find a good Web source, how do you record it? A working bibliography will help you organize and compile the resources you find, so that you can cite them as sources in the list of works cited. For Web resources, you should note the author or authors, title of the page, URL, date of publication, date of the last revision, date you accessed the resource, heading of any part or section where the relevant information is located, navigation instructions necessary to find the resource, and other pertinent information.

When you are compiling your information, you may want an e-mail address on the Web page to find the author. You may have to write to the person responsible for the Web site, called a Webmaster, and ask for the author's name. First, display the home page of the Web site to see if a directory or contact section is listed. If you do not find a directory or contact section, display the bottom of the Web page. Many Web pages include the e-mail address of the Webmaster at the bottom of the page.

Traditionally, index cards have been used to record relevant information about a work, and you still can use index cards to record Web research. However, several electronic means are now available for keeping track of the Web sites you visit and the information you find.

▶ You can e-mail pertinent information to yourself and store the messages in separate folders. Use one folder for each point or category you are researching.
▶ You can store the pertinent information in separate document files using copy and paste techniques. Use a separate file for each point or category you research.
▶ You can create a folder in the Favorites list and then place related favorites you find on the Web in that folder.
▶ You can print the promising Web page.

To demonstrate how to record relevant information about a Web resource, the following steps show how to copy information from the Carbohydrates in Nutrition page and paste it into a WordPad document. The copy and paste technique you will use was illustrated in Project 1 on page NN 1.48.

> ## More About
>
> ### Citing Web Sources
>
> All of the style guides mentioned in the text differ slightly from one another on the format of the citation used to cite a Web source. Check with your instructor for the accepted format your school uses. Check out the two most widely used style guides - Modern Language Association Web site (www.mla.org) and American Psychological Association (www.apa.org).

 ## To Record Relevant Information About a Research Source Using WordPad

1 **If the Carbohydrates in Nutrition page is not displaying in your browser, click Bookmarks on the menu bar and then click Carbohydrates in Nutrition. Click the Start button on the taskbar, point to Programs, point to Accessories on the Programs submenu, and then click WordPad on the Accessories submenu.**

Windows starts the WordPad application and the WordPad window opens (Figure 2-81). A Document - WordPad button displays on the taskbar.

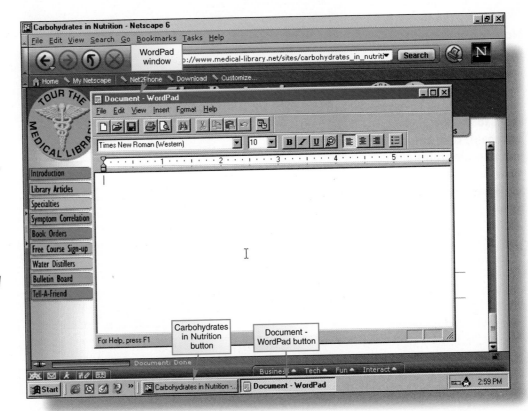

FIGURE 2-81

2 Click the Carbohydrates in Nutrition button on the taskbar to display the page and then point to the beginning of the title of the page. Drag to the bottom of the document. Right-click the selected text, and then point to Copy on the pop-up menu.

The text is selected and a pop-up menu displays (Figure 2-82).

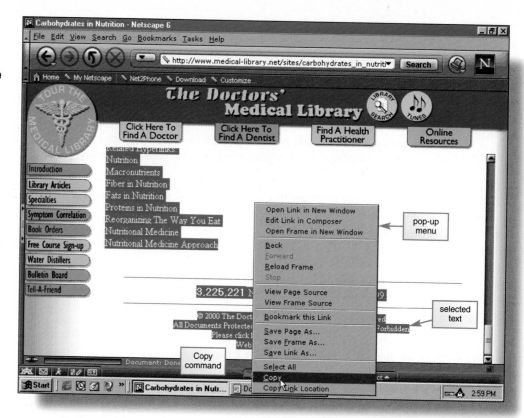

FIGURE 2-82

3 Click Copy and then click the Document - WordPad button on the taskbar. Right-click an empty area in the WordPad window and then click Paste on the pop-up menu. Scroll to the top of the document, click before the C in Carbohydrates and press the ENTER key. Click the blank line above the title.

Windows copies the selected text to the Clipboard, the Document - WordPad window displays, and Windows pastes the contents of the Clipboard to the WordPad document (Figure 2-83).

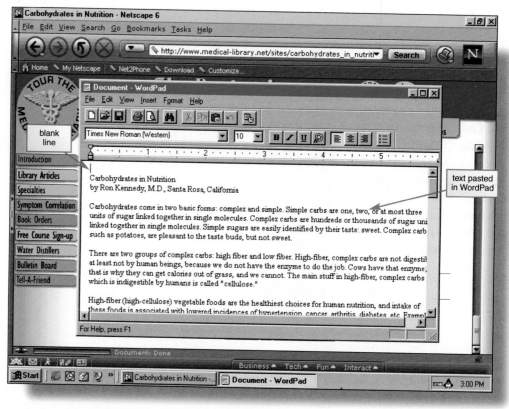

FIGURE 2-83

4 Click the Carbohydrates in Nutrition button. Double-click the Location field. Click Edit on the menu bar and then click Copy. Click the Document - WordPad button on the taskbar. Right-click the blank line above the title, and then click the Paste command.

The WordPad document displays as shown in Figure 2-84.

5 Insert a formatted floppy disk in drive A. Click the Save button on the toolbar. Type carbohydrates in nutrition in the File name text box. Click the Save in box arrow. Click 3½ Floppy (A:) in the Save in list. Click the Save button in the Save As dialog box. Click the Close button in the WordPad title bar to quit WordPad. Remove the floppy disk from drive A.

WordPad saves the WordPad document on the floppy disk in drive A using Carbohydrates in Nutrition as the file name, closes the WordPad window, and quits WordPad.

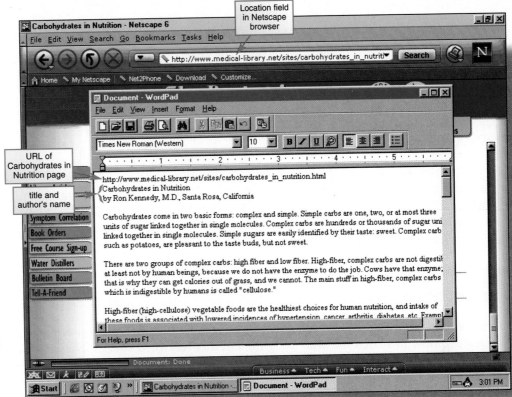

FIGURE 2-84

If you are using the electronic technique for evaluating a Web source (see Figure 2-80 on page NN 2.64), you can save the research information at the bottom of the worksheet document. Then, both the evaluation criteria and the research information for a particular Web page are stored in the same document.

Citing Web Sources

Figure 2-85 illustrates how to cite a Web resource using the MLA style. The example documents the source of the criteria for the Carbohydrates in Nutrition page discussed in the previous section.

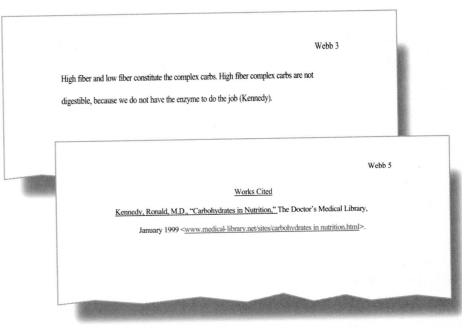

FIGURE 2-85

As you have learned in this project, the World Wide Web can be an informative and valuable source of information. By using proper searching and note-taking techniques, and asking the right questions about the usefulness of a Web resource, you can add to the information base you use to write a paper or speech. Always remember, however, that Web sources should complement, not replace, printed sources for locating information.

CASE PERSPECTIVE SUMMARY

Knowing how to use the Internet Keyword system, Netscape Search, Google, AltaVista, and Yahoo! to find information on the Web will be a valuable asset for the English research course, as well as any other college course that requires research. Also, knowing how to evaluate Web resources, create a working bibliography, and cite Web sources will simplify the complexities of putting a research paper together.

Project Summary

In this project, the seven general types of Web pages and the three general types of search tools were described. You learned how to search the Web using the Internet Keyword system, Netscape Search, Google, AltaVista, and Yahoo! You learned how to put together complex keywords using operators, commands, and special characters. You learned to search the Web for a business, images, and a map, and how to translate Web pages from one language to another. You learned how to evaluate a Web page as a potential source for research. In addition, you recorded relevant information about a potential source for future reference and learned how to write a citation for a Web resource.

What You Should Know

Having completed this project, you now should be able to perform the following tasks:

▶ Display the Netscape Search Directory *(NN 2.34)*
▶ Enter a Complex Keyword Using Netscape Search *(NN 2.24)*
▶ Evaluate a Web Resource *(NN 2.63)*
▶ Find Text on a Web Page *(NN 2.27)*
▶ Record Relevant Information About a Research Source Using WordPad *(NN 2.65)*
▶ Search for Keywords in Web Page Titles Using Netscape Search *(NN 2.26)*
▶ Search the Web Using Google *(NN 2.39)*
▶ Search the Web Using the AltaVista Multimedia Search for Images *(NN 2.49)*
▶ Search the Web Using the AltaVista Power Search *(NN 2.47)*
▶ Search the Web Using the AltaVista Simple Search *(NN 2.43)*
▶ Search the Web Using the Google Advanced Search *(NN 2.41)*

▶ Search the Web Using the Netscape Search Subject Directory *(NN 2.35)*
▶ Translate a Web Page from One Language to Another *(NN 2.59)*
▶ Use Multiple Search Engines to Search the Web *(NN 2.30)*
▶ Use Netscape Search to Find Web Pages *(NN 2.19)*
▶ Use the Choose Keyword Button to Speed Up a Search *(NN 2.17)*
▶ Use the Internet Keyword System to Display a List of Related Web Pages *(NN 2.14)*
▶ Use the Internet Keyword System to Display a Web Page *(NN 2.12)*
▶ Use the Yahoo! Yellow Pages to Locate Businesses *(NN 2.52)*
▶ Use Yahoo! Maps to Get Directions and Draw a Map *(NN 2.56)*

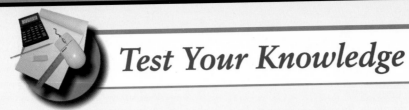

Test Your Knowledge

1 True/False

Instructions: Circle T if the statement is true or F if the statement is false.

T F 1. A portal Web page is designed to offer a variety of Internet services from a single convenient location.

T F 2. Gopher is a newsgroup.

T F 3. You can rely solely on the Web for research information because the Web does not lie.

T F 4. Search tools are hardware devices that help you find Web pages containing the information in which you are interested.

T F 5. An Internet Keyword system allows you to enter a name or word in the Location field to display a corresponding Web page.

T F 6. The Netscape Search search engine completes a Web-wide search before it passes the keyword to Google.

T F 7. A search tool that organizes Web pages in a hierarchical menu is called a subject directory.

T F 8. The word or phrase that describes the topic you are searching for is called a searchword.

T F 9. The two keywords: 1) physical and fitness; and 2) physical or fitness, mean one and the same to search engines.

T F 10. The Search panel must be in the basic mode for Netscape to use multiple search engines.

2 Multiple Choice

Instructions: Circle the correct response.

1. Web pages can be organized into several categories, including advocacy, business/marketing, personal, informational, other, and _____.
   a. news
   b. government
   c. FTP
   d. reference

2. To use the Internet Keyword system, enter the keyword in the Location field and _____.
   a. click the Search button
   b. press the ENTER key
   c. click the Google Search button
   d. press the ALT key

3. With Netscape Search, _____ is not a Boolean operator.
   a. and
   b. or
   c. and not
   d. within

4. To indicate that a certain word should not appear in a Web page, place _____ immediately before the word when defining the search criteria.
   a. +
   b. –
   c. "
   d. |

5. A search tool that does not require the use of a keyword to perform a search is called a(n) _____.
   a. subject directory
   b. power search
   c. advanced search
   d. simple search

(continued)

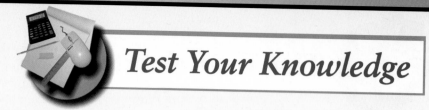

Test Your Knowledge

Multiple Choice *(continued)*

6. Search engines search indexes that are compiled using special programs called _____.
   a. autosearchers
   b. gophers
   c. directories
   d. spiders

7. URLs that no longer work are called _____.
   a. dead links
   b. sick links
   c. red links
   d. loose links

8. Which one of the following Netscape commands changes a page in the German language to English?
   a. Interpret
   b. Translate
   c. Decipher
   d. Decode

9. Which one of the following Netscape commands searches for text in the displayed page?
   a. Find
   b. Seek
   c. Locate
   d. Find in This Page

10. Which one of the following characters substitutes for any combination of characters at the end of a word in a keyword?
    a. circumflex (^)
    b. question mark (?)
    c. asterisk (*)
    d. plus sign (+)

3 Understanding Web Page Classifications

Instructions: Listed below are the seven general categories into which most Web pages fall. In the spaces provided, write a brief description of the indicated category. For each category, include two examples of groups, organizations, or other entities that may publish that type of page on the Web.

a. Advocacy: _____

_____

b. Business/marketing: _____

_____

c. Informational: _____

_____

d. News: _____

_____

e. Personal: _____

_____

f. Portal: _____

_____

g. Other: _____

_____

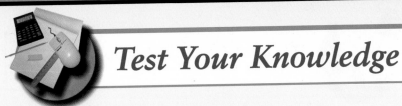

Test Your Knowledge

4 Understanding Web Page Evaluation Criteria

Instructions: Because most Web pages are not reviewed for accuracy, you should evaluate the usefulness of any Web resource you decide to use. Listed below are four criteria used to evaluate Web pages. In the spaces provided, list at least three pieces of information found on a Web page and related to the criterion that can be used to evaluate a Web page.

a. Authorship: _____

_____

b. Accuracy: _____

_____

c. Currency: _____

_____

d. Topic and Scope of Coverage: _____

_____

5 Understanding Complex Keywords

Instructions: Using Table 2-3 on page NN 2.27, write the keyword for each of the following.

a. Search only the phrase, George Washington, in the title of Web pages.

_____

b. Search for Web pages that include words that begin with the characters, jog.

_____

c. Search for Web pages that include one or more of the three words, pollution smog fumes.

_____

d. Search for Web pages that include the word, dog, or any one of commonly used synonyms.

_____

e. Search for Web pages that include the phrase, Viet Nam and Saigon, but not war and not conflict.

_____

f. Search for Web pages that include the phrase, Michael Jordan, and the term, baseball, but not basketball or golf.

_____

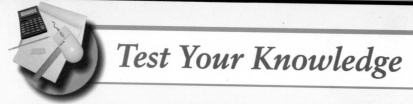

Test Your Knowledge

6 Online Practice Tests and Learning Games

Instructions: Start Netscape. Double-click the Location field, enter the URL scsite.com/nn6/practice.htm and then press the ENTER key to display the Netscape Navigator 6 Practice Test & Learning Games page (Figure 2-86). Complete the following tasks.

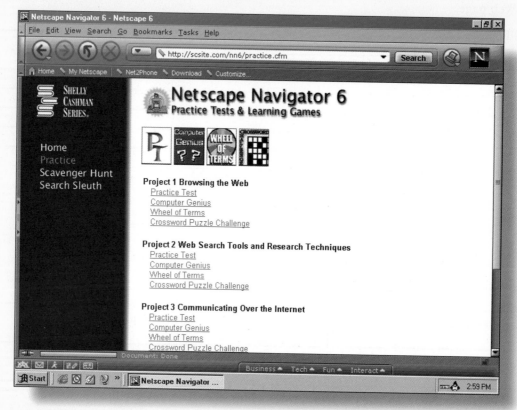

FIGURE 2-86

1. **Practice Test:** Click the Practice Test link under Project 2. Answer each question, enter your first and last name at the bottom of the page, and then click the Grade Test button. When the system displays the graded practice test, click Print on the File menu to print a hardcopy. Submit the printout to your instructor.
2. **Who Wants to be a Computer Genius:** Click the Computer Genius link under Project 2. Read the instructions, enter your first and last name at the bottom of the page, and then click the Play button. Submit your score to your instructor.
3. **Wheel of Terms:** Click the Wheel of Terms link under Project 2. Read the instructions, and then enter your first and last name and your school name. Click View High Scores to see other student scores. Close the High Scores window. Click the Play button. Submit your score to your instructor.
4. **Crossword Puzzle Challenge:** Click the Crossword Puzzle Challenge link under Project 2. Read the instructions, and then enter your first and last name. Click the Submit button. Solve the crossword puzzle. When you are finished, click the Submit button. When the crossword puzzle redisplays, click the Print button. Submit the printout to your instructor.

In the Lab

1 Using Netscape's Internet Keyword System

Instructions: Start Netscape. Use Netscape's Internet Keyword system to display company home pages or links to pages containing the desired information. (*Hint:* To use the Internet Keyword system, enter the keyword in the Location field and press the ENTER key.)

1. Display and print the home pages that display for the following keywords: ibm, stanford, abc, aol, united airlines. The Web page that displays for Stanford University (stanford) should resemble Figure 2-87.

2. Using Table 2-2 on page NN 2.16, display and print a Web page for the city where you live for each of the following: (a) real estate; (b) sports; (c) weather; (d) news; and (e) driving directions (use your home address and print the map). You may have to click a link for your city (or a larger city nearby) on a results page to display an appropriate page. If Netscape does not return any results, then use a larger city nearby.

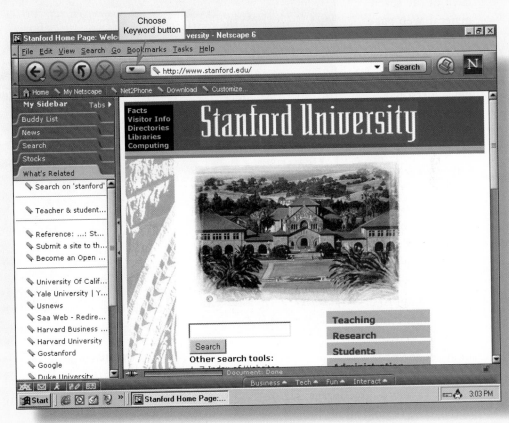

FIGURE 2-87

3. Use the Choose Keyword button (Figure 2-87) to display and print a Web page for the following: (a) stock quote for General Electric (GE); (b) stock quote for Merck (MRK); (c) local information.

2 Using Netscape Search

Instructions: Start Netscape. Use Netscape Search to display the information specified. (*Hint:* To use Netscape Search, double-click the Location field, type the keyword, and then click the Search button.)

(continued)

In the Lab

Using Netscape Search (continued)

1. Display and print one Web page that is representative of each of the seven general Web page types (advocacy, informational, business/marketing, news, personal, portal, and other) by using appropriate keywords. In some cases, you can use the type of Web page as the keyword. For others, you will need to determine a keyword that will lead you to an appropriate page. For example, to display an advocacy page you may want to

FIGURE 2-88

use the keyword, greenpeace. Figure 2-88 shows an example of an advocacy page belonging to the Greenpeace organization.

2. Using Table 2-3 on page NN 2.27, display and print the results page (first page of links returned) for each of the following:

   a. Search for the phrase, Abraham Lincoln. Print the first page under Reviewed Web Sites.

   b. Search for Web pages that include words that begin with the characters, box. Print the first page under Reviewed Web Sites on the sport of boxing.

   c. Search for Web pages that include one or more of the two words, music and melody.

   d. Search for Web pages that include the word, cat, or any one of three additional synonyms.

   e. Search for Web pages that include the phrase, World War II, the word, Italy but not Germany and not Africa. Print the first page under Reviewed Web Sites.

3. Re-enter the keywords in Step 2 a, b, c, and d. When the Netscape Search results display, click the Search again link on the results page to have Google complete a Web-wide search. Print the initial Google results page for each.

In the Lab

3 Searching the Web Using the Google Search Engine

Instructions: Start
Netscape. If necessary,
click the My Sidebar han-
dle to hide it. Double-click
the Location field, type
google.com and then
press the ENTER key to
display the Google home
page (Figure 2-89).

1. Find a page of inspi-
   rational quotations
   and print it.
2. Find the address,
   phone number, and
   e-mail address of your
   representative in the
   U.S. House of
   Representatives.
3. Find, display, and
   print Tiger Woods'
   home page. Rather
   than clicking the
   Google Search button,
   click the I'm Feeling Lucky button. If the results are not what you expected, re-enter the keyword and click
   the Google Search button.

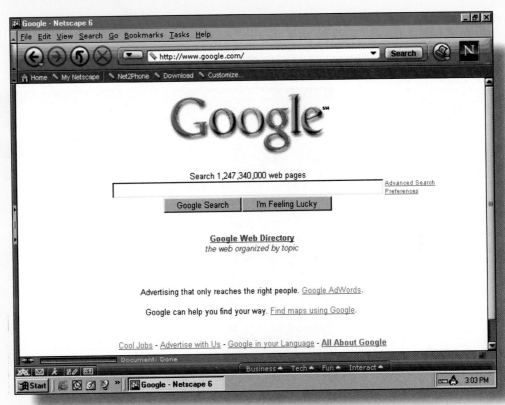

FIGURE 2-89

4. What is the current temperature in Moscow, Russia?
5. Who played Harvey Pell in the classic movie *High Noon*? Use the keyword, movie database, to get started.
6. What is the URL and address of the University of Chicago?
7. Use the Advanced Search link on the Google home page to find a page written in German on the phrase,
   "caribbean cruises"; exclude the word, miami; and exclude .gov sites. When the Google results display, click
   a link that has a German description and print the page. Use the Translate command on the View menu to
   translate the page to English. Print the page in English.

In the Lab

4 Search Sleuth

Instructions: Start Netscape. Double-click the Location field, enter the URL scsite.com/nn6/sleuth.htm and then press the ENTER key. When the Netscape Navigator 6 Search Sleuth Exercises page displays (Figure 2-90), select one or more of the following and complete the tasks outlined on the Web page.

1. Click the Encyclopedia Britannica link and the Clip Art Search link.
2. Click the Ask Jeeves link and the Direct Hit link.
3. Click the MetaCrawler link and the AltaVista link.
4. Click the Meta Tags link and the Go link.
5. Click the NorthernLight link and the Excite link.
6. Click the Yahoo! link and the Virtual Library link.
7. Click the Privacy link and the Switchboard.com link.

FIGURE 2-90

5 Searching the Web Using Multiple Search Engines

Part 1 Instructions: Start Netscape. If My Sidebar is hidden, click its handle on the left side of the screen. Click the Search tab. Complete the following tasks.

1. Place the My Sidebar Search panel in the advanced mode.
2. Select all the search engines in the Search panel in My Sidebar as shown in Figure 2-91.
3. Use the Search text box in the Search panel in My Sidebar to find Web pages that discuss the famous author, Upton Sinclair. Make sure all search engines are checked. Perform a Web-wide search.
4. When the results display, click each search engine button in the View by Search Engine area. Print the first page of results for each search engine. When was he born? What college did Upton Sinclair attend? When did he die? List three books he wrote.

In the Lab

5. Change the Search panel in My Sidebar back to the basic mode.

Part 2 Instructions:
Start Netscape. Click the Search the Web command on the Search menu (Figure 2-91). One at a time, use the search engines listed on the Net Search Page shown in Figure 2-91 to find Web pages that discuss the 2000 presidential election in Florida. Print the initial page of links that each search engine displays.

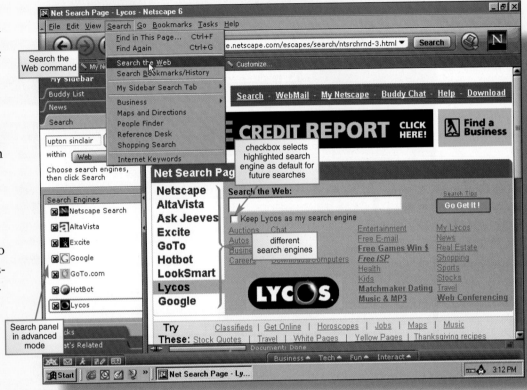

FIGURE 2-91

6 Searching the Web Using the AltaVista Search Engine

Instructions: Start Netscape. If necessary, click the My Sidebar handle to hide it. Double-click the Location field, type altavista.com and then press the ENTER key to display the AltaVista home page (Figure 2-92 on the next page).

1. Simple Search: Perform a Simple search using AltaVista for any one of the following topics: virtual reality, computer generated graphics, Java applets, MLA style, APA style, or extreme sports. Print the first results page returned by AltaVista. Find one or more informative Web sites about the topic you select. Using Word-Pad, copy information about the topic from the Web sites into a WordPad document and develop a short report about the topic. Add the URLs of the Web sites you used and your name to the end of the report. Print the WordPad document and the report.

2. Power Search: Use AltaVista's Power search tool to find links for the exact phrase, john grisham, in the titles of English language Web pages posted in the last six months. Show only one page per Web site in the results. Print the results page.

3. Multimedia Search: Use AltaVista's Multimedia search for Images to display images of the President of the United States. Do a title search for the exact phrase. Print the first results page. Copy one of the images to disk and then into WordPad. Print the results.

4. Advanced Search: Use AltaVista's Advanced Search tool to find links for the phrase, genetic engineering; exclude variations of corn and soybean. Print the first results page. Display and print a Web page on the keyword topic.

(continued)

In the Lab

Searching the Web Using the AltaVista Search Engine *(continued)*

FIGURE 2-92

7 Searching the Web Using the Yahoo! Subject Directory

Instructions: Start Netscape. If necessary, click the My Sidebar handle to hide My Sidebar. Double-click the Location field, type yahoo.com and then press the ENTER key to display the Yahoo! home page (Figure 2-93).

1. Use the Yahoo! subject directory to search for and print a Web page containing a graphic image of each of the following categories: cycling, sailing, snowboarding, tennis, and gymnastics. Click the Yahoo! Photography link and then the Picture Gallery link.

2. Use the Yahoo! subject directory to search for and print a Web page containing information on any three of the following topics: government spending, a historical event, life of a current political figure, an extreme weather event, asteroid collisions with the earth, an extraterrestrial sighting, biological weapons, or genetic engineering.

In the Lab

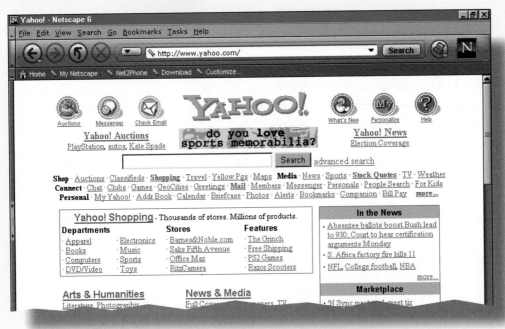

FIGURE 2-93

8 Scavenger Hunt

Instructions: Start Netscape. Double-click the Location field and type `scsite.com/nn6/scavenger.htm` to enter the URL. When the Netscape Navigator 6 Scavenger Hunt Exercises page displays (Figure 2-94), select one or more of the following and complete the tasks outlined on the Web page.

1. Click the Personal Productivity Software to Supercomputers link and the Web Servers to Protocols link.

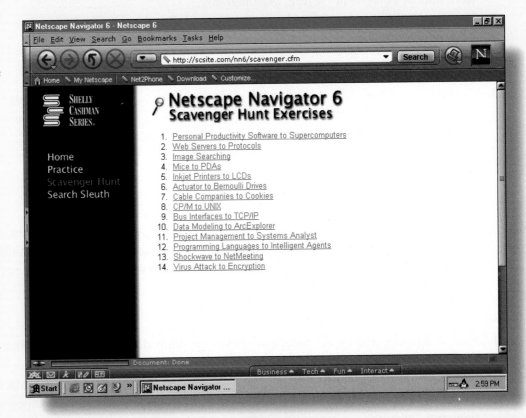

FIGURE 2-94

(continued)

In the Lab

Scavenger Hunt *(continued)*

2. Click the Image Searching link and the Mice to PDAs link.
3. Click the Inkjet Printers to LCDs link and the Actuator to Bernoulli Drives link.
4. Click the Cable Companies to Cookies link and the CP/M to UNIX link.
5. Click the Bus Interfaces to TCP/IP link and the Data Modeling to ArcExplorer link.
6. Click the Project Management to Systems Analyst link and the Programming Languages to Intelligent Agents link.
7. Click the Shockwave to NetMeeting link and Virus Attack to Encryption link.

9 Searching for Businesses, Maps, People, and Articles

Instructions: Use Yahoo! or a portal of your choice from Table 2-1 on page NN 2.8 to step through Parts 1 through 4.

Part 1: *Searching for a Business Address*

1. Use the Yellow Pages to search for the address and telephone number of each of the following businesses: Course Technology (Massachusetts), Microsoft Corporation (Washington), Flagler Museum (Florida), and Recreational Equipment (Seattle, Washington).
2. Use WordPad to create a list of business names, addresses, and telephone numbers.
3. Print the WordPad document and submit the document to your instructor.

Part 2: *Searching for a Map*

1. Create a map for each of the following places or landmarks: Salzburg (Austria), Eiffel Tower (France), Statue of Liberty (New York), Key West (Florida), and White House (District of Columbia). Print each map. Circle the place or landmark on the hardcopy of the map.
2. Find and print directions from Kennedy airport in New York to the Empire State Building, 350 Fifth Avenue, New York, NY 10118.

Part 3: *Searching for People*

1. Use the People Search link or a similar link to locate people with your last name. Print the first results page.
2. Use the People Search link or a similar link to locate a friend. Enter the last name and state in which the friend lives. Print the first results page. Click your friend's name on the results page and print a map of where he/she lives.

Part 4: *Searching for an Encyclopedia Article*

1. Find an encyclopedia on the Web, such as the Encyclopedia Brittanica at brittanica.com.
2. Use the encyclopedia site to find an article on one of the following topics: black widow spiders, blowfish (also called puffer or globefish), cobra snake, or killer bees (also called Africanized honey bees). Use WordPad to create a report that consists of the main article from the encyclopedia, the scientific classification, and a picture.

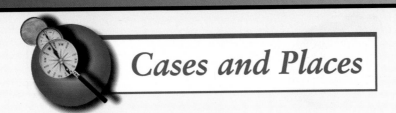

Cases and Places

The difficulty of these case studies varies:
▶ are the least difficult; ▶▶ are more difficult; and ▶▶▶ are the most difficult.

1 ▶ Many popular bands, singers, and musical groups have their own home pages on the Web. Using the Google search engine, find out when and where a singer of your choice will be playing next. Print their home page. Next, use the AltaVista search engine to find out when and where a band or musical group of your choice will be playing next. Print their home page. Do these pages qualify as informational Web pages? Write your answer and the reasons supporting your position on one of the printouts and then hand it in to your instructor.

2 ▶ You have been hired by a local bicycle shop to compare their store prices to the prices available on the Internet. Search the Internet for Web pages that sell bicycles and bicycle parts. Find at least 10 items being sold by three different online bicycle stores. Develop a price list to compare the prices of the 10 items and submit the price list to your instructor.

3 ▶ You recently graduated from college and took a job at a small investment firm. Your first job is to search for and compare the services of the major online brokers. Find five online brokers and compare their services, costs to buy and sell stocks, Web sites, and any other pertinent information. Print their home pages. Summarize your findings in a brief report.

4 ▶▶ Use the advanced mode on the Netscape Search panel in My Sidebar to find information on the topic, reviews of search engines. Using at least five search engines of your choice, find three different Web sources that review search engines. Record the relevant information. Write a brief report about which search engine you think is the best and why. Print the three pages, write the citation on the page using either the MLA or APA style, and then submit the pages to your instructor.

5 ▶▶ A gopher is a computer system that allows computer users to find files on the Internet. Some federal, state, and local government agencies continue to use a gopher site to provide information and distribute documents and forms. Use the AltaVista Power search tool to find one government agency (search only .gov sites) that provides gopher services (search for gopher), learn to use its gopher, and write a brief report about the gopher. Include instructions to follow to use the gopher, documents you found using the gopher, and whether you like or disliked this method of finding information on the Internet.

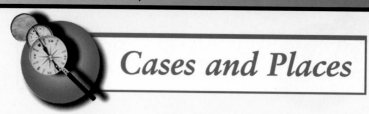

Cases and Places

6 ▶▶▶ Computer security is a major concern for systems administrators. A very important first line of defense is a user name and password. Choosing good passwords is important for security issues. Using the search engine of your choice, find three different Web sources that describe criteria for creating a good password. Record the relevant information necessary for citing the sources using the MLA or APA style. Print the three pages, write the citation on the page using either the MLA or APA style, and then submit the pages to your instructor.

7 ▶▶▶ The World Wide Web and the Internet provide another source for information in addition to libraries, encyclopedias, and reference materials. Finding useful resources on the Web can be challenging for reasons such as unknown authorship, lack of verification of the materials, and the ever-changing nature of the Web. Choose a topic of interest to you and then narrow down a research topic. Using the Web and Internet resources, find at least five sources of information on the topic. Evaluate the five sources using the evaluation criteria discussed in Project 2. Print the Web resources and then submit them to your instructor along with your evaluations.

Netscape Navigator 6

P R O J E C T

3

Communicating, Scheduling, and Contact Management with Netscape

You will have mastered the material in this project when you can:

O B J E C T I V E S

- Start Netscape Mail
- Open, read, print, reply to, and delete electronic mail messages
- Compose and send electronic mail messages
- Open an attachment in an electronic mail message
- Subscribe and unsubscribe to a newsgroup
- Read, post, and print newsgroup articles
- Expand and collapse a thread
- Start Netscape Address Book
- Create, edit, and delete an Address Book entry
- Add, edit, and delete a name from the Buddy List
- Send and reply to an Instant Message to someone on your Buddy List
- Start WebCalendar
- Describe the components of the WebCalendar window
- Enter one-time and recurring appointments
- Add events to WebCalendar using the Event Directory
- Display WebCalendar in Day, Week, and Month views
- Print WebCalendar
- Understand Netscape Composer
- Listen to music from the Web

Electronic Communication

Around the World At Once

I n the not-so-distant past, say a century or so ago, communication took two basic forms: verbal or written. Because telephones, telegraphs, radios, and television did not exist yet, hand-written letters were the main form of long-distance communication. Imagine a Civil War general trying to make informed decisions and devise strategy based on information that is days, or even weeks, old. Imagine receiving news of the birth of a child or the death or illness of a loved one weeks or months after the event.

Today, communication is virtually instantaneous. This immediacy is due to electronic devices that would have been denounced as science fiction not long ago. Chief among the communication advances is e-mail. Using e-mail, families can receive birth announcements moments after — or even during — the blessed event. Students can send their semester grades to their parents as soon as the grades are posted. Any momentous, or not-so-momentous, news can be relayed to anyone, any time, and anywhere via the Internet.

Now, nearly 80 percent of Internet users communicate with e-mail, and this service is one of the major reasons they became users. They send more than three billion messages

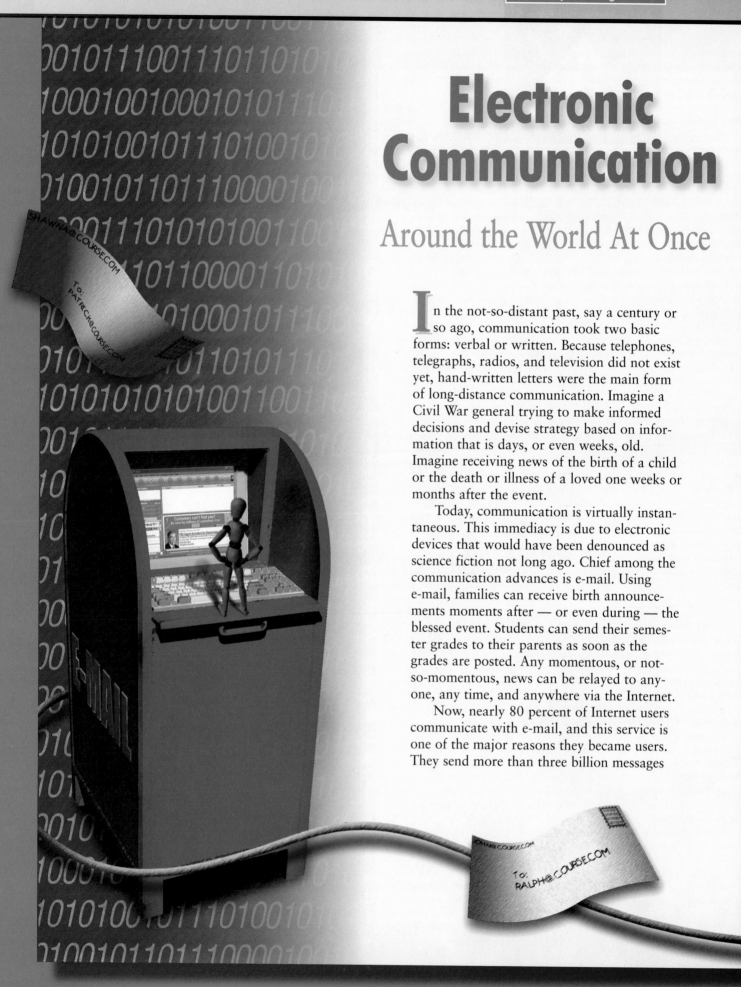

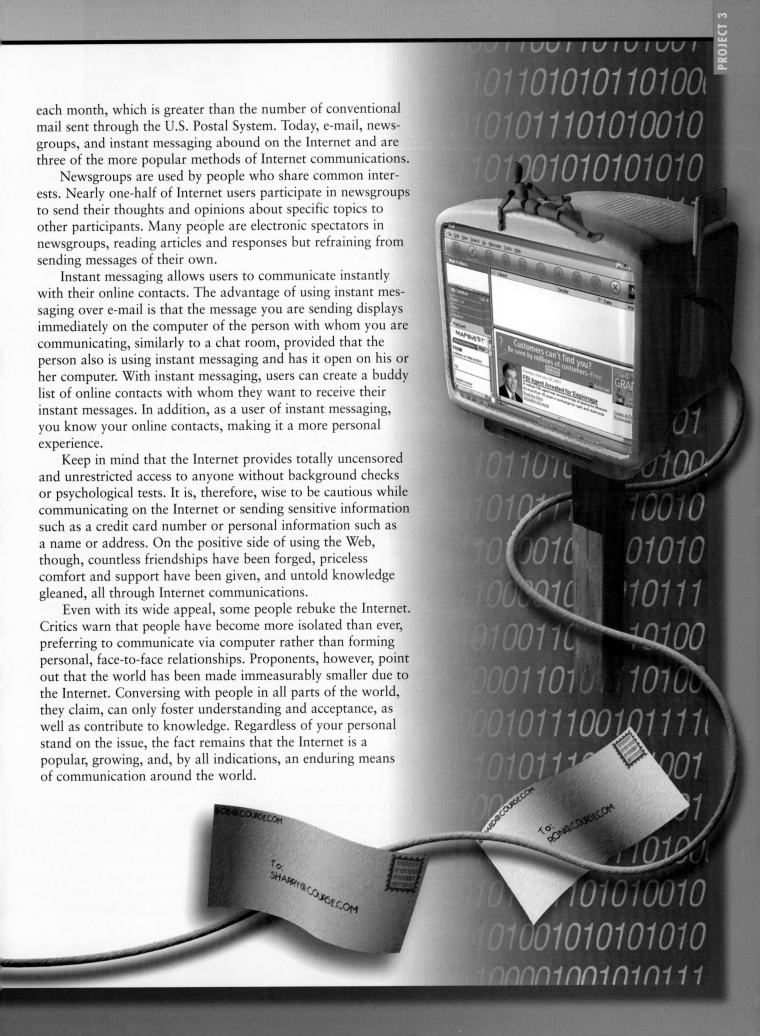

each month, which is greater than the number of conventional mail sent through the U.S. Postal System. Today, e-mail, news-groups, and instant messaging abound on the Internet and are three of the more popular methods of Internet communications.

Newsgroups are used by people who share common interests. Nearly one-half of Internet users participate in newsgroups to send their thoughts and opinions about specific topics to other participants. Many people are electronic spectators in newsgroups, reading articles and responses but refraining from sending messages of their own.

Instant messaging allows users to communicate instantly with their online contacts. The advantage of using instant messaging over e-mail is that the message you are sending displays immediately on the computer of the person with whom you are communicating, similarly to a chat room, provided that the person also is using instant messaging and has it open on his or her computer. With instant messaging, users can create a buddy list of online contacts with whom they want to receive their instant messages. In addition, as a user of instant messaging, you know your online contacts, making it a more personal experience.

Keep in mind that the Internet provides totally uncensored and unrestricted access to anyone without background checks or psychological tests. It is, therefore, wise to be cautious while communicating on the Internet or sending sensitive information such as a credit card number or personal information such as a name or address. On the positive side of using the Web, though, countless friendships have been forged, priceless comfort and support have been given, and untold knowledge gleaned, all through Internet communications.

Even with its wide appeal, some people rebuke the Internet. Critics warn that people have become more isolated than ever, preferring to communicate via computer rather than forming personal, face-to-face relationships. Proponents, however, point out that the world has been made immeasurably smaller due to the Internet. Conversing with people in all parts of the world, they claim, can only foster understanding and acceptance, as well as contribute to knowledge. Regardless of your personal stand on the issue, the fact remains that the Internet is a popular, growing, and, by all indications, an enduring means of communication around the world.

Netscape Navigator 6

Communicating, Scheduling, and Contact Management with Netscape

PROJECT

3

CASE PERSPECTIVE

Dapeka Patel is president of the Computer Club at Chesterton Community College. As a busy college student, she is concerned about scheduling club meetings and keeping the other club members informed about upcoming meetings and events. She recently read about Netscape and thinks it would be the perfect tool both to communicate over the Internet and to maintain her personal schedule and contacts.

You work part-time at the Help desk in the school's computer lab and are quite familiar with Netscape's features. Dapeka has visited the Help desk requesting that you help her set up her Netscape Mail, Instant Messenger, Address Book, and WebCalendar. She would like to use Netscape Mail to manage her e-mail account, Instant Messenger to keep in contact with the other officers of the Computer Club, and WebCalendar to schedule her classes, meetings, and other events. Dapeka feels that having all of her communication and schedules in one place should help her manage her time efficiently and make it easier to keep club members abreast of upcoming meetings and events. With your help, she can accomplish this goal.

Introduction

In Projects 1 and 2, you used Netscape to search for information on the World Wide Web. In addition to searching for information, you also may use Netscape to communicate with other individuals and manage your personal contacts and schedule. Communication services included in Netscape include Netscape Mail, which allows you to send and receive electronic mail and read and post messages to a newsgroup; and Instant Messenger, which permits you to engage in real-time messaging with family, friends, or coworkers. Netscape also provides you with the means to organize your contacts with Address Book and to organize your personal schedule with WebCalendar. In addition, Composer allows you to create Web pages, and Radio allows you to listen to music from the Web.

> **NOTE:** You must have a valid Netscape username and password to successfully complete this project.

Electronic Mail (E-Mail) Messages

Electronic mail (e-mail) has become an important means of exchanging messages and files among business associates and friends. Businesses find that using e-mail to send documents electronically saves both time and money. Parents with students away at college or relatives who are scattered across the country find that exchanging e-mail messages is an inexpensive and easy way to stay in touch with their family members. In fact, exchanging e-mail messages is one of the more widely used features of the Internet.

Besides exchanging e-mail messages, another popular method of sharing information among individuals is to use Internet newsgroups. An **Internet newsgroup** contains articles and messages about many varied and interesting topics.

Netscape Mail allows you to receive and store incoming e-mail messages, compose and send e-mail messages, and read and post messages to Internet newsgroups.

Starting Netscape Mail

After starting Netscape, you can start Netscape Mail using the Mail button on the Task toolbar in the Netscape window. Perform the following steps to start Netscape Mail.

To Start Netscape Mail

1 Point to the Mail button on the Task toolbar (Figure 3-1).

More About

Electronic Mail Addresses

Many search engines contain an electronic mail search feature. For example, AltaVista (www.altavista.com) allows you to search for a person or e-mail address using People Finder (http://worldpages. altavista.com/whitepages). In addition, AltaVista allows you to search for a business using YellowPages (http://worldpages. altavista.com/).

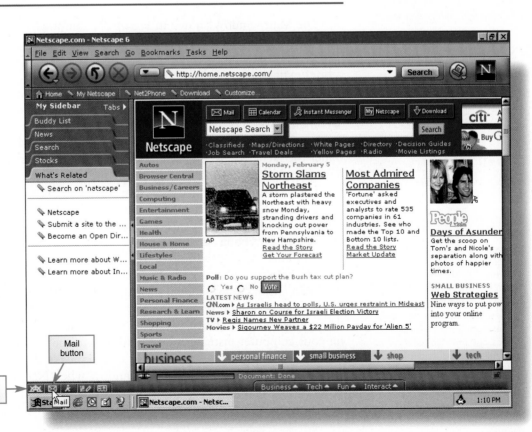

FIGURE 3-1

2 Click the Mail button. When the Mail window opens, maximize the window and, if necessary, click the My Sidebar handle to hide My Sidebar. Click the Netscape for Computer Club message displayed in the Inbox.

The Netscape Mail window opens (Figure 3-2). The window contains the folders list, message list, and preview pane.

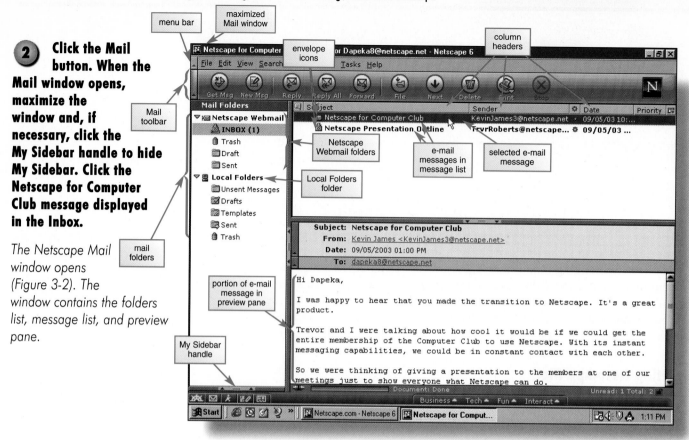

FIGURE 3-2

The Mail window shown in Figure 3-2 contains a number of elements. Below the title bar and the menu bar is a Mail toolbar containing buttons specific to Mail (Get Msg, New Msg, Reply, and so on). Table 3-1 contains the Mail toolbar buttons and a brief explanation of their functions.

The Mail window is divided into three frames. The **folders list** in the upper-left frame contains the Netscape Webmail folder, the four mail folders contained in the Webmail folder, Local Folders folder, and the five mail folders contained in the Local Folders folder. Four standard mail folders (Inbox, Trash, Draft, and Sent) display under the Netscape Webmail folder when you first start Mail. You cannot rename or delete the Inbox or Trash folders; you can, however, create additional folders.

The **Inbox folder** is the destination for incoming mail. The **Trash folder** contains messages that you have moved to the Trash folder from other folders. As a safety precaution, you can retrieve messages from the Trash folder if you later decide to keep them. Emptying the Trash folder removes the messages permanently. The **Draft folder** retains copies of messages that you are not yet ready to send. The **Sent folder** retains copies of messages you have sent.

Folders can contain e-mail messages, faxes, and files created in other applications. Folders in bold type followed by a number in parentheses (**Inbox (1)**) indicate the number of messages in the folder that are unopened. Other folders may display on your computer instead of or in addition to the folders shown in Figure 3-2.

The contents of the Inbox folder automatically display in the **message list** at the top of the upper-right frame of the window when Netscape Mail starts. Five column headers display above the message list. A thread icon displays to the left of the first header. Entries in the columns below the second header (Subject), third header

Table 3-1 Mail Toolbar Buttons and Functions

BUTTON	FUNCTION
Get Msg	Gets new messages for the current account.
New Msg	Opens the Message Compose window used to compose a new e-mail message.
Reply	Opens a window used to reply to an e-mail message. The e-mail address, original subject of the e-mail message preceded by the Re: entry, and the original e-mail message display in the window.
Reply All	Opens a window used to reply to an e-mail message. The e-mail address of all recipients, subject of the e-mail message preceded by the Re: entry, and the original e-mail message display in the window.
Forward	Opens a window used to forward an e-mail message to another recipient. The original subject of the e-mail message preceded by the Fwd: entry and the original e-mail message display in the window.
File	Allows you to move messages between folders.
Next	Moves to the next unread message.
Delete	Deletes the selected e-mail message in the message list by moving the message to the Trash folder.
Print	Prints the selected e-mail message in the message list.
Stop	Stops the current action.

(Sender), and fifth header (Date) indicate the subject of the e-mail, the e-mail author's name or e-mail address, and date and time the message was received. Collectively, these three entries are referred to as the **message heading**. A green star in the fourth column indicates the message is marked as unread. An exclamation point icon in the column below the sixth header indicates the e-mail message has been marked high priority by the sender and should be read immediately. The folder icon at the far right of the column headers allows you to delete or add columns.

An envelope with a green arrow icon in the Subject column and a message heading that displays in bold type identifies an unread e-mail message. In Figure 3-2, the second e-mail message contains an envelope with a green arrow icon and a message heading that displays in bold type. The icon and bold message heading indicate the e-mail message has not been read (opened).

The envelope with the green arrow icon is one of two icons, called **message list icons**, that display in the Subject column. A plain closed envelope icon indicates the message has been read.

The lower-right frame contains a **preview pane** containing a portion of the selected e-mail message (Kevin James) in the message list. When only a portion of an e-mail message displays in the preview pane, the vertical scroll bar allows you to view the hidden part of the message.

More About

Message Headings

You can change the column widths of the column headers in the message list by dragging the vertical line between two column headers. To change the size of the two areas, drag the vertical line that separates the folders list and contacts list from the message list and preview pane.

More About

Reading E-Mail Messages

Many people do not have the Mail window open when they are using Netscape Navigator. When they receive a new e-mail message, Netscape displays a down-pointing arrow over the Mail button on the Task toolbar. Netscape removes the icon when you read the message.

Opening and Reading E-Mail Messages

In Figure 3-2 on page NN 3.6, the highlighted message heading of the Kevin James message displays in the message list, and a portion of the e-mail message displays in the preview pane. If you wish to view the entire e-mail message in a separate window, you must open the e-mail message. Perform the following step to open the e-mail message from Kevin James.

 Steps **To Open (Read) an E-Mail Message**

1 **Double-click the Netscape for Computer Club message and then maximize the Mail window. Point to the Print button.**

The maximized Mail window opens (Figure 3-3). The window contains a menu bar, a Mail toolbar, identifying information about the e-mail message, and a message pane.

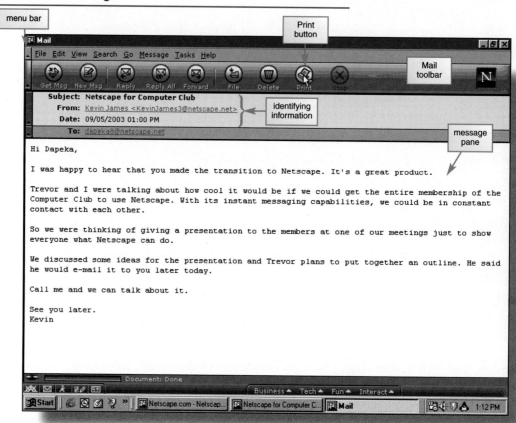

FIGURE 3-3

Other Ways

1. Select message heading, on File menu click Open
2. Right-click in message, click Open Message in New Window on shortcut menu
3. Select message heading, press CTRL+O

When you double-click a message in the message list, Mail displays the message in a separate window, and no longer displays the message heading in bold type.

Below the title bar and menu bar shown in Figure 3-3 is the Mail toolbar. This toolbar contains the buttons needed to work with opened e-mail messages. Refer to Table 3-1 on the previous page for a brief explanation of their functions.

Printing an E-Mail Message

You can print the contents of an e-mail message before or after opening the message. The following steps describe how to print an opened e-mail message.

To Print an Opened E-Mail Message

1 **Click the Print button on the Mail toolbar. When the Print dialog box displays, point to the OK button.**

The Print dialog box displays (Figure 3-4).

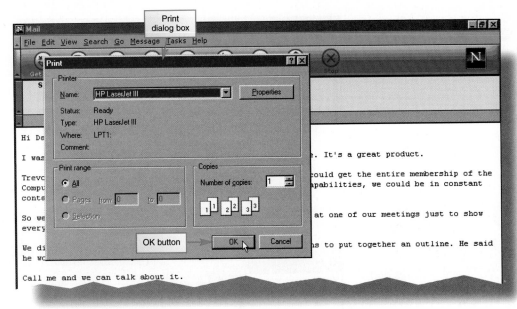

FIGURE 3-4

2 **Click the OK button.**

The printed message consists of Subject, From, Date, and To entries, and the e-mail message (Figure 3-5).

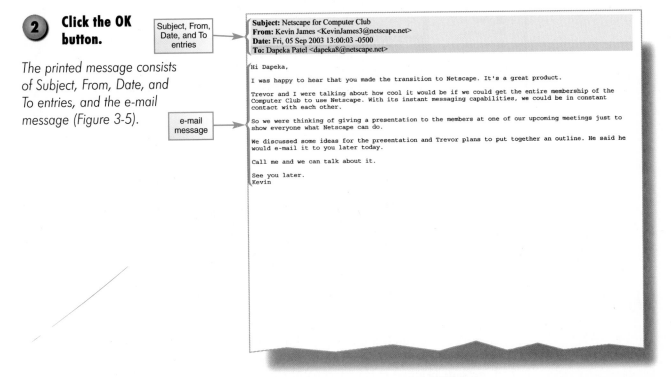

FIGURE 3-5

Closing an E-Mail Message

When you have finished opening and reading an e-mail message, you can close the window containing the e-mail message by performing the steps on the next page.

Other **Ways**

1. On File menu click Print, click OK button
2. Press CTRL+P, press ENTER

To Close an E-Mail Message

1 **Point to the Close button on the title bar (Figure 3-6).**

FIGURE 3-6

2 **Click the Close button. Point to the Reply button.**

The Mail window closes and the Inbox window redisplays (Figure 3-7).

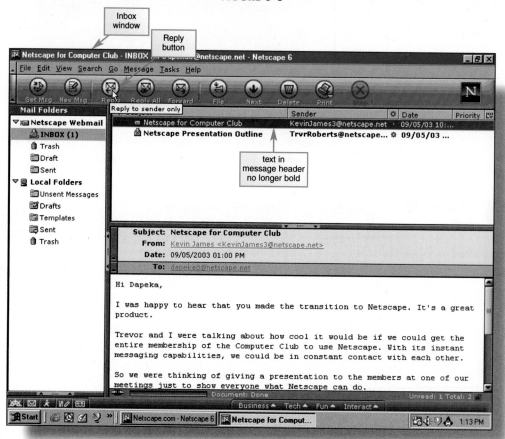

FIGURE 3-7

 Ways

1. On File menu click Close
2. Press CTRL+W

When you double-click a message in the message list, Mail opens the message and displays its contents in a separate window. When you close the window, the e-mail message heading in the message list no longer displays in bold type, which indicates the e-mail message has been opened.

Replying to an E-Mail Message

After closing the e-mail message from Kevin James, you decide to compose and send an e-mail reply to Kevin James. The Reply button on the Mail toolbar allows you to reply quickly to an e-mail message using the sender's e-mail address. Perform the following steps to reply to Kevin James.

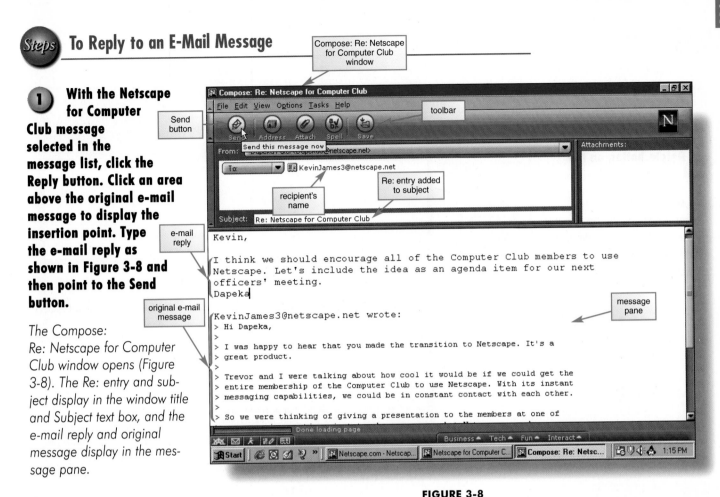

Steps To Reply to an E-Mail Message

1 **With the Netscape for Computer Club message selected in the message list, click the Reply button. Click an area above the original e-mail message to display the insertion point. Type the e-mail reply as shown in Figure 3-8 and then point to the Send button.**

The Compose: Re: Netscape for Computer Club window opens (Figure 3-8). The Re: entry and subject display in the window title and Subject text box, and the e-mail reply and original message display in the message pane.

FIGURE 3-8

2 **Click the Send button.**

The Compose: Re: Netscape for Computer Club window closes, and moves the message to the Sent folder.

Other Ways

1. On Message menu click Reply
2. Press CTRL+R

In Figure 3-8, the KevinJames3@netscape.net e-mail address displays in the To text box, and the original e-mail message is identified by the words, KevinJames3@netscape.net wrote:. In addition, a toolbar displays below the menu bar. Table 3-2 shows the buttons on the toolbar and their functions.

Deleting an E-Mail Message

After reading and replying to an e-mail message, you may wish to delete the original e-mail message from the message list. Deleting a message removes the e-mail from the Inbox folder. If you do not delete unwanted messages, large numbers of messages in the Inbox folder make it difficult to find and read new messages, and it wastes disk space. Perform the steps on the next page to delete the e-mail message from Kevin James.

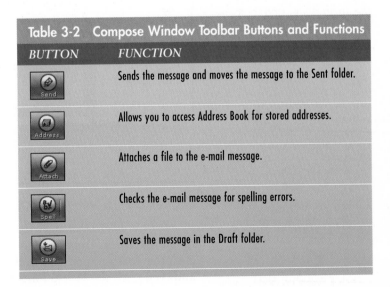

Table 3-2 Compose Window Toolbar Buttons and Functions	
BUTTON	**FUNCTION**
Send	Sends the message and moves the message to the Sent folder.
Address	Allows you to access Address Book for stored addresses.
Attach	Attaches a file to the e-mail message.
Spell	Checks the e-mail message for spelling errors.
Save	Saves the message in the Draft folder.

To Delete an E-Mail Message

1 **If necessary, click the Netscape for Computer Club message in the message list. Point to the Delete button on the Mail toolbar.**

The selected message heading displays in the message list and a portion of the e-mail message displays in the preview pane (Figure 3-9).

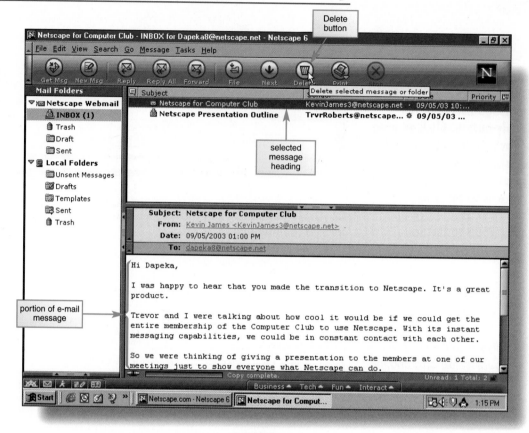

FIGURE 3-9

2 **Click the Delete button. Point to the New Msg button.**

Mail moves the Netscape for Computer Club e-mail message from the Inbox folder to the Trash folder and removes the e-mail entry from the message list (Figure 3-10).

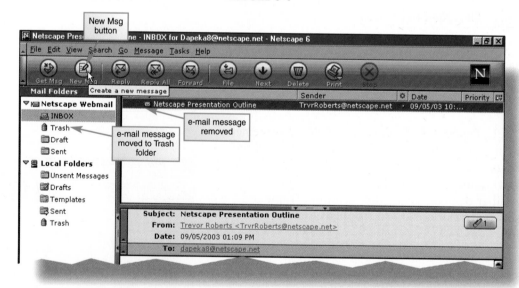

FIGURE 3-10

Other **Ways**

1. Drag e-mail message to Trash folder in folders list
2. On Edit menu click Delete Message
3. Right-click e-mail message, click Delete on shortcut menu

As you delete messages from the Inbox, the number of messages in the Trash folder increases. To permanently delete an e-mail message from the Trash folder, click the Trash folder icon in the folders list, select the message in the message list, and then click the Delete button on the Mail toolbar.

Composing a New E-Mail Message

In addition to opening and reading, replying to, and deleting e-mail messages, you may wish to compose and send a new e-mail message. When you compose an e-mail message, you must know the e-mail address of the recipient of the message, enter a brief one-line subject that identifies the purpose or contents of the message, and type the message itself.

Perform the following steps to compose an e-mail message to Marci Jacobs, the secretary of the Computer Club.

More About

Replying to an E-Mail Message

Some people who receive reply e-mail messages do not want the original e-mail message to display with the reply message. To remove the message from all e-mail replies, click Tools on the menu bar, click Options, click the Send tab, click the Include message in reply check box, and then click the OK button.

Steps **To Compose an E-Mail Message**

1. **Click the New Msg button.**

The Compose window opens (Figure 3-11). The window contains a menu bar, toolbar, two text boxes, the Attachments area, and the message pane. The insertion point is located in the To text box.

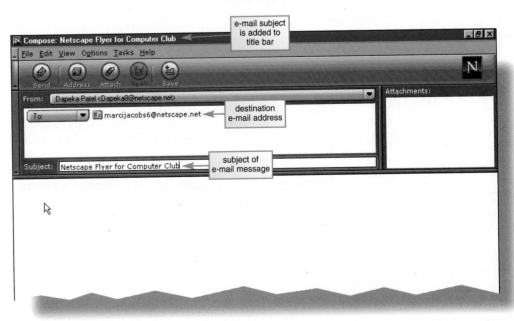

FIGURE 3-11

2. **Type** marcijacobs6 @netscape.net **in the To text box, click the Subject text box, and then type** Netscape Flyer for Computer Club **in the Subject text box.**

The destination e-mail address displays in the To text box, and the subject of the message displays in the Subject text box (Figure 3-12). The title bar of the Compose window now displays the subject of the e-mail message.

FIGURE 3-12

3 Press the TAB key. Type the e-mail message as shown in Figure 3-13.

The e-mail message displays in the message pane (Figure 3-13).

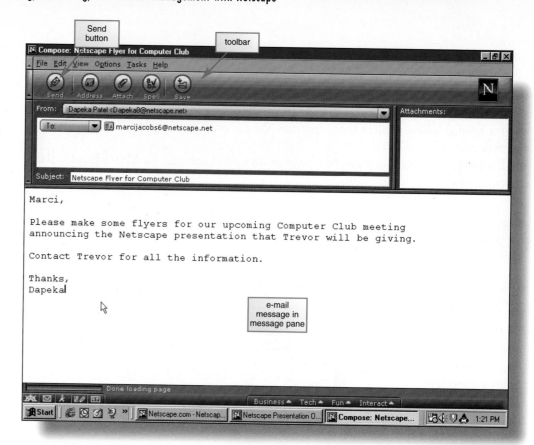

FIGURE 3-13

The Compose window shown in Figure 3-13 contains a toolbar containing buttons specific to composing a new e-mail message. The buttons on the toolbar are explained in Table 3-2 on page NN 3.11.

Sending an E-Mail Message

After composing an e-mail message, send the message by performing the following step.

TO SEND AN E-MAIL MESSAGE

1 Click the Send button on the Mail toolbar.

The Compose window closes, and then Mail stores the message in the Sent folder.

Opening an Attachment in an E-Mail Message

The remaining message in the message list, Netscape Presentation Outline, contains an attachment. The attachment icon displayed in the preview pane in Figure 3-14 indicates this. The following steps describe how to open and view an attachment.

About

Personalizing an E-Mail Message

You can personalize an e-mail message using smileys (smiley faces) in your message. For example, the :-) smiley means I am happy/I am smiling; the :-(smiley means I am sad/I am unhappy; the :-D smiley means I am laughing; and the :-O smiley means I am surprised.

To Open and View an Attachment

1 **Select the Netscape Presentation Outline message.**

A portion of the Netscape Presentation Outline message displays in the preview pane (Figure 3-14).

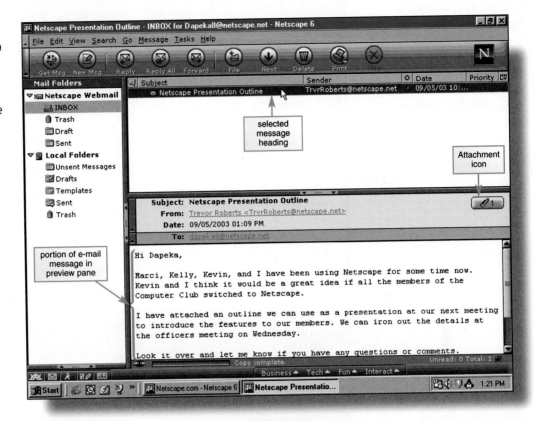

FIGURE 3-14

2 **Double-click the selected message to open the Mail window. With the window maximized, click the Attachment icon and then point to Netscape Presentation Outline.doc.**

The Mail window opens, and the Netscape Presentation Outline.doc attachment is selected (Figure 3-15).

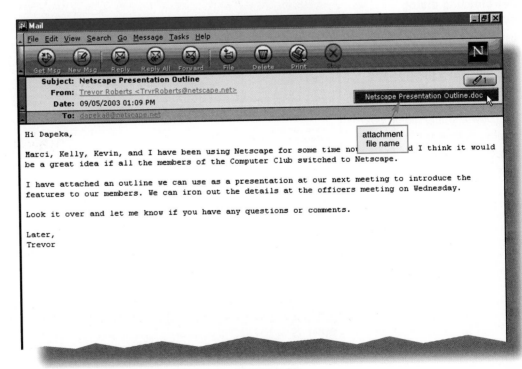

FIGURE 3-15

3 **Click Netscape Presentation Outline.doc. When the Open/Save Attachment dialog box displays, click Open it and then point to the OK button.**

The Open/Save Attachment dialog box displays (Figure 3-16).

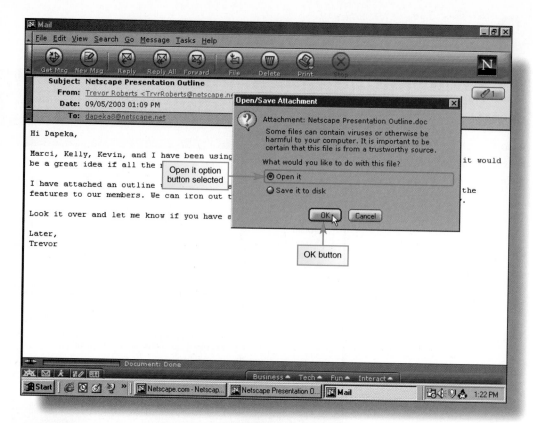

FIGURE 3-16

4 **Click the OK button. When the Downloading dialog box displays, click Open using, make certain Word displays in the Choose text box, and then point to the OK button.**

The Downloading dialog box displays with Word as the default application for this attachment (Figure 3-17).

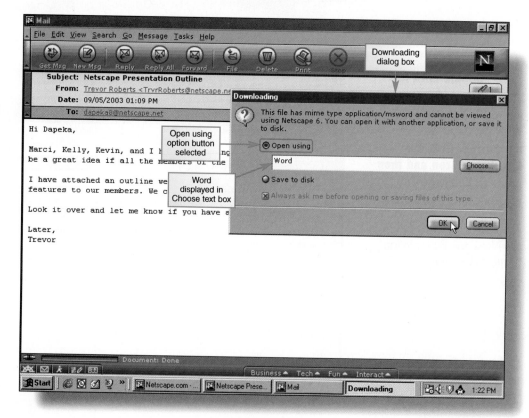

FIGURE 3-17

5 Click the OK button.

The Microsoft Word window opens with the Netscape Presentation Outline document displayed (Figure 3-18).

6 Click the Close button on the Word title bar to close Word.

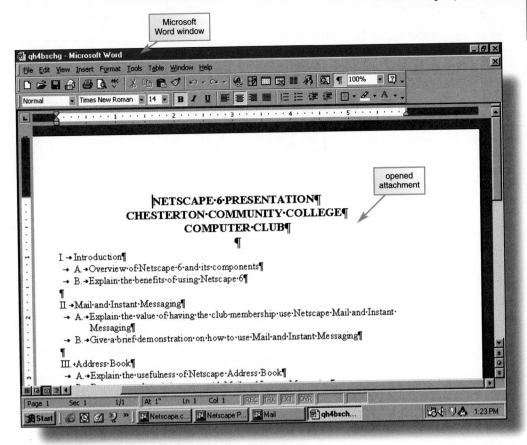

FIGURE 3-18

File attachments can be anything from spreadsheets to pictures. Netscape gives you the option of viewing the attachment as you read the e-mail, or you can save it to a file to view at another time.

Quitting Netscape Mail

When you have finished reading, replying to, and sending e-mail messages, you should quit Netscape Mail by performing the following step.

TO QUIT NETSCAPE MAIL

1 Click the Close button on the Inbox window's title bar.

The Netscape home page redisplays.

Internet Newsgroups

Besides exchanging e-mail messages, another popular method of communicating over the Internet is to read and place messages in a newsgroup. A **newsgroup** is one of a collection of news and discussion groups that you can access via the Internet. Each newsgroup is devoted to a particular subject. A special computer, called a **news server**, contains related groups and newsgroups.

More *About*

Newsgroup Articles

Many newsgroup articles contain pictures, movies, and sound clips. Check the newsgroup name for the words: pictures, movies, or audio.

To participate in a newsgroup, you must use a program called a **newsreader**. The newsreader enables you to access a newsgroup to read a previously entered message, which is called an **article**; or you can add an article, which is called **posting**. A newsreader also keeps track of which articles you have read and have not read. In this project, you will use Netscape Mail, which is a newsreader, to read and post articles.

Newsgroup members often post articles in reply to other articles — either to answer questions or to comment on material in the original articles. These replies often cause the author of the original article, or others, to post additional articles related to the original article. This process can be short-lived or go on indefinitely, depending on the nature of the topic and the interest of the participants. The original article and all subsequent related replies are called a **thread**. Figure 3-19 shows some articles and threads from a newsgroup called netscape.public.general.

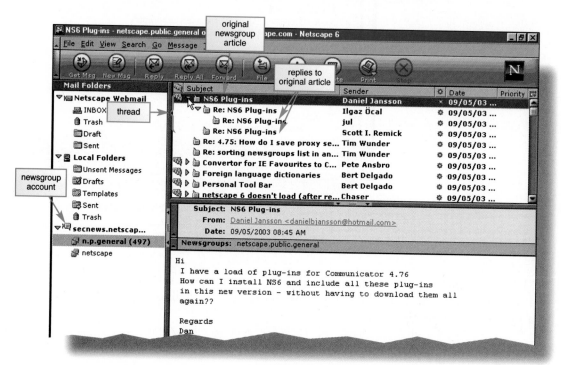

FIGURE 3-19

Table 3-3	Newsgroup Prefixes
PREFIX	**DESCRIPTION**
alt	Groups on alternative topics
biz	Business topics
comp	Computer topics
gnu	GNU Software Foundation topics
ieee	Electrical engineering topics
info	Information about various topics
misc	Miscellaneous topics
news	Groups pertaining to newsgroups
rec	Recreational topics
sci	Science topics
talk	Various conversation groups

Newsgroups exist on products from vendors such as Netscape and IBM; on subjects such as recipes, gardening, and music; or on just about any other topic you can imagine. A **newsgroup name** consists of a prefix and one or more subgroup names. For example, the comp.software newsgroup name consists of a **prefix** (comp), which indicates the subject of the newsgroup is computers; a period (.); and a **subgroup name** (software), which indicates the subject is further narrowed down to a discussion of software. A list of some prefix names and their descriptions are shown in Table 3-3.

The newsgroup prefixes found in Table 3-3 are not the only ones used. Innovative newsgroups are being created every day. Many colleges and universities have their own newsgroups on topics such as administrative information, tutoring, campus organizations, and distance learning.

In addition, some newsgroups are supervised by a **moderator**, who reads each article before it is posted to the newsgroup. If the moderator thinks an article is appropriate for the newsgroup, he or she posts the article for all members to read.

Accessing Newsgroups Using Netscape Help

Before accessing the articles in a newsgroup or posting an article to a newsgroup, you must establish a newsgroup account on your computer. A **newsgroup account** allows access to the news server with the same name. The newsgroup account secnews.netscape.com displays in Figure 3-19.

The secnews.netscape.com account is available through Netscape Help. Perform the following steps to establish an account with this newsgroup.

Local Newsgroups

Many schools have created local newsgroups where you can ask technical questions and get information about current events. Look for newsgroup names containing the school's name.

 To Access a Newsgroup Using Netscape Help

1 **Click Help on the menu bar and then point to Feedback Center.**

The Help menu displays (Figure 3-20).

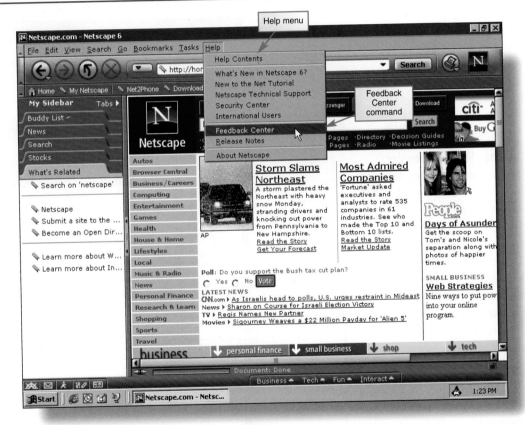

FIGURE 3-20

2 **Click Feedback Center. Scroll down until the Chat with others about Netscape 6 section displays and then point to the Security link.**

The Netscape 6 Feedback Center page displays (Figure 3-21) with a list of newsgroups for various Help topics.

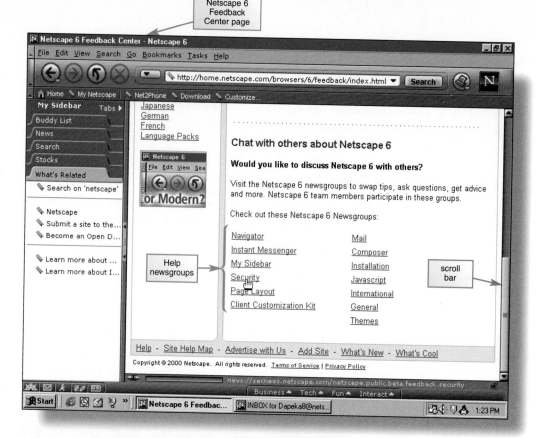

FIGURE 3-21

3 **Click the Security link. When the Account Wizard Identity dialog box displays, enter your name and e-mail address and then click the Next button three times until the Account Wizard Congratulations dialog box displays. Click the Finish button. When the Mail window opens, maximize it if necessary and then click the secnews.netscape.com folder.**

The Mail window opens and the secnews.netscape.com folder is selected (Figure 3-22). You must enter information only in the Account Wizard Identity dialog box. The remainder of the dialog boxes contains default values that you will use for this exercise.

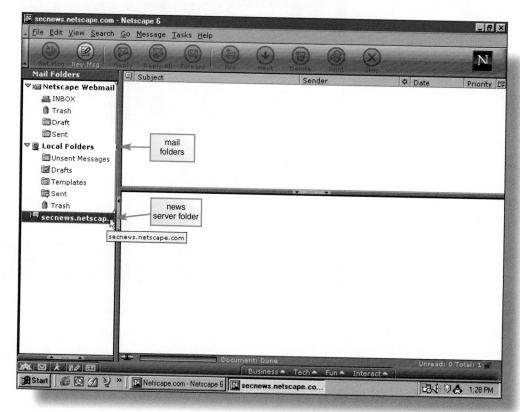

FIGURE 3-22

Now that you have set up an account for the secnews.netscape.com news server, the next step will be to view the available newsgroups within that server and then subscribe to a newsgroup. When you **subscribe** to a newsgroup, the newsgroup name displays in the folder list, making it easy to return to the newsgroup.

Subscribing to a Newsgroup

Several hundred newsgroups may be listed under a news server. Searching for a previously visited newsgroup or scrolling through the newsgroup to find a previously visited newsgroup can be time-consuming. To quickly find a previously visited newsgroup, Netscape Mail allows you to subscribe to a newsgroup. **Subscribing to a newsgroup** permanently adds the newsgroup name to the folders list. This allows you to return quickly to the newsgroup by clicking the newsgroup name in the folders list instead of searching or scrolling to find the newsgroup name. Perform the following steps to subscribe to the netscape.public.general newsgroup.

 To Subscribe to a Newsgroup

① **With the secnews. netscape.com folder selected, click File on the menu bar and then point to Subscribe.**

The File menu displays (Figure 3-23).

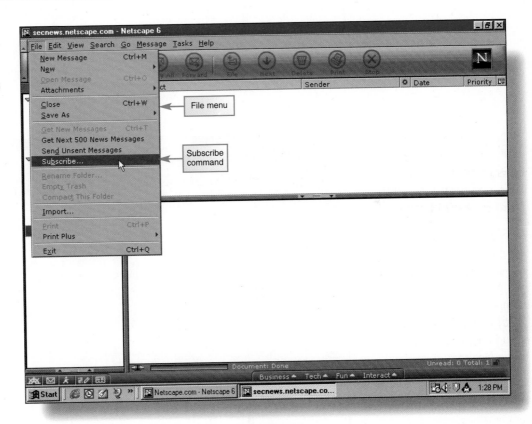

FIGURE 3-23

2 **Click Subscribe.**
When the Subscribe
dialog box displays, click
the arrow next to netscape
and then click the arrow
next to
netscape.public.

The Subscribe dialog
box displays with a list
of available newsgroups
under the secnews.netscape.
com server (Figure 3-24).

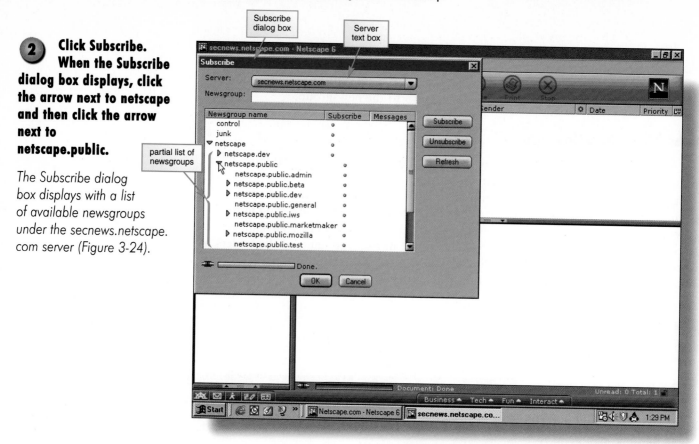

FIGURE 3-24

3 **Select the netscape.**
public.general
newsgroup. Click the
Subscribe button and then
point to the OK button.

A check mark displays next to
the netscape.public.general
newsgroup, indicating that
you have chosen to subscribe
to this newsgroup (Figure
3-25). The selected news-
group name also displays
in the Newsgroup text box.

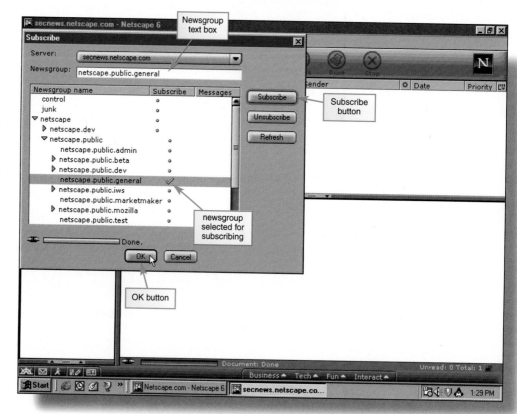

FIGURE 3-25

4 **Click the OK button. When the Subscribe dialog box closes, point to the n.p.general folder in the folders list.**

The Mail window opens. The n.p.general folder displays in the folders list, and a list of messages displays in the message list (Figure 3-26).

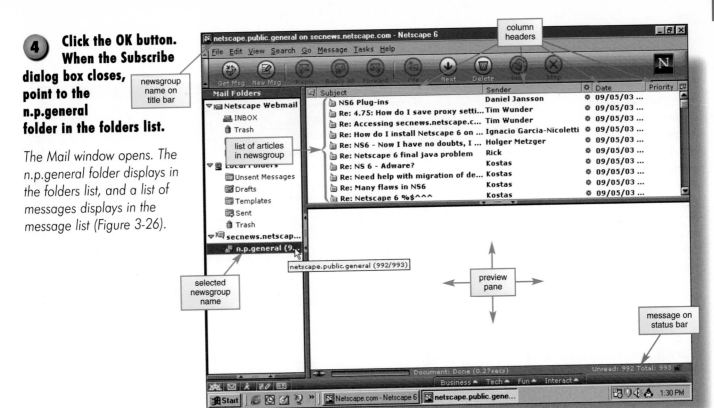

FIGURE 3-26

The upper-right frame (message list) contains column headers and a list of the original articles, or postings, in the netscape.public.general newsgroup. Each original article consists of the subject of the article, sender name, and date the article was sent.

When you select an article in the message list, the text of the article displays in the preview pane. In Figure 3-26, the preview pane indicates no message is selected.

The status bar at the bottom of the Mail window indicates that 993 articles have been retrieved, and 992 articles have not been read.

Reading Newsgroup Articles

The entries in the Subject column in the message list allow you to look at the subject of an article before deciding to read the article. Perform the step on the next page to read the NS6 Plug-ins article.

Other Ways

1. Right-click news server folder, click Subscribe

More About

Column Headers

You can change the widths of columns in the message list by dragging the vertical line between two column headers. Likewise, you can drag the vertical line that separates the folders list and contacts list from the message list and preview pane to change the size of the two areas.

Steps   To Read a Newsgroup Article

1   **Click the thread icon to view which articles contain threads and then click the NS6 Plug-ins article. Point to the right-pointing arrow to the left of the of NS6 Plug-ins article.**

The contents of the article display in the preview pane (Figure 3-27). A header in the preview pane contains the subject of the article, the name of the person who posted the article, the date the article was posted, and the newsgroup name.

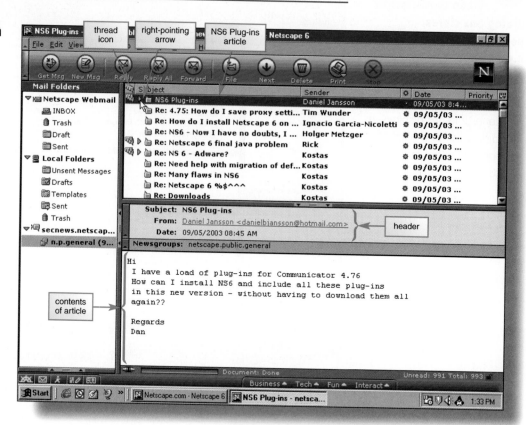

FIGURE 3-27

By clicking the thread icon, you displayed icons next to the articles that contain threads. The next section explains how to view these threads.

Expanding a Thread

When a multiple newsgroup icon and a right-pointing arrow display to the left of an article in the message list, the article is part of a thread and can be expanded. **Expanding a thread** displays the replies to the original article indented below the original article and changes the right-pointing arrow to a down-pointing arrow. To expand the NS6 Plug-ins thread and view the replies to the article, complete the following step.

Steps To Expand a Thread

1 **Click the right-pointing arrow to the left of the NS6 Plug-ins article and then click the first reply below the original article.**

The right-pointing arrow to the left of the original article changes to a down-pointing arrow, and two replies display below the original article (Figure 3-28). The Re: entry displays to the left of each reply, the first reply is selected, and the text of the first reply displays in the preview pane.

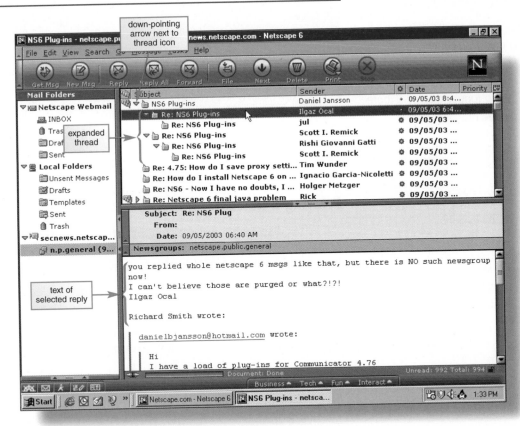

FIGURE 3-28

Other Ways

1. On View menu point to Messages, click Expand All Threads

Collapsing a Thread

When you expand a thread, a down-pointing arrow replaces the right-pointing arrow to the left of the original article. Sometimes, after reading the replies within a thread, you will want to collapse the thread. **Collapsing the thread** removes the replies from the thread, displays the original article in the preview pane, and changes the down-pointing arrow to the left of the original article back to a right-pointing arrow. To collapse the NS6 Plug-ins thread, perform the following steps.

Steps To Collapse a Thread

1 **Point to the arrow to the left of the original NS6 Plug-ins article (Figure 3-29).**

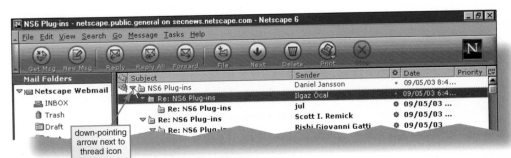

FIGURE 3-29

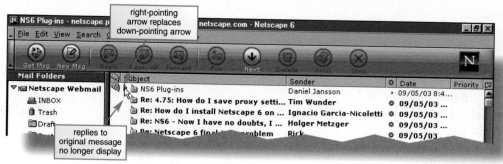

2 **Click the down-pointing arrow.**

The arrow to the left of the original article changes back to a right-pointing arrow, and the replies to the original article no longer display (Figure 3-30).

FIGURE 3-30

Printing a Newsgroup Article

After displaying and reading an article, you may wish to print the article. The printout is similar to the printout that results when you print an e-mail message (see Figure 3-5 on page NN 3.9). Perform the following steps to print the contents of the original NS6 Plug-ins article.

TO PRINT A NEWSGROUP ARTICLE

1 Select the appropriate newsgroup article.

2 Click the Print button on the Mail toolbar.

3 Click the OK button in the Print dialog box.

The printed message consists of Subject, From, Date, and Newsgroups entries and the body of the message (Figure 3-31). The Newsgroups entry contains the newsgroup name, and the Subject entry contains the article name.

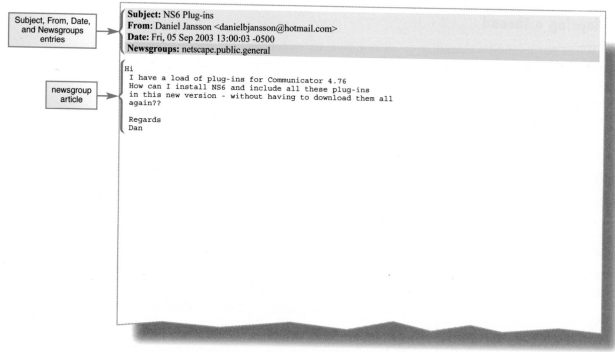

FIGURE 3-31

Posting a Newsgroup Article

At some point in time, you may wish to **post**, or send, a reply to a newsgroup article. The steps on the following pages show how to submit a newsgroup article for posting to the netscape.public.test newsgroup. This is a newsgroup for miscellaneous purposes. Posting to this newsgroup will not disturb any other newsgroup articles.

Before you can post a reply to the netscape.public.test newsgroup, you must first subscribe to the newsgroup. Perform the following steps to subscribe to the netscape.public.test newsgroup.

TO SUBSCRIBE TO A NEWSGROUP

1. Select the secnews.netscape.com folder in the folders list, and then click Subscribe on the File menu.

2. When the Subscribe dialog box displays, click netscape.public.test, click the Subscribe button, and then click the OK button.

The n.p.test folder displays in the folder list (see Figure 3-32).

After displaying the articles in the netscape.public.test newsgroup, post a test article to the newsgroup. Use the words, Test Message, as the subject of the article to indicate that the article is a test and can be disregarded by anyone browsing the newsgroup. Perform the following steps to post a test article.

More About

Newsgroups

Instructors use newsgroups in courses taught over the Internet. An instructor posts a question and students respond by posting an article. Students can read the articles in the thread to be aware of all responses and subscribe to the newsgroup to return to it quickly.

 To Post a Newsgroup Article

1. **Point to the New Msg button on the Mail toolbar (Figure 3-32).**

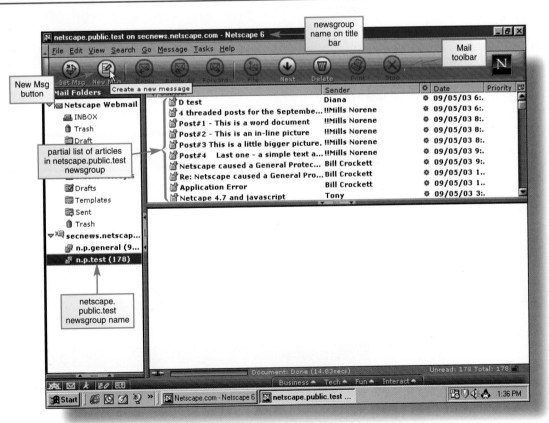

FIGURE 3-32

② **Click the New Msg button and then maximize the Compose window.**

The Compose window opens (Figure 3-33). The window contains a menu bar, a toolbar, three text boxes, a Formatting toolbar, and a message pane. The News-group text box contains the newsgroup name (netscape.public.test), and the Subject text box contains the insertion point.

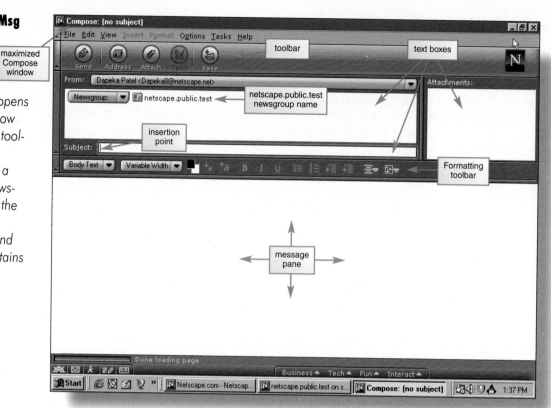

FIGURE 3-33

③ **Type** Test Message **in the Subject text box, press the TAB key, type** Please ignore this message. I am learning to post a message to a newsgroup. **as the message, and then point to the Send button.**

The subject displays on the title bar and in the Subject text box, and the message displays in the message pane (Figure 3-34). The subject indicates that this is a test message and can be disregarded.

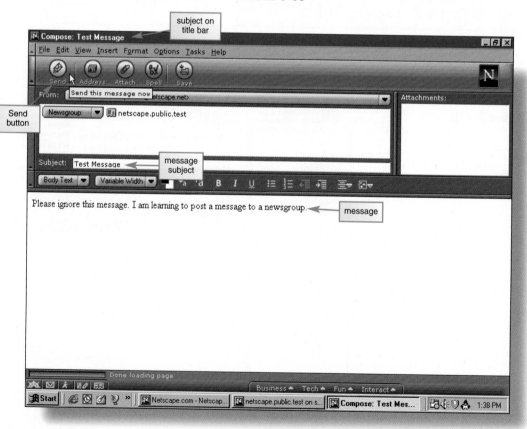

FIGURE 3-34

4 **Click the Send button. When the Mail window redisplays, scroll down until the new posting is visible and then click the new posting.**

The Compose window closes and the Mail window redisplays (Figure 3-35). The Test Message article displays in the message list, and the contents of the message display in the preview pane.

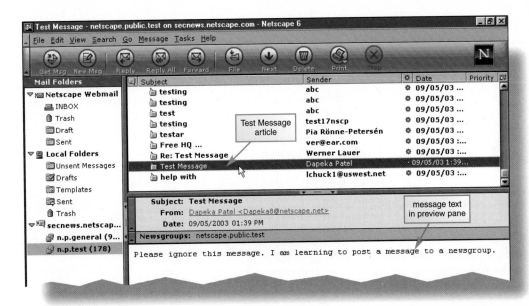

FIGURE 3-35

Other Ways

1. On File menu click New Message
2. Press CTRL+M

Displaying the Articles in a Newsgroup after Subscribing to the Newsgroup

Earlier in this project, you subscribed to the netscape.public.general newsgroup. After subscribing to a newsgroup, you can view the articles in the newsgroup by clicking the newsgroup name in the folders list without having to search or scroll to find the articles in the newsgroup. Perform the following step to view the articles in the netscape.public.general newsgroup.

 **To Display the Articles in a Newsgroup**

 1 **Click n.p.general in the folders list.**

The netscape.public.general newsgroup name is selected in the folders list, and the articles in the newsgroup display in the message list (Figure 3-36).

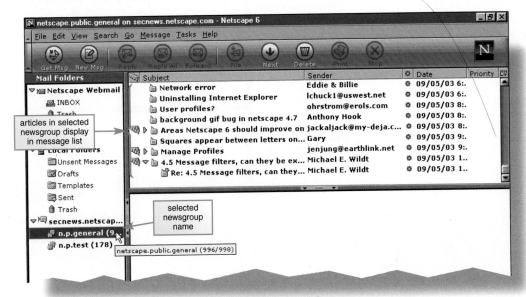

FIGURE 3-36

Unsubscribing from a Newsgroup

When you no longer need quick access to a newsgroup, you can cancel the subscription to the newsgroup, a process called **unsubscribing**, and then remove the newsgroup name from the folders list. Perform the following steps to unsubscribe from the netscape.public.general newsgroup.

 To Unsubscribe from a Newsgroup

1 Select the netscape. public.general newsgroup name in the folders list and then point to the Delete button on the Mail toolbar (Figure 3-37).

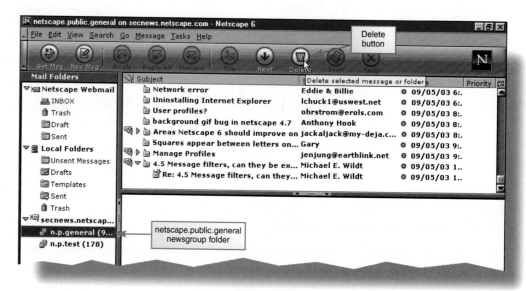

FIGURE 3-37

2 Click the Delete button.

The newsgroup name is removed from the folders list, indicating the subscription to the newsgroup has been cancelled (Figure 3-38).

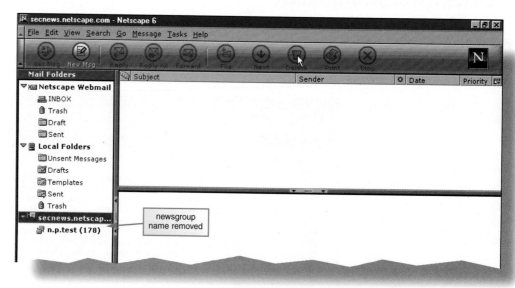

FIGURE 3-38

 **Other Ways**

1. On Edit menu click Delete Folder

Quitting Netscape Mail

When you have finished working with newsgroups, you should quit Netscape Mail, as shown in the following step.

TO QUIT NETSCAPE MAIL

 Click the Close button on the Netscape Mail title bar.

The Mail window closes, and the Netscape home page redisplays.

Address Books

The **Address Book** application of Netscape allows you to store information about individuals or companies. Netscape provides you with two address books: Personal Address Book and Collected Addresses. The **Personal Address Book** is where you enter your own contacts. **Contacts** are people with whom you communicate for school, business, social, or personal reasons. The **Collected Addresses** address book collects e-mail addresses from incoming and outgoing messages. Incoming addresses are stored as soon as you open a message; outgoing addresses are stored as soon as you send a message. Netscape address books allow you to store names, addresses, e-mail addresses, and more. Once the information has been entered, your address book can be retrieved, sorted, edited, organized, or printed.

When you open the Address Book window, information about each contact displays on an address card. Each address card includes fields such as name, address, various telephone numbers, as well as e-mail and Web page addresses.

The following sections describe how to create, edit, and print a contact list containing the contacts shown in Table 3-4.

Table 3-4 Contact Information

NAME	E-MAIL ADDRESS	ADDRESS	TELEPHONE
Kevin James	kevinjames3@netscape.net	5721 O'Hara Dr. Valparaiso, IN 46385	(219) 555-1234
Trevor Roberts	trvrroberts@netscape.net	8315 W. 5th St. Chesterton, IN 46304	(219) 555-6543
Kelly Higgins	kellyhigginsnet@netscape.net	9823 Sandpiper Dr. Griffith, IN 46319	(219) 555-8527
Marci Jacobs	marcijacobs6@netscape.net	5645 Central Ave. Portage, IN 46368	(219) 555-9514

Adding Entries to the Address Book

The following steps describe how to enter the data in Table 3-4 in the Address Book.

 To Add an Entry in the Address Book

1 **Point to the Address Book button on the Task toolbar (Figure 3-39).**

FIGURE 3-39

2 **Click the Address Book button to open the Address Book window. If the Instant Message dialog box displays, click the Cancel button. Instant messaging is covered later in this project. When the Address Book window opens, if necessary, maximize it. Click the My Sidebar handle to close My Sidebar and then point to the New Card button on the toolbar.**

The Address Book window displays the address book folders in the folders list, a contact listing pane, a contact detail pane, and a toolbar (Figure 3-40).

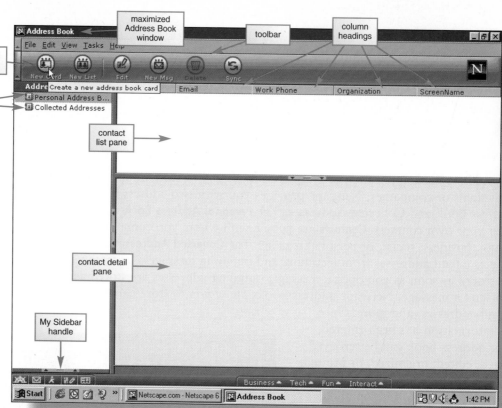

FIGURE 3-40

3 **Click the New Card button.**

The New Card dialog box displays (Figure 3-41). This dialog box allows you to enter general contact information.

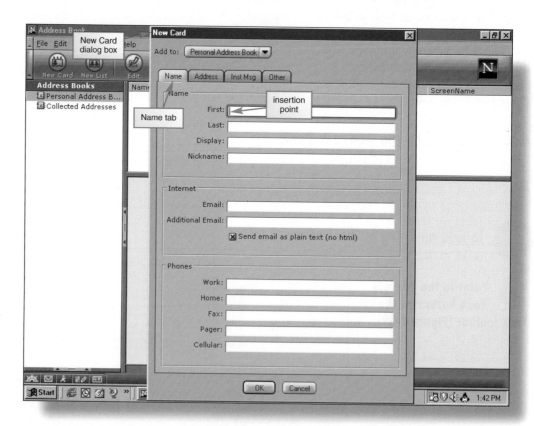

FIGURE 3-41

4 In the New Card dialog box, type Kevin in the First text box in the Name area. Press the TAB key and then type James in the Last text box. Press the TAB key until the insertion point displays in the Email text box. Type kevinjames3 @netscape.net then press the TAB key until the insertion point is positioned in the Home text box in the Phones section. Type (219) 555-1234 and then point to the Address tab.

The New Card dialog box contains the e-mail address and home telephone number for Kevin James (Figure 3-42).

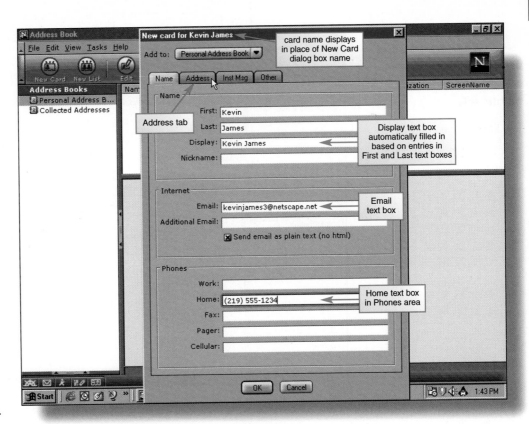

FIGURE 3-42

5 Click the Address tab and then click in the Address text box. Type 5721 O'Hara Dr. in the Address text box. Click the City text box, type Valparaiso and then tab to the State text box. Type IN and then press the TAB key to move the insertion point to the Zip text box. Type 46385 and then point to the OK button.

The Address sheet displays Kevin James' address (Figure 3-43).

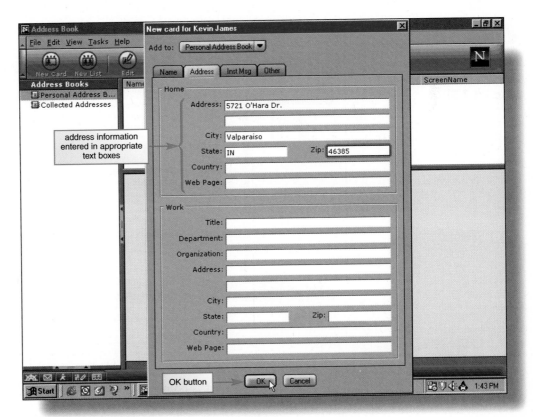

FIGURE 3-43

6 **Click the OK button. When the Address Book window redisplays, click Kevin James in the contact list.**

The Kevin James address book card displays (Figure 3-44).

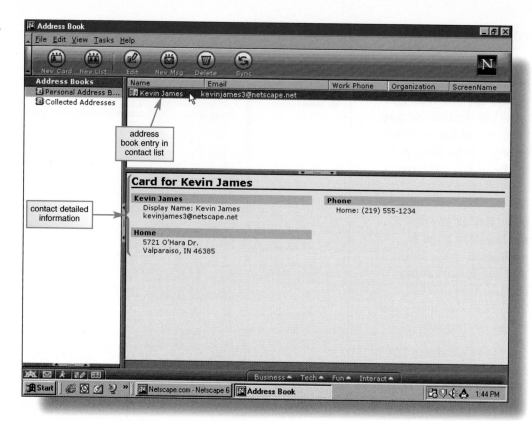

FIGURE 3-44

7 **Repeat Steps 3 through 6 to enter the three remaining contacts in Table 3-4 on page NN 3.31.**

The completed address book should look like Figure 3-45.

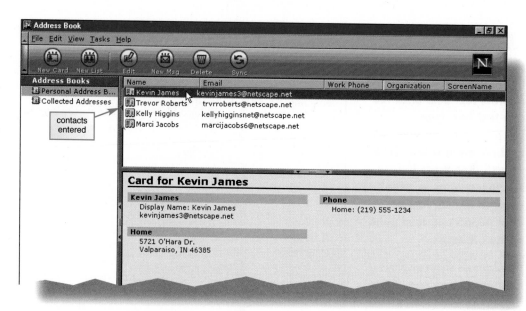

FIGURE 3-45

Other Ways

1. On menu bar click Tasks, click Address Book
2. In Address Book window click New Address Book Card on File menu
3. Press CTRL+5

Once the contact list is complete, it can be viewed, edited, or updated at any time. To display and edit the information for a contact, double-click the entry to display the Address Card dialog box. Clicking the different tabs allows you to enter information about a contact, such as Web page addresses and work telephone numbers.

Sorting the Address Book

Netscape allows you to sort your address book entries in one of four ways: Name, E-Mail Address, Work Phone, or Organization. For the list created in this project, it will be sufficient to sort them alphabetically by name. The following steps illustrate this procedure.

 To Sort Address Book Entries

1 **Click View on the menu bar and then point to Sort by. Point to Name on the Sort by submenu.**

The View menu and the Sort by submenu display (Figure 3-46).

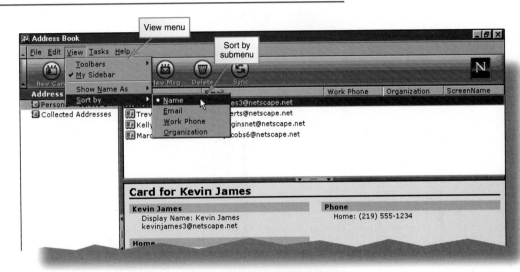

FIGURE 3-46

2 **Click Name.**

The address entries display sorted by the person's first name (Figure 3-47).

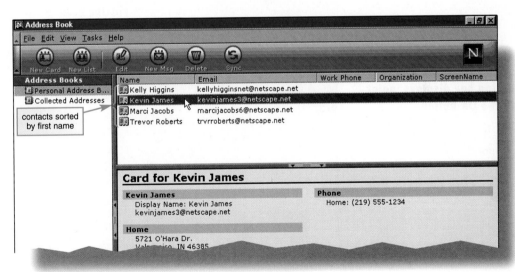

FIGURE 3-47

Printing an Address Book Card

Printing an address book card is an easy way to obtain a hard copy of information about a person you frequently contact. The printed card can be used for business mailings, invitations to social gatherings, or even a telephone or Christmas card list. The steps on the next page describe how to print an address book card.

Steps | **To Print an Address Book Card**

1 Select the Kelly Higgins address book entry, click File on the menu bar, and then point to Print Card.

The Kelly Higgins entry is selected, and the File menu displays (Figure 3-48).

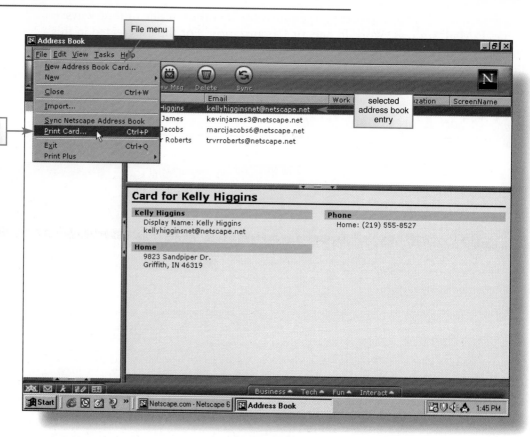

FIGURE 3-48

2 Click Print Card. When the Print dialog box displays, point to the OK button.

The Print dialog box displays (Figure 3-49).

3 Click the OK button.

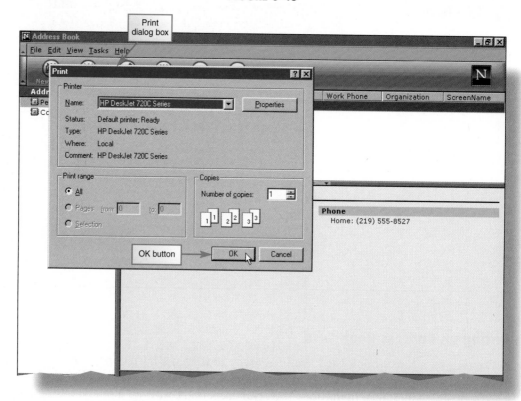

FIGURE 3-49

4 Repeat Steps 1 through 3 to print the remaining Address Book entries.

The printed Address Book cards should look like the printouts shown in Figure 3-50.

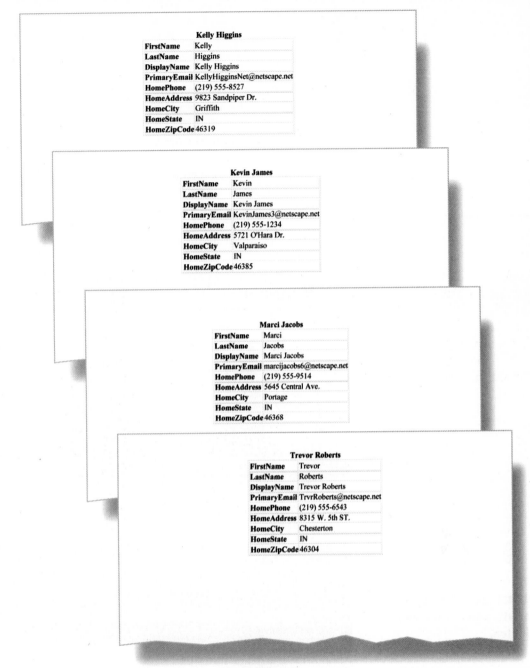

Kelly Higgins

FirstName	Kelly
LastName	Higgins
DisplayName	Kelly Higgins
PrimaryEmail	KellyHigginsNet@netscape.net
HomePhone	(219) 555-8527
HomeAddress	9823 Sandpiper Dr.
HomeCity	Griffith
HomeState	IN
HomeZipCode	46319

Kevin James

FirstName	Kevin
LastName	James
DisplayName	Kevin James
PrimaryEmail	KevinJames3@netscape.net
HomePhone	(219) 555-1234
HomeAddress	5721 O'Hara Dr.
HomeCity	Valparaiso
HomeState	IN
HomeZipCode	46385

Marci Jacobs

FirstName	Marci
LastName	Jacobs
DisplayName	Marci Jacobs
PrimaryEmail	marcijacobs6@netscape.net
HomePhone	(219) 555-9514
HomeAddress	5645 Central Ave.
HomeCity	Portage
HomeState	IN
HomeZipCode	46368

Trevor Roberts

FirstName	Trevor
LastName	Roberts
DisplayName	Trevor Roberts
PrimaryEmail	TrvrRoberts@netscape.net
HomePhone	(219) 555-6543
HomeAddress	8315 W. 5th ST.
HomeCity	Chesterton
HomeState	IN
HomeZipCode	46304

FIGURE 3-50

Other **Ways**

1. Press CTRL+P

Quitting Address Book

Once you have finished adding or editing your Address Book entries, you should quit Netscape Address Book, as shown in the following step.

TO QUIT NETSCAPE ADDRESS BOOK

1 Click the Close button on the Address Book title bar.

The Address Book window closes, and the Netscape home page redisplays.

Instant Messenger

One of the more useful communication tools offered by Netscape is Instant Messenger. **Instant Messenger** allows you to communicate instantly with your online contacts. The advantage of using Instant Messenger over e-mail is that the message you are sending displays immediately on the machine of the person with whom you are communicating, provided that person has Instant Messenger open on his or her machine.

With Instant Messenger, you create a **buddy list** of online contacts that you want to receive your instant messages. The Instant Messenger Buddy List also allows you to see which contacts are or are not online.

Before using Instant Messenger, you first must activate Instant Messenger. The following steps illustrate how to open and activate Netscape Instant Messenger.

Steps To Start Netscape Instant Messenger

1 Point to the Instant Messenger button on the Task toolbar (Figure 3-51).

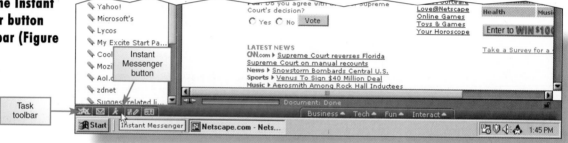

FIGURE 3-51

2 Click the Instant Messenger button. When the Instant Messenger Setup wizard starts, point to the Next button.

The first Instant Messenger Setup Wizard dialog box displays (Figure 3-52).

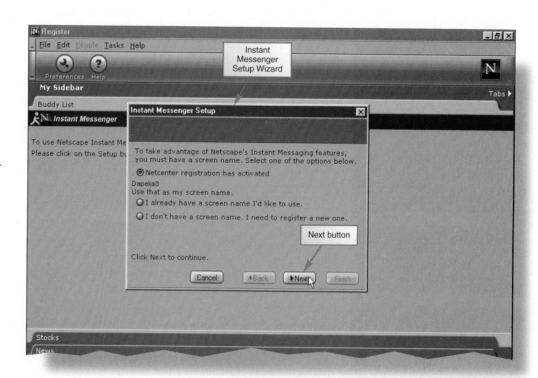

FIGURE 3-52

3 Click the Next button and then click the Finish button. When the Sign On window opens, maximize the window and then click in the Password text box.

The Sign On window opens (Figure 3-53).

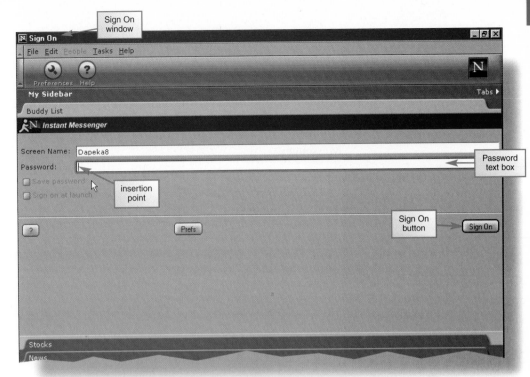

FIGURE 3-53

4 Type your password in the Password text box and then click the Sign On button. When the Buddy List Window opens, point to the List Setup tab.

The maximized Buddy List Window opens (Figure 3-54).

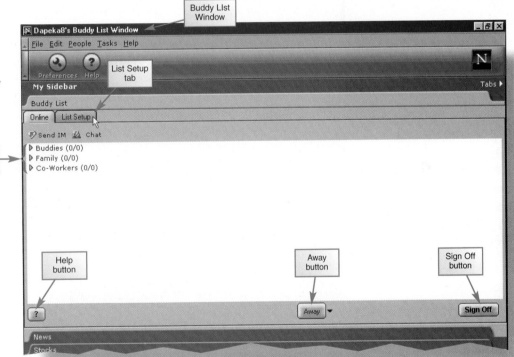

FIGURE 3-54

Other Ways

1. Click Buddy List tab on My Sidebar
2. On Tasks menu click Instant Messenger
3. Press CTRL+3

With Instant Messenger activated, you are ready to build a buddy list. To add someone to your buddy list, you must know his or her screen name. A **screen name**, or user name, is the unique name a person uses when they log on to Netscape; for example, Dapeka's screen name is Dapeka8. Netscape has two methods of adding people to its Buddy List: through Instant Messenger itself and through Address Book. Both methods are shown in this project. The following steps show how to add one of the authors of this book, Jeff Webb, to the Buddy List using Instant Messenger.

Steps **To Add a Buddy in Instant Messenger**

① **Click the List Setup tab. Point to the Add Buddy button.**

The List Setup sheet displays (Figure 3-55). This sheet allows you to add to, delete from, or group names on the Buddy List.

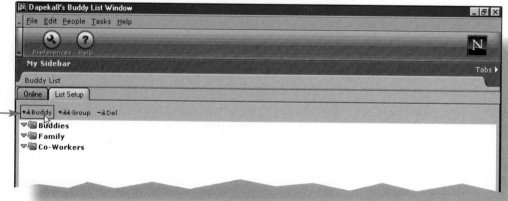

FIGURE 3-55

② **Click the Add Buddy button. When the Add Buddy dialog box displays type** JWebbJJ **in the Buddy Name text box. Make sure the Buddies check box is selected and then point to the OK button.**

The Add Buddy dialog box displays (Figure 3-56). Netscape provides three groups to choose from when deciding where to place your Buddy List entries.

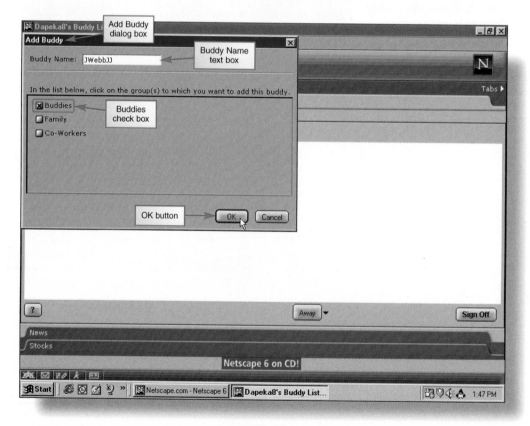

FIGURE 3-56

3 Click the OK button. When the Buddy List window redisplays, point to the Online tab.

The Buddy List window redisplays with the JWebbJJ entry in the Buddies folder (Figure 3-57).

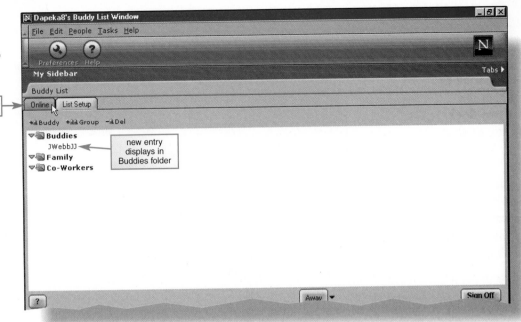

FIGURE 3-57

4 Click the Online tab.

The Online sheet displays showing zero of one contact online (Figure 3-58).

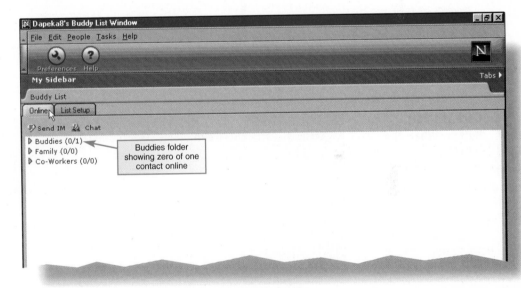

FIGURE 3-58

When you add a person to the Buddy List, Netscape automatically enters them in the Address Book. The reverse also holds true: if you add a person's screen name in the Address Book, Netscape automatically adds it to the Buddy List. Earlier in this project, you added four names to the Address Book. Table 3-5 shows the screen names for those four people.

The steps on the next page illustrate how to go into the Address Book and add those four individuals' screen names, which also adds them to the Buddy List.

Other Ways

1. On People menu click Add a Buddy

Table 3-5	Screen Names for Contacts
CONTACT	SCREEN NAME
Kevin James	KevinJames3
Trevor Roberts	TrvrRoberts
Kelly Higgins	KellyHigginsNet
Marci Jacobs	MarciJacobs6

To Add a Buddy Using Address Book

1 **Open the Address Book** by clicking the Address Book button on the task bar. When the Address Book window opens, if necessary, maximize it. Select Kevin James in the contact list and then point to the Edit button on the toolbar.

The Address Book window opens with the four previously entered contacts (Figure 3-59).

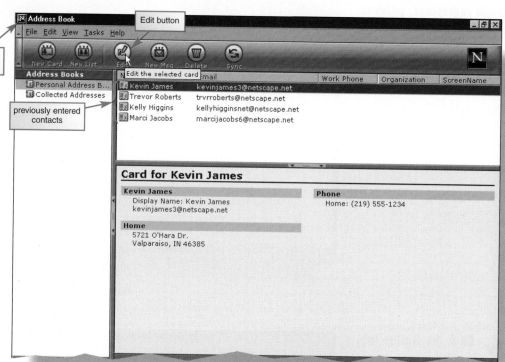

FIGURE 3-59

2 **Click the Edit button. When the Card for Kevin James dialog box displays, point to the Inst Msg tab.**

The address book card for Kevin James displays (Figure 3-60).

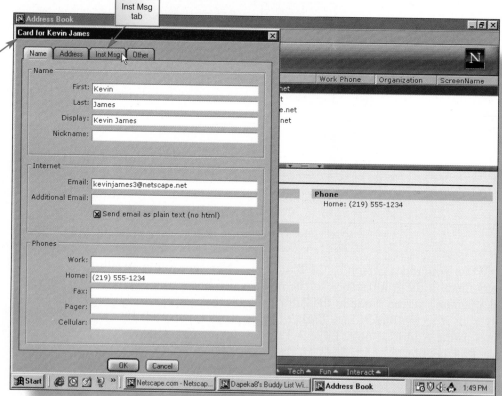

FIGURE 3-60

3 Click the Inst Msg tab. When the Inst Msg sheet displays, click the Screen Name text box and type `KevinJames3` to enter the first screen name. Make certain the Buddies check box is selected and then point to the OK button.

The Inst Msg page displays with the screen name for Kevin James entered (Figure 3-61).

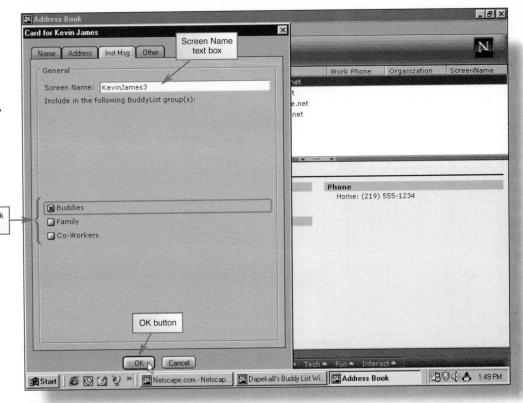

FIGURE 3-61

4 Click the OK button and then close the Address Book window by clicking the Close button on its title bar. When the Buddy List window redisplays, point to the List Setup tab.

The Address Book window is closed, and the Buddy List window redisplays showing zero of two contacts online (Figure 3-62).

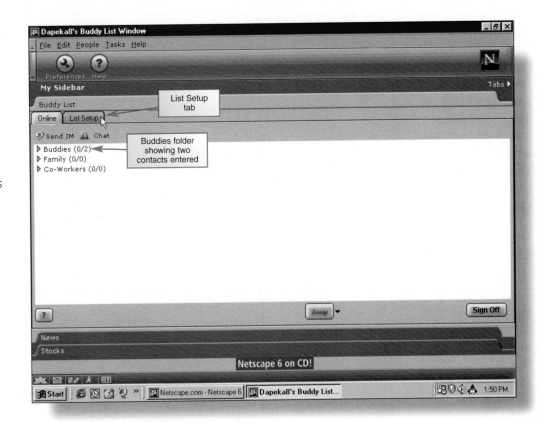

FIGURE 3-62

5 **Click the List Setup tab.**

The List Setup sheet displays with the new entry in the Buddies folder (Figure 3-63).

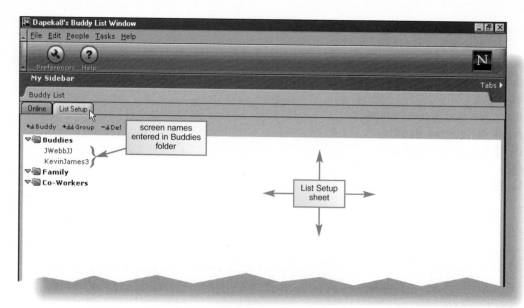

FIGURE 3-63

6 **Repeat Steps 1 through 4 and refer to Table 3-5 on page NN 3.41 to enter the remaining screen names.**

The completed Buddy List displays as shown in Figure 3-64.

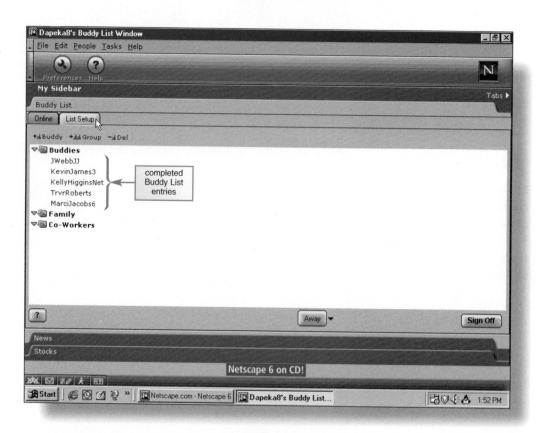

FIGURE 3-64

Other **Ways**

1. In Address Book, click Edit Card on Edit menu

Now that the Buddy List is complete, you can use Instant Messenger to communicate with your online contacts.

Communicating with Instant Messenger

In order to use Instant Messenger, the person with whom you want to communicate must be online and have Instant Messenger activated on his or her machine. The Buddy List shown in Figure 3-65 indicates that MarciJacobs6 (Marci Jacobs) is online. Perform the following steps to engage in a conversation using Instant Messenger.

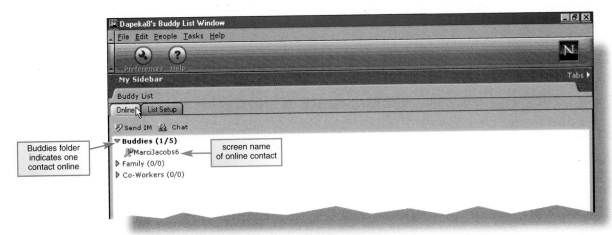

FIGURE 3-65

 To Communicate Using Instant Messenger

1. **Select MarciJacobs6 in the Buddy List and then point to the Send IM button.**

MarciJacobs6 is selected (Figure 3-66).

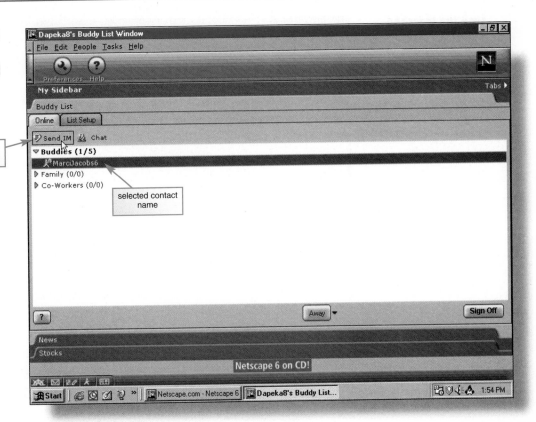

FIGURE 3-66

2 Click the Send IM button. Maximize the Instant Message window.

The Instant Message window opens (Figure 3-67). The window contains a toolbar, message area, and a Formatting toolbar.

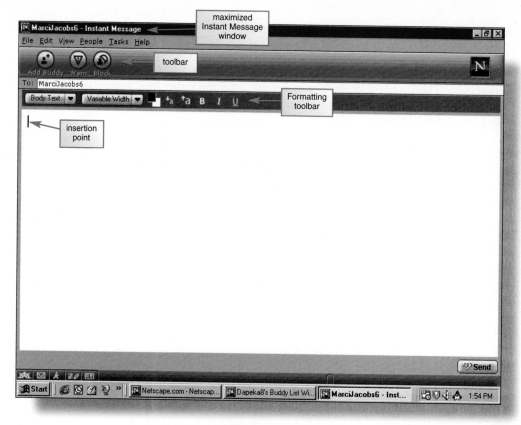

FIGURE 3-67

3 Type the message shown in Figure 3-68 and then point to the Send button.

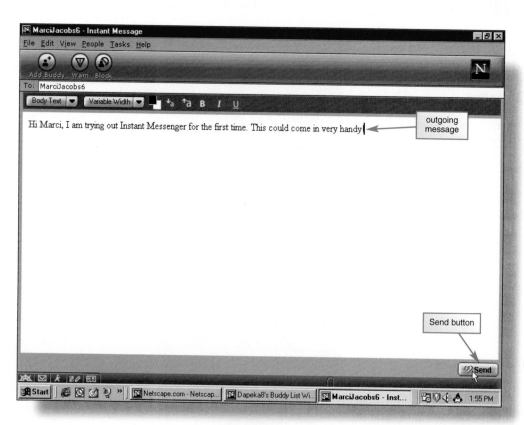

FIGURE 3-68

Click the Send button.

The Instant Message window now is split into two panes (Figure 3-69). The top pane, which is the message display pane, displays the sent message; the bottom pane, which is the message compose pane, is used to compose messages.

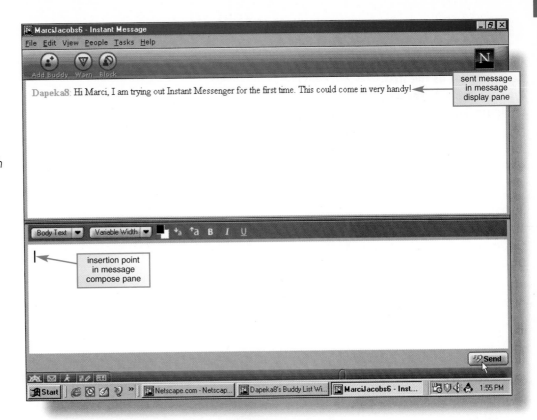

FIGURE 3-69

5 **MarciJacobs6 has replied to your message. Repeat Steps 3 and 4 to send the message shown in Figure 3-70.**

MarciJacobs6 reply displays in the message display pane below the original message (Figure 3-70).

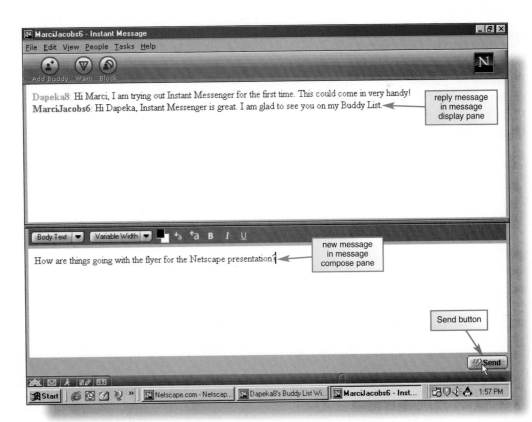

FIGURE 3-70

6 Reply to MarciJacobs6 second message in the same manner as the first. Type the reply as shown in Figure 3-71.

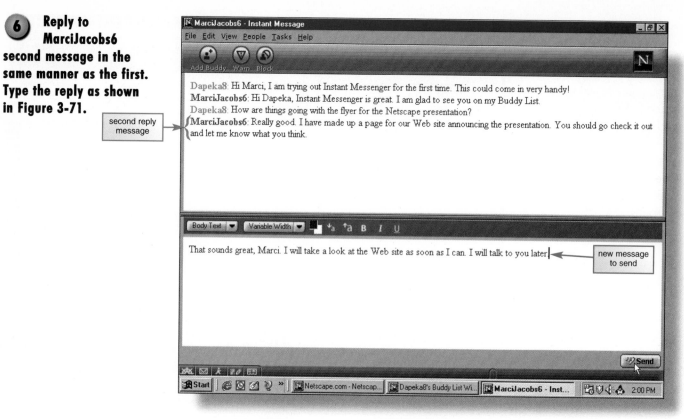

FIGURE 3-71

7 After MarciJacobs6 last reply, she signs off and no longer is available for instant messaging. Point to the Close button on the Instant Message title bar.

A message displays indicating that MarciJacobs6 has signed off and is no longer online (Figure 3-72).

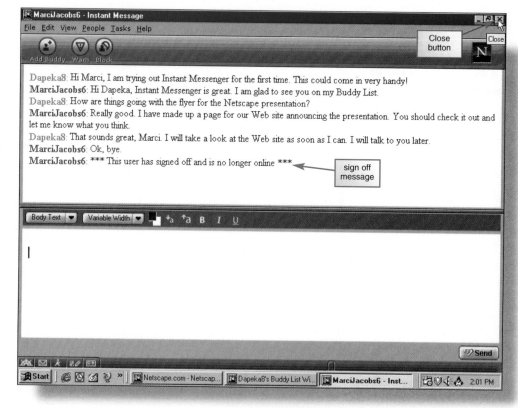

FIGURE 3-72

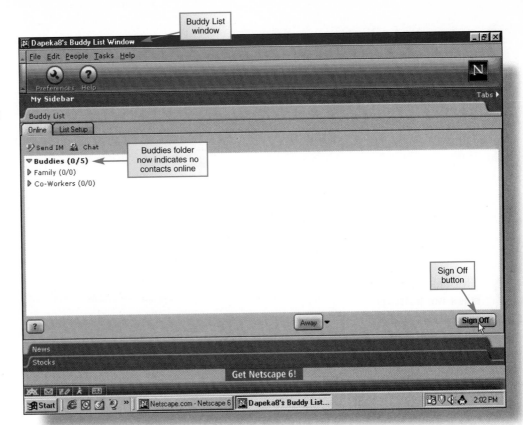

FIGURE 3-73

8. **The instant messaging session is complete. Close the Instant Message window by clicking the Close button on the title bar. Point to the Sign Off button.**

The Instant Message window closes, and the Buddy List window redisplays showing no contacts online (Figure 3-73).

When you have finished using Instant Messenger, you should sign off and close Instant Messenger. Perform the following steps to sign off and close Instant Messenger.

TO SIGN OFF AND QUIT INSTANT MESSENGER

 Click the Sign Off button (see Figure 3-73).

2 Click the Close button in the Sign On window.

The Sign On window closes, and the Netscape window redisplays.

WebCalendar

WebCalendar, an application contained in Netscape, is an effective time-management program that helps you organize your busy schedule in a structured, readable manner. WebCalendar allows you to create, display, and maintain your own calendar online. For example, you can add appointments, ideas, and events to your calendar. You can display the calendar from any location, because it is stored on Netscape's server.

Starting WebCalendar

To start WebCalendar, Netscape must be running. Perform the steps on the next page to start WebCalendar.

Steps **To Start WebCalendar**

1 **If necessary, click the My Sidebar handle to hide My Sidebar. Click Interact on the Task toolbar and then point to Calendar.**

The Interact menu displays (Figure 3-74).

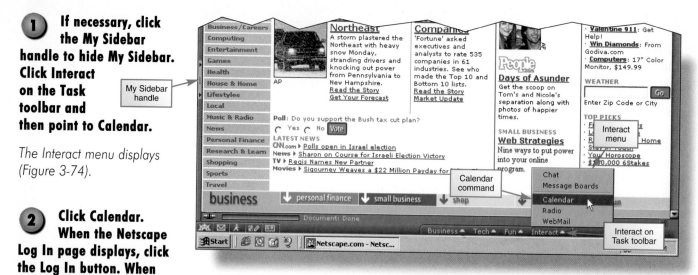

FIGURE 3-74

2 **Click Calendar. When the Netscape Log In page displays, click the Log In button. When the Netscape Member Sign In page displays, enter your user name and password. Click the Sign In button. When the Calendar Activation page displays, enter your zip code and then click the I Accept the Terms of Service button. When the Welcome page displays, click the Go to your Calendar button. Click the No thanks button in the horoscope area.**

The Netcenter WebCalendar page displays.

3 **When the Netcenter WebCalendar page displays, if necessary click the Day tab.**

*The WebCalendar page displays in Day view (Figure 3-75). The **Day view** allows you to enter information for one day at a time. Your calendar will display the current system date, rather than the date shown in Figure 3-75.*

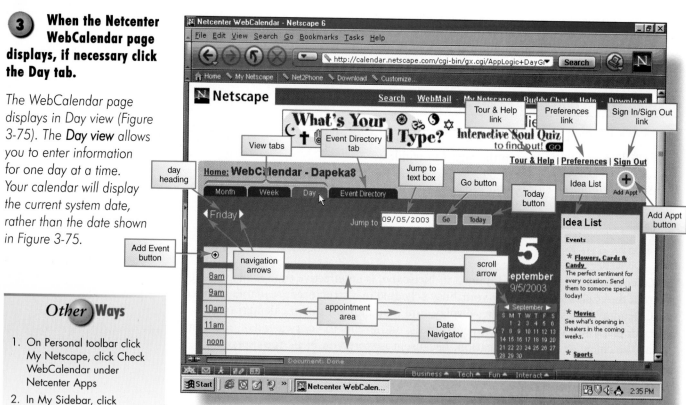

FIGURE 3-75

Other Ways

1. On Personal toolbar click My Netscape, click Check WebCalendar under Netcenter Apps
2. In My Sidebar, click Calendar tab, if necessary click Tabs to add Calendar tab

WebCalendar allows you to display your calendar in day, week, or month view. If you add an appointment in one view, it automatically will appear in the other views. The next section describes the WebCalendar page features.

The Netcenter WebCalendar Page

The **Netcenter WebCalendar page** shown in Figure 3-75 includes a variety of features to help you work efficiently. The main elements of the Netcenter WebCalendar page are the Date Navigator, the appointment area, the Event Directory, and the Idea List.

DATE NAVIGATOR The **Date Navigator** includes a miniature calendar of the current month with monthly scroll arrows. When you click the monthly scroll arrows, WebCalendar moves forward or backward one month. You also can click the day of the month to display the appointment area for any day in the month.

APPOINTMENT AREA The **appointment area** contains a day heading and, under the day heading, time slots for the current view. The date displays in the Jump to text box and above the Date Navigator. By default, workday time slots are set from 8:00 A.M. to 7:00 P.M. in one-hour increments.

Scheduled items, such as appointments or events, display in the appointment area. An **appointment** is a calendar entry that you create, such as business meetings, anniversary reminders, or social plans. An **event** is an individual entry that you can add to the event area above the time slots. Events or appointments with no scheduled time appear immediately above the first time slot.

VIEW TABS When you click the **Month, Week,** or **Day tab**, Netscape displays different views of WebCalendar.

EVENT DIRECTORY When you click the **Event Directory tab**, Netscape displays the Event Directory sheet. The **Event Directory sheet** includes interesting events and event schedules, such as your favorite teams' schedules, local movies, and Initial Public Offering (IPO) announcements. You can add any event to your WebCalendar by browsing through an event category and selecting the events you want on the dates you need.

IDEA LIST The **Idea List** contains links to some of the categories found on the Event Directory sheet. Clicking a link in the Idea List displays a corresponding Event Directory sheet. You then can add the dates of these events to WebCalendar automatically. The Idea List changes daily with new event ideas.

NAVIGATION TOOLS Just below the View tabs are buttons and a Jump to text box to navigate the calendar. Use the navigation arrows on either side of the day heading to move back or go forward a day. Use the **Jump to** text box and **Go button** to enter any valid date. Use the **Today button** to display today's calendar.

ADD APPT BUTTONS AND OTHER LINKS To the right of the View tabs in Day view and Week view is the Add Appt button. The **Add Appt button** allows you to add appointments.

Above the Add Appt button are the Tour & Help, Preferences, and Sign In/Sign Out links. The **Tour & Help link** displays WebCalendar Help. The **Preferences link** lets you change the WebCalendar default settings. The **Sign In/Sign Out link** toggles between letting you sign in and sign out.

Entering Appointments Using the Appointment Window

This section describes how to enter the appointments in Table 3-6 into your WebCalendar for September 5, 2003. When you enter an appointment into a time slot that is not visible in the current view, WebCalendar automatically adjusts your view to include that time slot. Once you enter an appointment, you can perform ordinary editing actions.

Table 3-6	Appointments for September 5, 2003	
TIME	APPOINTMENT	DURATION
8:00 am	Get class list at registrar	1 hr
9:30 am	Pick up books at bookstore	1 hr
12:00 pm	Lunch with friends	1 hr
4:00 pm	Computer Club orientation	2 hr

Perform the following steps to enter the appointments in Table 3-6 using the appointment area.

To Enter Appointments in WebCalendar

1 **Double-click the Jump to text box. Type** 9/5/03 **and then click the Go button. Point to the 8am link.**

WebCalendar displays September 5, 2003 in Day view (Figure 3-76).

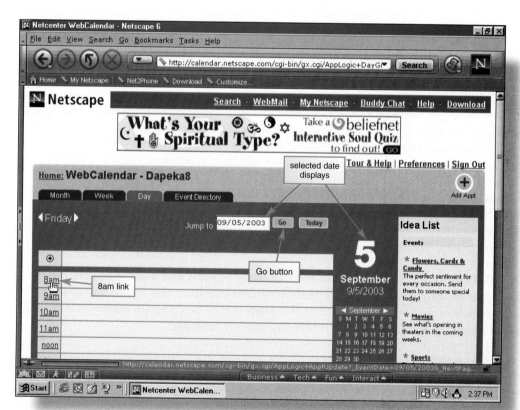

FIGURE 3-76

② **Click the 8am link.**

The Calendar Appointment page displays (Figure 3-77). The insertion point is in the Title text box in the Appointment Information area.

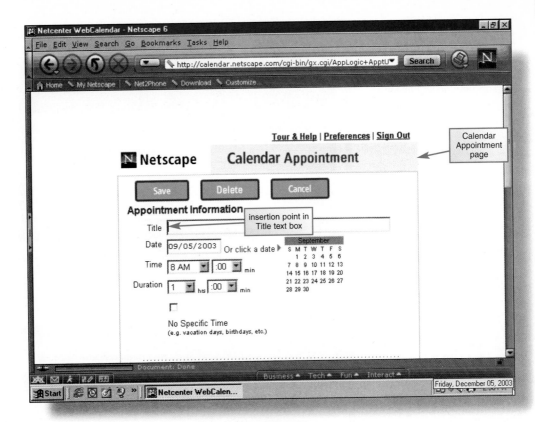

FIGURE 3-77

③ **Type** Get class list at registrar **in the Title text box. Confirm that the time and duration are correct then point to the Save button in the Calendar Appointment area.**

The title, time, and duration display in the appropriate text boxes (Figure 3-78).

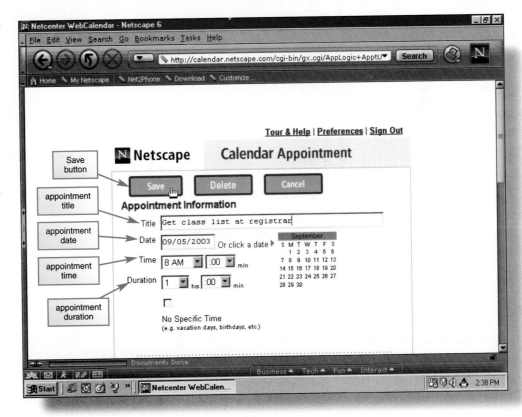

FIGURE 3-78

4 **Click the Save button.**

WebCalendar returns to Day view. The new appointment displays in the 8am timeslot (Figure 3-79).

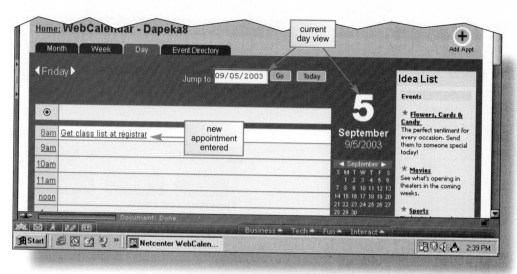

FIGURE 3-79

5 **Repeat Steps 2 through 4 and refer to Table 3-6 on page NN 3.52 to add the remaining appointments.**

The schedule for Friday, September 5, 2003 displays in the appointment area with the four new appointments entered (Figure 3-80).

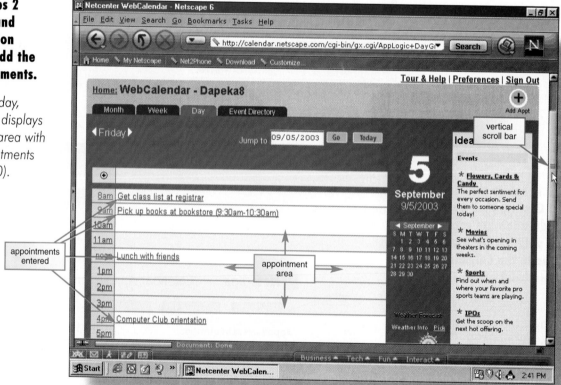

FIGURE 3-80

Other Ways

1. Click Add Appt button

Press the TAB key to move through the items on the Appointment page (see Figure 3-78), or click any text or list box to make a change.

When you scroll down the Appointment page, two other areas display: Tell a Friend, and Notes & Repeat. The **Tell a Friend section** allows you to e-mail appointment or meeting information to one or several people. The **Notes & Repeat section** lets you enter personal notes you may have about a specific appointment and set the appointment as recurring (repeating). In the next set of steps, recurring appointments are added to the calendar.

Recurring Appointments

Many appointments are **recurring**; that is, they repeat or occur at regular intervals. For example, a class held every Monday and Wednesday from 9:00 A.M. to 10:00 A.M. is a recurring appointment. Having to type these recurring appointments for each occasion would be very time-consuming. By designating an appointment as recurring, the appointment needs to be added only once; recurrence then is specified for the days on which it occurs.

Table 3-7	Recurring Appointments				
TIME	DURATION	APPOINTMENT	OCCURRENCE	START DATE	END DATE
9:00 am	1 hr	Operating Systems	Every Monday and Wednesday	September 8, 2003	December 12, 2003
10:30 am	1 hr	Data Communications	Every Monday, Wednesday, and Friday	September 8, 2003	December 12, 2003
3:00 pm	2 hr	Computer Club	Every Monday	September 8, 2003	December 12, 2003

Perform the following steps to enter the recurring appointments in Table 3-7.

 To Enter Recurring Appointments in WebCalendar

1 With the calendar for 9/8/2003 displaying, click the 9am link then type Operating Systems in the Title text box. Scroll down until the Notes and Repeat section displays (Figure 3-81).

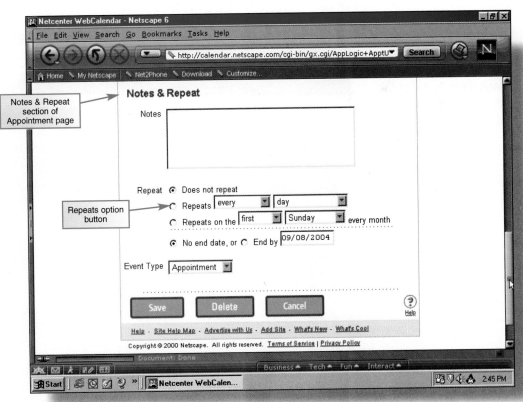

FIGURE 3-81

② **Click Repeats in the Repeat area. Click the day box arrow and then click Mon & Wed. Click the End by option button. Select the date in the text box and type** 12/12/2003 **as the end by date. Point to the Save button.**

The Notes and Repeat area displays as shown in Figure 3-82.

③ **Click the Save button.**

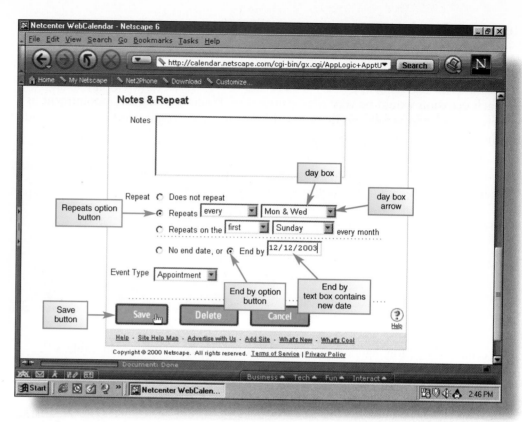

FIGURE 3-82

④ **Repeat Steps 1 through 3 and refer to Table 3-7 on the previous page to enter the remaining recurring appointments.**

The schedule for Monday, September 8, 2003 is complete (Figure 3-83). A recurrence symbol displays beside each recurring appointment.

FIGURE 3-83

WebCalendar • NN 3.57

PROJECT 3

The navigation arrows above the appointment area and the Jump to text box allow easy movement and display of a specific date in the appointment area. Once a specific date is displayed, appointments can be entered on that date. Using the navigation arrows to move through the calendar is demonstrated in the next section.

Entering Appointments for Another Day

Now that the Monday schedule is complete, the next step is to enter appointments for Tuesday. To do so, Tuesday must display in the appointment area. The following steps show how to move to the next day using the navigation arrows above the appointment area and then enter the recurring appointments in Table 3-8.

More About

The Recurring Icon

The recurring icon can be applied to appointments, events, and meetings. Double-click the item to open its dialog box and then click Repeats in the Repeat area.

Table 3-8 Additional Recurring Appointments

TIME	APPOINTMENT	DURATION	OCCURRENCE	END DATE
9:30 am	Sociology	1 hr	Every Tuesday	December 12, 2003
1:30 pm	Psychology	1 hr	Every Tuesday and Thursday	December 12, 2003

 To Enter Appointments for Another Day

1 Point to the right navigation arrow next to Monday above the appointment area (Figure 3-84).

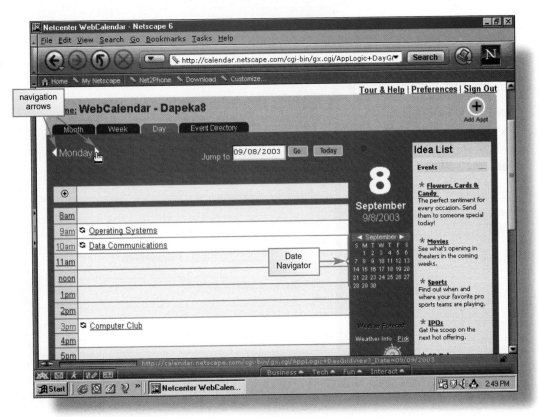

FIGURE 3-84

2 **Click the right navigation arrow.**

WebCalendar displays the calendar for Tuesday, September 9, 2003 (Figure 3-85).

FIGURE 3-85

3 **One at a time, enter the recurring appointments provided in Table 3-8 on the previous page for Tuesday, September 9, 2003.**

The schedule for Tuesday, September 9, 2003 displays (Figure 3-86).

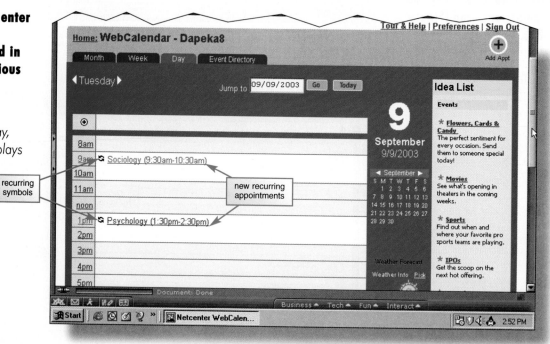

FIGURE 3-86

Other **Ways**

1. Click desired date in Date Navigator
2. Enter date in Jump to text box, click Go button

The Notes & Repeat section provides daily, weekly, monthly, or yearly recurrence patterns. WebCalendar also provides three options for the range of recurrence. Appointments can recur every week or choice of weeks for one or multiple days. An appointment can be set to occur up to a certain date. If the recurring appointment is ongoing, such as office hours, you can select the **No end date option button**.

An appointment can be set as recurring when first entered, or, if you decide to make a one-time appointment recurring later, click the appointment and then click the Repeat option button. You can edit recurring appointments to add new days, omit certain days, or change other recurrence details. Editing recurring appointments is covered in the next section.

Editing Appointments

Because schedules often need to be rearranged, WebCalendar allows you to edit your appointments. To edit an appointment, click the appointment in the appointment area and make corrections on the Calendar Appointment page. All occurrences of a recurring appointment can be changed, or a single occurrence can be altered.

Appointments sometimes are canceled and must be deleted from the schedule. For example, the schedule created thus far in this project contains an appointment on Thursday, November 27, 2003. Because November 27 is Thanksgiving Day, however, no classes will meet, and the scheduled appointment needs to be deleted. The following steps describe how to delete an appointment from the calendar.

 To Delete an Appointment

1 **Type** 11/27/03 **in the Jump to text box and then click the Go button. Scroll down until the Psychology appointment displays and then point to Psychology in the 1pm timeslot.**

WebCalendar displays the calendar for Thursday, November 27 (Figure 3-87).

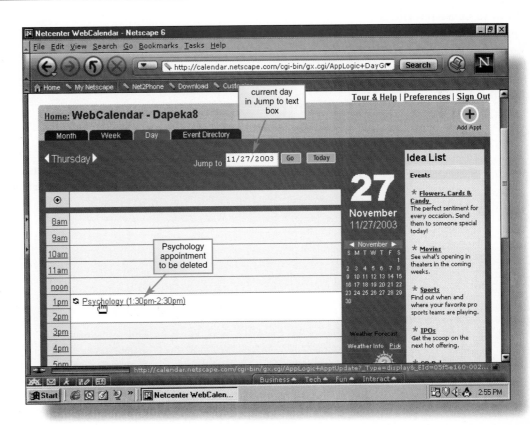

FIGURE 3-87

2 **Click Psychology to display the Calendar Appointment page. Scroll down to display all the options in the Apply These Changes To: area and then click This occurrence only (Figure 3-88).**

By selecting the This occurrence only option button, no other occurrences for this appointment will be affected.

3 **Click the Delete button.**

The Psychology appointment is deleted from Thursday, November 27, 2003. All other occurrences of the appointment remain in the calendar.

4 **Repeat Steps 1 through 3 to delete the Data Communications appointment from Friday, November 28, 2003.**

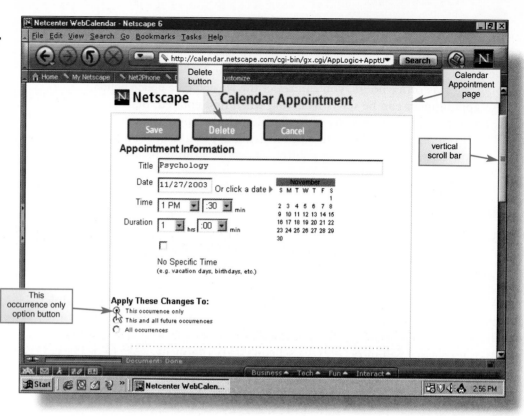

FIGURE 3-88

Adding Events Using the Event Directory

The **Event Directory** allows you to add a wide assortment of events or event schedules to your calendar, such as CD releases, sports schedules, civic holidays, and local festivals. The following steps show how to enter civic holidays to the calendar.

To Add an Event to the Calendar Using the Event Directory

1 If necessary, return to September 8, 2003. Point to the Event Directory tab above the appointment area (Figure 3-89).

FIGURE 3-89

2 Click the Event Directory tab. Scroll down until the Holidays topic displays and then point to the All Holidays link.

The lower portion of the Event Directory displays (Figure 3-90).

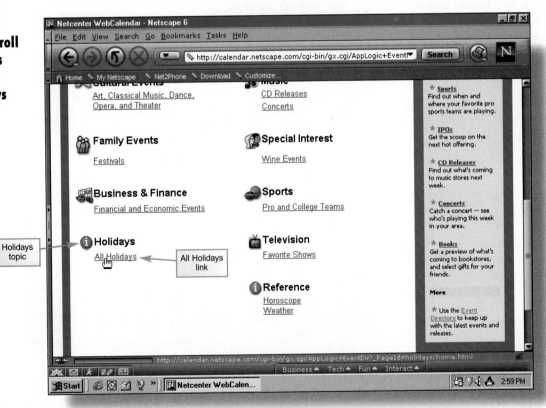

FIGURE 3-90

3 **Click the All Holidays link. When the Holidays page displays, click the U.S. link below the Civic and Cultural heading. When the next Holidays page displays, scroll down until the Christmas Day (Civic) holiday displays.**

A list of civic and cultural holidays displays (Figure 3-91).

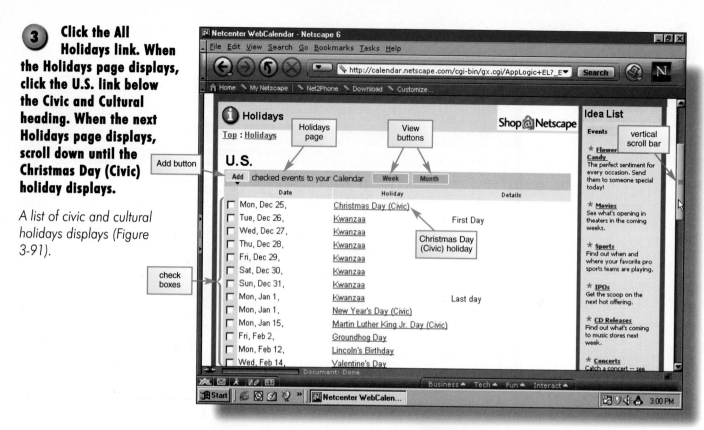

FIGURE 3-91

4 **Select the Christmas Day, New Year's Day, and Martin Luther King, Jr. Day check boxes and then point to the Add button above the first check box.**

Check marks display next to the selected holidays (Figure 3-92).

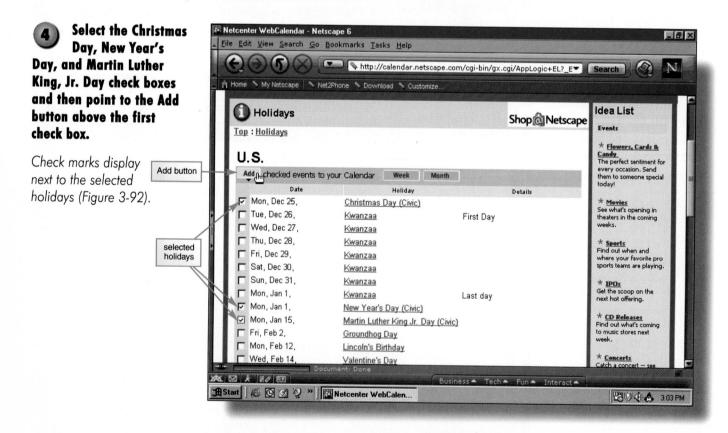

FIGURE 3-92

5 Click the Add button. Point to the Day tab.

The Holiday list displays with a message stating that the selected holidays have been successfully added to the calendar (Figure 3-93).

6 Click the Day tab to return to WebCalendar.

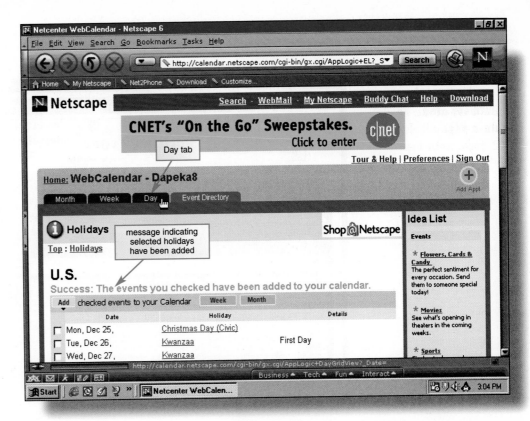

FIGURE 3-93

Other Ways

1. Click Event Directory link in Idea List

Netscape maintains civic holidays only for the current year. Because the previous example uses a future year (2003) in relation to when this book was written, the civic holidays may not fall on the dates shown in this exercise.

Clicking the Day or Month view buttons at the top of the Holidays page displays the available holidays in either a weekly or monthly calendar view. You can select the holidays in the same manner used in the default view.

Displaying the WebCalendar in Week and Month Views

WebCalendar can display calendars in three different views: Day, Week, and Month. Thus far, this project has demonstrated only the Day view. Although the screen displays quite differently in Week and Month views, the same tasks can be performed as in Day view.

WEEK VIEW The advantage of displaying a calendar in **Week view** is that you can see how many appointments are scheduled for any given week. In Week view, the seven days of the selected week display in the appointment area. The steps on the next page describe how to display the WebCalendar with the previously entered appointments in Week view.

Steps To Change to Week View

1 Point to the Week tab above the appointment area (Figure 3-94).

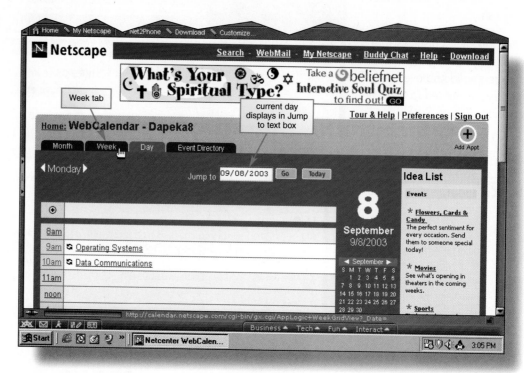

FIGURE 3-94

2 Click the Week tab. If necessary, use the Jump to text box to display the calendar for the week of September 8, 2003. Point to the Month tab.

The week of September 8, 2003 displays showing all the appointments for that week (Figure 3-95).

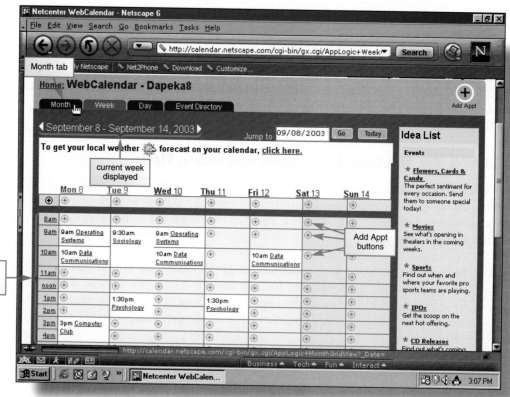

FIGURE 3-95

The navigation arrows above the appointment area allow backward or forward movement one week at a time. As in Day view, click an appointment to view and edit appointment details.

MONTH VIEW The **Month view** resembles a standard monthly calendar page and displays your WebCalendar for an entire month. Appointments are listed in each date frame in the calendar. The following steps illustrate how to display the WebCalendar in Month view.

Steps **To Change to Month View**

1 **Click the Month tab. If necessary, use the Jump to text box to display the calendar for the month of September 2003.**

The month of September 2003 displays showing all the appointments for that month (Figure 3-96).

2 **Click the Day tab to return to Day view. If necessary, display the calendar for September 8, 2003.**

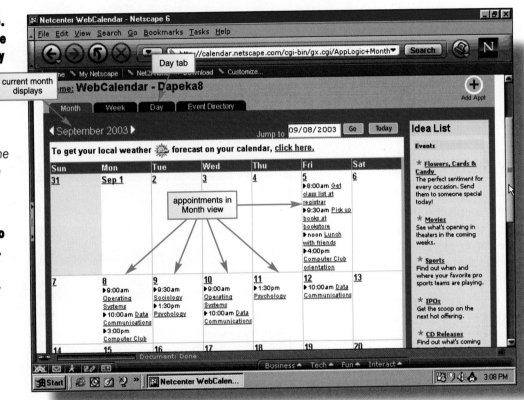

FIGURE 3-96

Use the navigation arrows above the appointment area to move the Month view forward and backward one month at a time. As in Day and Week views, you can add, edit, or delete appointments in Month view.

Printing a WebCalendar

The steps on the next page describe how to print your WebCalendar from Day view. Because WebCalendar prints exactly what is displayed, the printing method is the same for all views.

Steps To Print the WebCalendar in Day View

1 **Click the Print button on the Navigation toolbar. When the Print dialog box displays, point to the OK button.**

The Print dialog box displays (Figure 3-97).

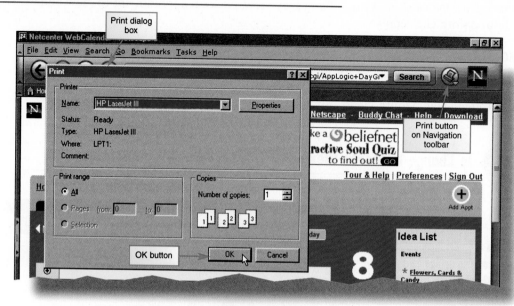

FIGURE 3-97

2 **Click the OK button.**

The daily schedule of appointments for Monday, September 8, 2003 prints on the printer. The printout should display as shown in Figure 3-98.

FIGURE 3-98

 Other Ways

1. On File menu click Print
2. Press CTRL+P

Quitting WebCalendar

To quit WebCalendar, complete the following step.

TO QUIT WEBCALENDAR

1 Click the Close button on the title bar.

Creating Web Pages (Netscape Composer)

With the growing popularity of the Internet, the need to develop a presence on the World Wide Web has become increasingly important for businesses, schools, government, and other organizations. Whether you create a personal Web page to brag about your hobbies and achievements or create a more sophisticated Web site for use in business, the ability to create a Web page has become a popular and profitable skill. In fact, many new employees are expected to have knowledge of the Internet and Web page creation.

Although many software programs are available today that allow you to create Web pages, all Web pages are created using a special formatting language called **hypertext markup language (HTML)**. HTML consists of special instructions, called **tags** or **markups**, which are used to create a Web page. Figure 3-99a shows the hypertext markup language used to create the Web page shown in Figure 3-99b. The instructions indicate to the Web browser software, in this case, Netscape, how each Web page should look and how it relates to other Web pages.

Fortunately, you do not have to know the HTML language or its instructions to create a Web page. The capability to create a Web page is available within Netscape using a tool called Composer.

More About

Web Authoring Tools

Other Web page creation programs, such as Hotdog and HotMetal, are available free from public access FTP sites.

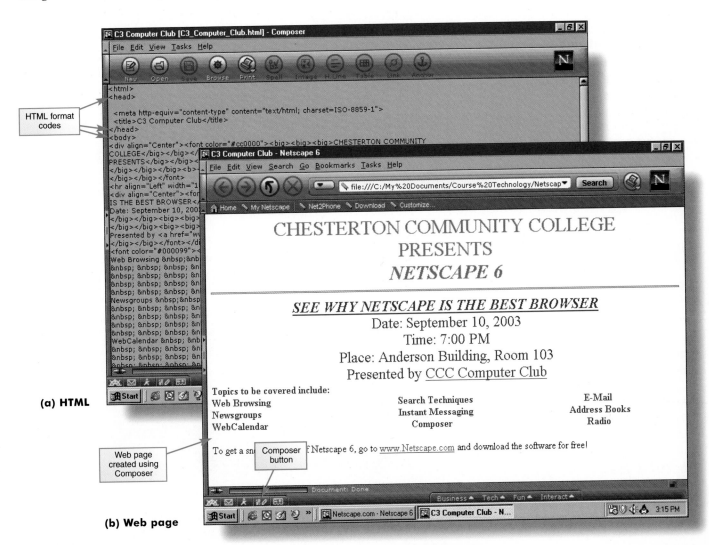

(a) HTML

(b) Web page

FIGURE 3-99

 More About

Composer

With Composer you can create a hyperlink to a Web page on another computer connected to the Web, to a Web page on the same computer, or to a location within the same Web page.

Netscape Composer

Netscape Composer is a Web page editor that allows you to use the power of HTML to create and format Web pages. With the capabilities of Composer, you can create a personal Web page such as the Computer Club flyer shown in Figure 3-99b (on the previous page). Before creating a Web page, you must start Composer using the Composer button on the Task toolbar.

The Composer window illustrated in Figure 3-99b contains a menu bar, a toolbar, a Formatting toolbar, and a display area where the Web page on which you are working displays. The toolbar contains buttons that are useful when creating and editing Web pages.

Netscape Radio

Netscape Radio allows you to listen to 16 different music channels via the Internet. After opening Radio, you can select a channel based on music preference (Classical, Country, The 80's, and so on). Perform the following steps to open Netscape Radio.

Steps **To Open Netscape Radio**

1 **Click the Interact button on the Task toolbar and then point to Radio on the Interact pop-up menu.**

The Interact pop-up menu displays (Figure 3-100).

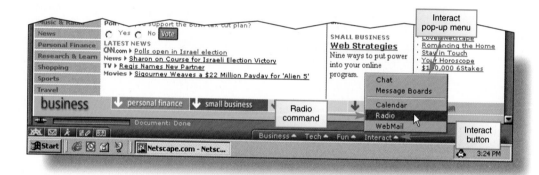

FIGURE 3-100

2 **Click Radio. If the plug-in test page displays, click the Yes button if you hear music. If you do not hear music, you may have to download RealPlayer8 in order for Radio to work properly.**

The Netscape Radio window displays (Figure 3-101). The window contains a volume control slide, a channel bar, a channel list to select additional channels, an information box that has information on the current artist and song, and a search text box to search for information on a particular artist.

FIGURE 3-101

Using Netscape Radio

With Radio opened, you can listen to any one of 16 channels based on your listening preference. If you do not see a channel to your liking on the channel bar, you can click the More Channels box arrow to display a list of additional channels. Perform the following step to select a channel and listen to Radio.

 To Listen to Netscape Radio

 With the Netscape Radio window displayed, click the Oldies button on the channel bar.

The Radio window displays the current artist and song title in the information box (Figure 3-102). The song shown in the information box should be playing on your computer. While listening to Radio, you may adjust the volume using the volume control slide.

FIGURE 3-102

Quitting Netscape Radio

Once you have finished listening to music, you should quit Netscape Radio, as shown in the following step.

TO QUIT NETSCAPE RADIO

 Click the Close button on the Netscape Radio – Netscape 6 title bar.

The Netscape Radio window closes.

Quitting Netscape

When you have finished using Netscape, you should quit Netscape by performing the following step.

TO QUIT NETSCAPE

Click the Close button on the Netscape title bar.

The Netscape window closes, and the Windows desktop displays.

CASE PERSPECTIVE SUMMARY

Dapeka Patel's school and meeting schedule, including all her classes and other engagements, are entered in her calendar. With your help, she has identified and scheduled all of her recurring appointments, organized her contacts in her address book, and set up her buddy list for instant messaging. She now feels prepared to handle her busy workload.

Project Summary

In this project, you learned to use Mail to read, reply to, delete, compose, and send e-mail messages. You also used Mail to display newsgroups, read and post articles, expand and collapse a thread, and subscribe and unsubscribe to a newsgroup. You also learned how to use Address Book to create a contact list. Using Instant Messenger you learned to add a contact to your buddy list, and send and reply to an instant message. You learned how use WebCalendar to enter appointments, create recurring appointments, schedule events, and print your calendar. The capabilities of Composer to create a Web page were discussed. Finally, you used Radio to listen to music over the Internet.

What You Should Know

Having completed this project, you now should be able to perform the following tasks.

- Access a Newsgroup Using Netscape Help *(NN 3.19)*
- Add a Buddy in Instant Messenger *(NN 3.40)*
- Add a Buddy Using Address Book *(NN 3.42)*
- Add an Event to the Calendar Using the Event Directory *(NN 3.61)*
- Add an Entry in the Address Book *(NN 3.31)*
- Change to Month View *(NN 3.65)*
- Change to Week View *(NN 3.64)*
- Close an E-Mail Message *(NN 3.10)*
- Collapse a Thread *(NN 3.25)*
- Communicate Using Instant Messenger *(NN 3.45)*
- Compose an E-Mail Message *(NN 3.13)*
- Delete an Appointment *(NN 3.59)*
- Delete an E-Mail Message *(NN 3.12)*
- Display the Articles in a Newsgroup *(NN 3.29)*
- Enter Appointments for Another Day *(NN 3.57)*
- Enter Appointments in WebCalendar *(NN 3.52)*
- Enter Recurring Appointments in WebCalendar *(NN 3.55)*
- Expand a Thread *(NN 3.25)*
- Listen to Netscape Radio *(NN 3.69)*
- Open (Read) an E-Mail Message *(NN 3.8)*
- Open and View an Attachment *(NN 3.15)*
- Open Netscape Radio *(NN 3.68)*
- Post a Newsgroup Article *(NN 3.27)*
- Print a Newsgroup Article *(NN 3.26)*
- Print an Address Book Card *(NN 3.36)*
- Print an Opened E-Mail Message *(NN 3.9)*
- Print the WebCalendar in Day View *(NN 3.66)*
- Quit Netscape *(NN 3.70)*
- Quit Netscape Address Book *(NN 3.37)*
- Quit Netscape Mail *(NN 3.17 and NN 3.31)*
- Quit Netscape Radio *(NN 3.70)*
- Quit WebCalendar *(NN 3.67)*
- Read a Newsgroup Article *(NN 3.24)*
- Reply to an E-Mail Message *(NN 3.11)*
- Send an E-Mail Message *(NN 3.14)*
- Sign Off and Quit Instant Messenger *(NN 3.49)*
- Sort Address Book Entries *(NN 3.35)*
- Start Netscape Instant Messenger *(NN 3.38)*
- Start Netscape Mail *(NN 3.5)*
- Start WebCalendar *(NN 3.50)*
- Subscribe to a Newsgroup *(NN 3.21 and NN 3.27)*
- Unsubscribe from a Newsgroup *(NN 3.30)*

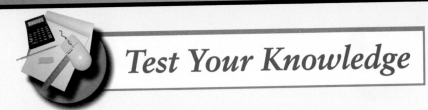

Test Your Knowledge

1 True/False

Instructions: Circle T if the statement is true or F if the statement is false.

T F   1. A news server is a collection of news and discussion groups that you can access via the Internet.

T F   2. Hypertext markup language (HTML) is the language used to create a Web page.

T F   3. Subscribing is the process of posting an article to a newsgroup.

T F   4. Screen names entered in the Address Book automatically are added to your Buddy List.

T F   5. You can send an instant message to someone even when they are not online.

T F   6. You can sort your Address Book entries by screen name.

T F   7. The Draft folder is the destination for incoming mail.

T F   8. The Event Directory contains links to some of the categories found in the Idea List.

T F   9. WebCalendar entries can be edited only in Day View.

T F   10. A thread is the original newsgroup article and all subsequent related replies to the article.

2 Multiple Choice

Instructions: Circle the correct response.

1. The place where e-mail messages are stored until you read them is the _____ folder.
   - a. Sent Items
   - b. Draft
   - c. Inbox
   - d. Outbox

2. A bold message heading indicates you have not _____ the e-mail message.
   - a. composed
   - b. replied to
   - c. read
   - d. sent

3. Alt, comp, news, rec, and sci are examples of _____.
   - a. subgroup names
   - b. threads
   - c. prefixes
   - d. suffixes

4. Selecting a newsgroup you wish to visit frequently is called _____.
   - a. saving
   - b. posting
   - c. subscribing
   - d. unsubscribing

5. The secnews.netscape.com name is an example of a _____.
   - a. subscription
   - b. thread
   - c. news server
   - d. newsgroup article

6. The _____ Address Book is where you enter your own contacts.
   - a. My Addresses
   - b. Collected Addresses
   - c. Personal
   - d. Favorite

7. The _____ page is where you can add or delete names to your Buddy List.
   - a. List Setup
   - b. Online
   - c. Contacts
   - d. Edit

8. Scheduled items, such as appointments or events, display in the _____ area.
   - a. schedule
   - b. task
   - c. appointment
   - d. event

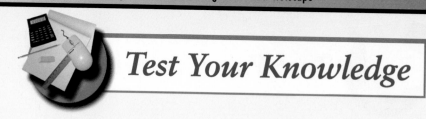

Test Your Knowledge

9. The software you use to create a Web page is _____.
   - a. Composer
   - b. Netscape
   - c. Mail
   - d. Instant Messenger
10. In Netscape _____, you can listen to any one of 16 channels based on your listening preference.
    - a. Composer
    - b. Radio
    - c. TV
    - d. Navigator

3 Opening and Reading an E-Mail Message

Instructions: Figure 3-103 illustrates the Mail window. In the spaces provided, list the steps to open and read the new e-mail message from Kelly Higgins and then send a reply to her. The return e-mail should contain a subject and a message.

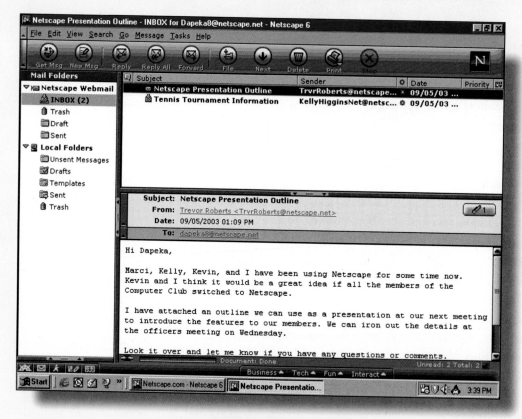

FIGURE 3-103

Step 1: _____

Step 2: _____

Step 3: _____

Step 4: _____

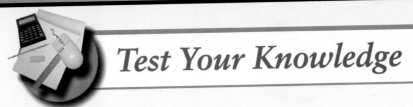

Test Your Knowledge

4 Online Practice Tests and Learning Games

Instructions: Start Netscape. Double-click the Location field, enter the URL scsite.com/nn6/practice.htm and then press the ENTER key to display the Netscape Navigator 6 Practice Tests & Learning Games page (Figure 3-104). Complete the following tasks.

FIGURE 3-104

1. Practice Test: Click the Practice Test link under Project 3. Answer each question, enter your first and last name at the bottom of the page, and then click the Grade Test button. When the system displays the graded practice test, click Print on the File menu to print a hard copy. Submit the printout to your instructor.
2. Who Wants to be a Computer Genius: Click the Computer Genius link under Project 3. Read the instructions, enter your first and last name at the bottom of the page, and then click the Play button. Submit your score to your instructor.
3. Wheel of Terms: Click the Wheel of Terms link under Project 3. Read the instructions, and then enter your first and last name and your school name. Click View High Scores to see other student scores. Close the High Score window. Click the Play button. Submit your score to your instructor.
4. Crossword Puzzle Challenge: Click the Crossword Puzzle Challenge link under Project 3. Read the instructions, and then enter your first and last name. Click the Submit button. Solve the crossword puzzle. When you are finished, click the Submit button. When the crossword puzzle redisplays, click the Print button. Submit the printout to your instructor.

In the Lab

1 Sending E-Mail Messages

Instructions: Start Netscape and perform the following tasks with a computer.

1. Double-click the Location field. Type www.senate.gov and then press the ENTER key to display the Web page shown in Figure 3-105.

FIGURE 3-105

2. Find and display the e-mail address of one of the Senators from your state.
3. Click the Mail button on the Task toolbar, and then click the New Msg button to open the Compose window.
4. Using the e-mail address of the Senate member you obtained in Step 2, compose a mail message to your Senator about some issue that is important to you.
5. Ask your instructor for his or her e-mail address and type it in the Cc: text box. Send a carbon copy of the message to your instructor. Print a copy of the message and submit it to your instructor.
6. Close all open windows.

In the Lab

2 Creating a Contact List

Instructions: Create a contact list containing the people listed in Table 3-9. Use the Custom 1: text box in the Other sheet to enter the student's grade level. When the list is complete, print each Address Card and then delete the entries. Submit the printouts to your instructor.

Table 3-9 Contact Information				
NAME	ADDRESS	TELEPHONE	E-MAIL	GRADE LEVEL
Beth Clark	8451 Colonial	(219) 555-5145	bclark@isp.com	Junior
Javier Hernandez	3581 Clay	(219) 555-1345	jhernandez@isp.com	Sophomore
Elana Goldberg	5689 Porter	(219) 555-0650	agoldberg@isp.com	Freshman
David Springer	7812 Wexford	(219) 555-0741	dspringer@isp.com	Senior
Chris Thomas	257 W. 5th	(219) 555-4736	cthomas@isp.com	Senior
Judy Price	648 Calumet	(219) 555-4346	jprice@isp.com	Sophomore

3 Creating a Calendar

Instructions: Perform the following tasks.

1. Enter the appointments listed in Table 3-10.
2. Print the calendar for the month of June and submit it to your instructor.
3. Save the Month view to a floppy disk and then delete all the appointments.
4. Close all open windows.

Table 3-10 Appointment Information		
DESCRIPTION	DATE	TIME
Staff Meeting	Every Monday from May 5, 2003 - June 30, 2003	9:00 am - 10:00 am
Shipping System Complete	June 6, 2003	
Customer Training Session	June 10 and 12, 2003	8:30 am - 4:30 pm
Manufacturing System Due	June 18, 2003	
Paul's Birthday	June 20, 2003	
Telephone Meeting with Susan	June 25, 2003	9:30 am - 10:00 am
Discuss New Projects	June 27, 2003	11:30 am - 1:00 pm
Meeting with Bob	June 30, 2003	3:00 pm - 4:00 pm
Teach Class	Every Monday from May 5, 2003 – June 30, 2003	7:00 pm - 9:30 pm

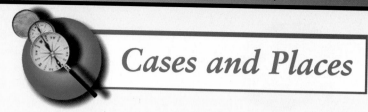

Cases and Places

> The difficulty of these case studies varies:
> ▶ are the least difficult; ▶▶ are more difficult; and ▶▶▶ are the most difficult.

1 ▶ Several Web sites are available that allow you to enter a person's name and search for information about the individual. Using a search engine, locate three of these sites. Use your name, a friend's name, and a relative's name to search for information using all three sites you find. Print the information you find, write your name on the printouts, and then submit them to your instructor.

2 ▶ Create a personal schedule for the next month. Include any work and class time, together with study time. Use recurring appointments where appropriate. All-day activities should be scheduled as events. Print a copy of your schedule in Month view and submit it to your instructor.

3 ▶▶ Create a contact list of your family, friends, and colleagues. Include their names, addresses, telephone numbers, and e-mail addresses, if any. Enter the name of the organization each one works for, if appropriate. For family, list their birthdays and wedding anniversaries using the Other tab. Submit a printout of each contact to your instructor.

4 ▶▶ Create a calendar that contains the following holidays: New Year's Day, Valentine's Day, St. Patrick's Day, Independence Day, Halloween, Veterans Day, Christmas Eve, and Christmas Day. For the first five holidays, indicate that you will be out of the office all day. Also, add events for several birthday or anniversary celebrations. Print the calendar in Month view and submit the pages to your instructor.

5 ▶▶ Using computer magazines, advertising brochures, the Internet, or other resources, compile information about two other e-mail programs. In a brief report, compare the two programs and Netscape Mail. Include the differences and similarities, how to obtain the software, the functions and features of each program, and so forth. Submit the report to your instructor.

6 ▶▶▶ Many colleges and universities maintain their own news servers containing school related newsgroups. Locate a school that has a news server. Explore the news server, determine how many newsgroups are on the server, locate five newsgroups that are of interest to you, determine the number of articles in each newsgroup, and read several articles in each newsgroup. Write a brief report summarizing your findings. Submit the report to your instructor

Netscape Navigator 6

APPENDIX A
Netscape Navigator Preferences

Introduction

Netscape has settings that control how it looks, feels, and reacts to different situations. The settings are called **preferences**. When you install Netscape, the preferences are assigned default values. You can view and modify the preferences by using the **Preferences command** on the Edit menu (Figure A-1). For example, through this command you can change the appearance of your browser; change the home page that displays; delete History files; change the default search engine; customize the Mail, Composer, and Instant Messenger applications; view cookies; and much more.

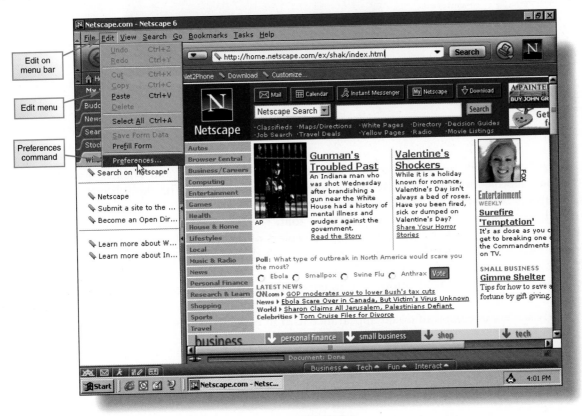

FIGURE A-1

When you invoke the Preferences command, Netscape displays the **Preferences dialog box** (Figure A-2 on the next page). Clicking an item in the **Category list** on the left side of the Preferences dialog box displays a different set of preferences on the left, which you then can change. The arrows to the left of an item in the Category list, such as Navigator or Composer, means the category has subcategories. For example, in Figure A-2 Appearance has three subcategories.

The Appearance Category

The **Appearance category** (Figure A-2) allows you to choose which Netscape components to display when you double-click the Netscape icon on the desktop. The default setting is Navigator (the browser). Other choices include Composer and Netscape Mail.

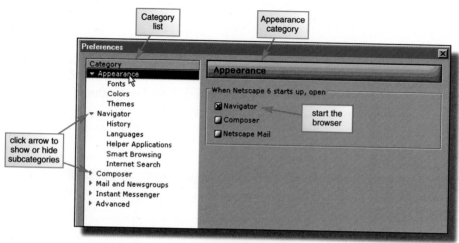

FIGURE A-2

The Appearance category (Figure A-3a) has three subcategories: Fonts, Colors, and Themes. As shown in Figure A-3b, the **Fonts subcategory** allows you to set the font name and font size. The check box at the bottom of the first area instructs Netscape to use the font settings as shown, rather than the Web page font. This can be especially beneficial if you prefer viewing a larger or smaller font.

The **Colors subcategory** (Figure A-3c) lets you change the colors of the text, links, and visited links. The lower check box in Figure A-3c instructs Netscape to use the colors shown, rather than the colors defined in the displayed Web page.

The **Themes subcategory** (Figure A-3d) allows you to change the look and feel of Netscape. In Figure A-3d you can choose from two themes: Modern and Classic. Modern, the default, is the theme that has been used in this book. Classic gives Netscape the traditional appearance used in earlier versions of the software.

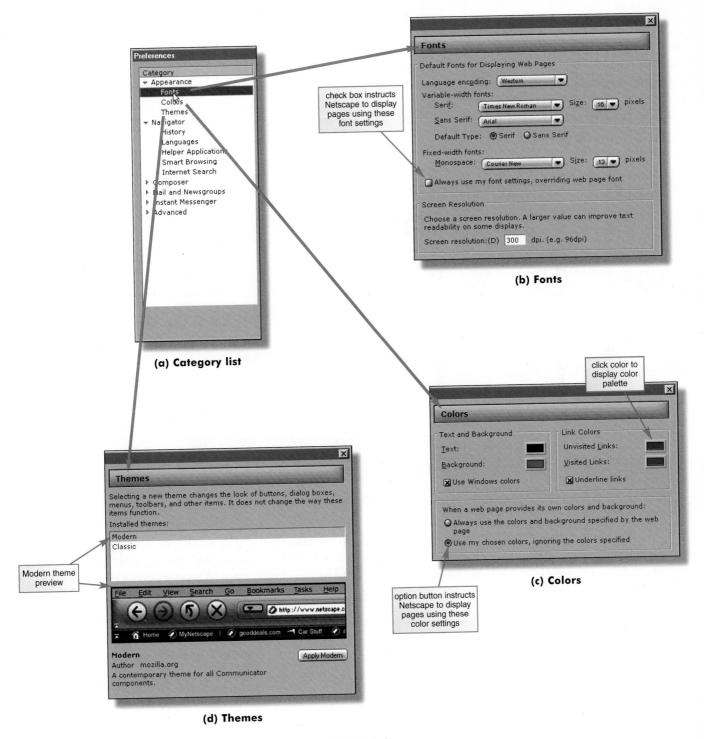

(a) Category list

check box instructs Netscape to display pages using these font settings

(b) Fonts

click color to display color palette

(c) Colors

Modern theme preview

option button instructs Netscape to display pages using these color settings

(d) Themes

FIGURE A-3

The Navigator Category

The **Navigator category** (Figure A-4) determines what the browser will display at start-up. Three choices are provided: blank page, home page, and last page visited. In Figure A-4, the Home page option is selected. You can use this category to change the home page to another Web page by changing the URL in the Location field in the Home Page area. Another way to change the home page is to display the page you wish to use as the home page and drag the URL in the Location field to the Home button on the Personal toolbar.

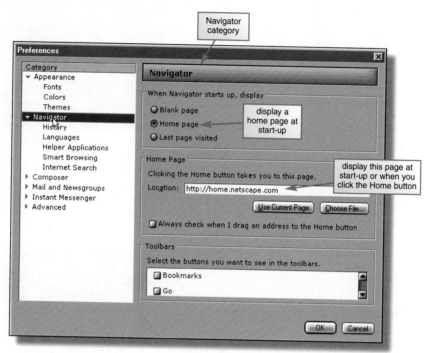

FIGURE A-4

The Navigator category has five subcategories (Figure A-5): History, Languages, Helper Applications, Smart Browsing, and Internet Search. The **History subcategory** (Figure A-5b) has two buttons: one to clear the History list and one to clear the Location field list. You also can use the History subcategory to instruct Netscape how long URLs should remain in the History list.

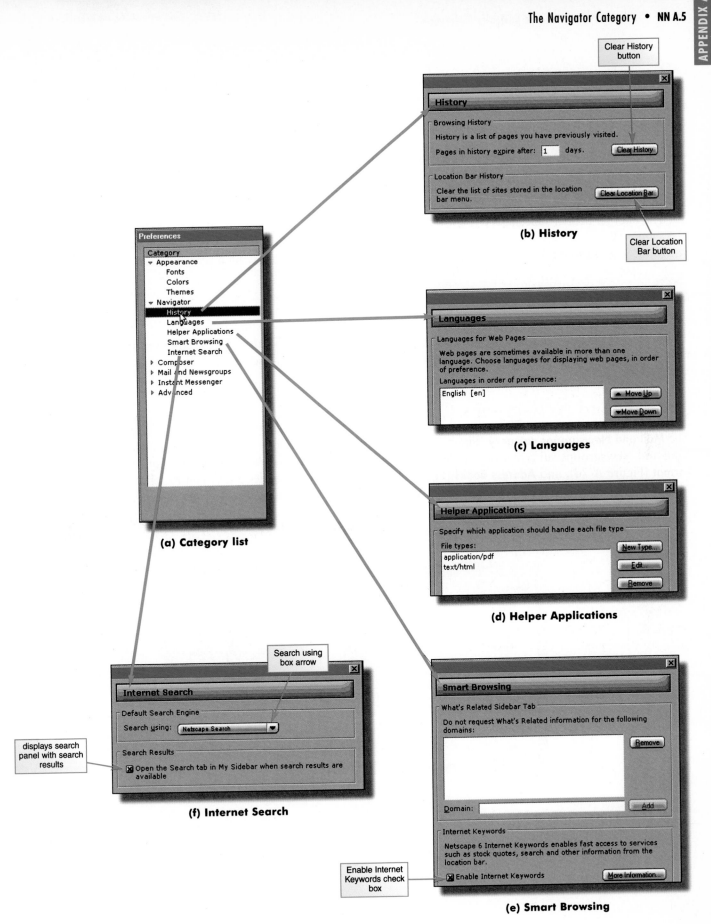

Clear History button

History

Browsing History
History is a list of pages you have previously visited.
Pages in history expire after: 1 days.   Clear History

Location Bar History
Clear the list of sites stored in the location bar menu.   Clear Location Bar

(b) History

Clear Location Bar button

Preferences

Category
▼ Appearance
    Fonts
    Colors
    Themes
▼ Navigator
    History
    Languages
    Helper Applications
    Smart Browsing
    Internet Search
▶ Composer
▶ Mail and Newsgroups
▶ Instant Messenger
▶ Advanced

(a) Category list

Languages

Languages for Web Pages
Web pages are sometimes available in more than one language. Choose languages for displaying web pages, in order of preference.
Languages in order of preference:

English [en]   ▲ Move Up
                 ▼ Move Down

(c) Languages

Helper Applications

Specify which application should handle each file type
File types: New Type...
application/pdf
text/html   Edit...

                                Remove

(d) Helper Applications

Search using box arrow

Internet Search

Default Search Engine
Search using: Netscape Search ▼

Search Results
☒ Open the Search tab in My Sidebar when search results are available

displays search panel with search results

(f) Internet Search

Smart Browsing

What's Related Sidebar Tab
Do not request What's Related information for the following domains:

                                Remove

Domain: Add

Internet Keywords
Netscape 6 Internet Keywords enables fast access to services such as stock quotes, search and other information from the location bar.
☒ Enable Internet Keywords   More Information...

Enable Internet Keywords check box

(e) Smart Browsing

FIGURE A-5

Use the **Languages subcategory** (Figure A-5c on the previous page) to set the order of languages that you want Netscape to use to display a page when it is available in more than one language. The **Helper Applications subcategory** (Figure A-5d) allows you to assign applications to file extensions so that Netscape knows what application to start to display a file.

The **Smart Browsing subcategory** (Figure A-5e on the previous page) includes three important parts. At the top, you can instruct Netscape not to update the What's Related panel in My Sidebar for the listed URLs. In the Internet Keywords area, you can toggle the Internet Keyword system on and off. Finally, you can toggle the URL AutoComplete on and off. The AutoComplete option will complete a previously visited URL (not shown in the Smart Browsing window).

The **Internet Search subcategory** (Figure A-5f on the previous page) lets you select the search engine that Netscape will use when you click the Search button on the Navigation toolbar. You also can tell Netscape whether you want it to automatically display the Search panel in My Sidebar following a search.

Composer Category

The **Composer category** lets you set preferences for the Composer application. The Composer application is beyond the scope of this book, and thus the Composer preferences will not be discussed.

Mail and Newsgroups Category

The **Mail and Newsgroups category** (Figure A-6) allows you to specify the appearance of the Mail window. The four Mail and Newsgroups subcategories are **Message Display** (Figure A-7b), **Message Composition** (Figure A-7c), **Send Format** (Figure A-7d), and **Address Books** (Figure A-7e). These subcategories allow you to tell Netscape how you want e-mails to display, how to reply to e-mails, how to compose e-mails, how to send e-mails, and how to update address books with e-mail addresses.

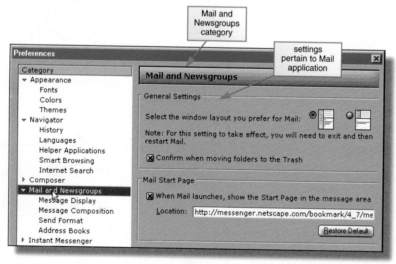

FIGURE A-6

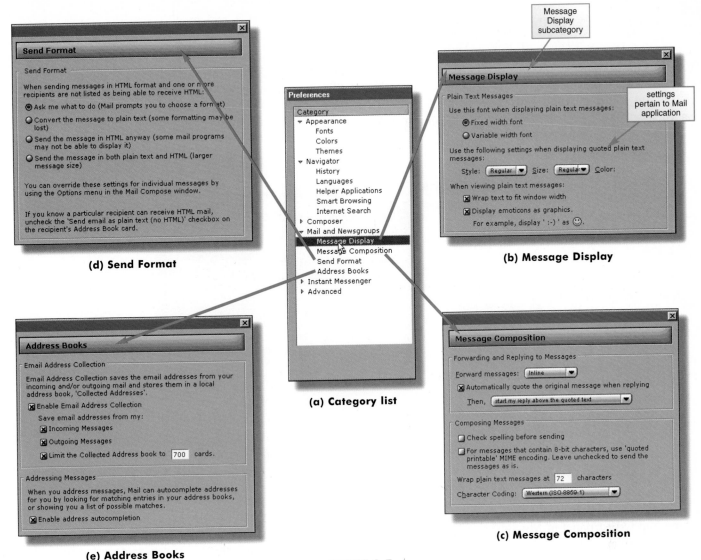

(d) Send Format

(b) Message Display

(a) Category list

(e) Address Books

(c) Message Composition

FIGURE A-7

Instant Messenger Category

The **Instant Messenger category** (Figure A-8) lets you set preferences for the Instant Messenger application. The four Instant Messenger subcategories are Privacy, Notification, Away, and Connection. The **Privacy subcategory** (Figure A-9b) lets you specify who can contact you. The **Notification subcategory** (Figure A-9c) includes settings that allow you to customize how you want to be notified when an instant message comes in. For example, you can have Netscape play a sound when a buddy signs on.

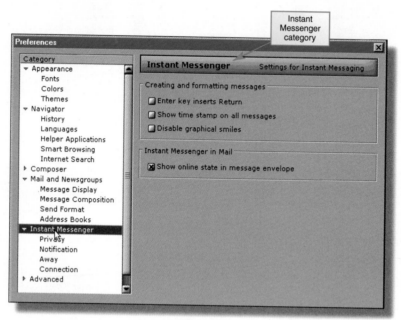

FIGURE A-8

The **Away subcategory** (Figure A-9d) includes several messages that you can display by clicking the Away arrow in the Buddy List panel in My Sidebar. When you choose an away message, your buddies online at the time will see the icon change to the left of your name in their Buddy List panel. You can use the Away subcategory to add and remove messages that you want sent when your system is on, but you are unavailable.

The **Connection subcategory** (Figure A-9e) identifies the host server that the Instant Messenger application uses to send and receive messages.

Advanced Category

The **Advanced category** (Figure A-10 on page NN A.10) lets you enable or disable Java and JavaScript for your browser. Programmers use Java and JavaScript to add functionality to Web pages. If you disable these languages, then functionality, such as moving objects or forms, will not work when you display the page. The nine Advanced subcategories are shown in Figure A-11 on pages NN A.10 and NN A.11 and include Cookies, Images, Forms, Passwords, Cache, Proxies, Software Installation, Mouse Wheel, and Desktop Integration.

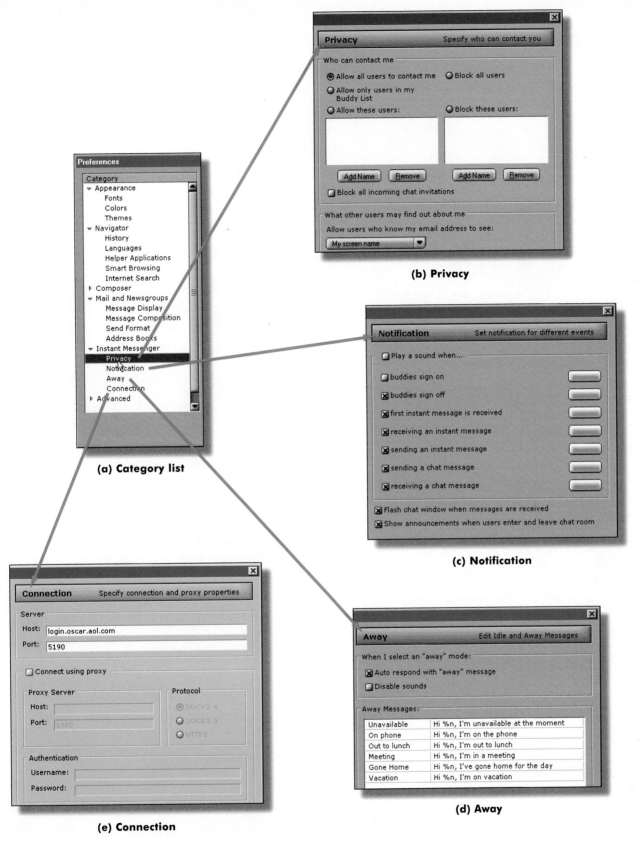

(a) Category list

(b) Privacy

(c) Notification

(d) Away

(e) Connection

FIGURE A-9

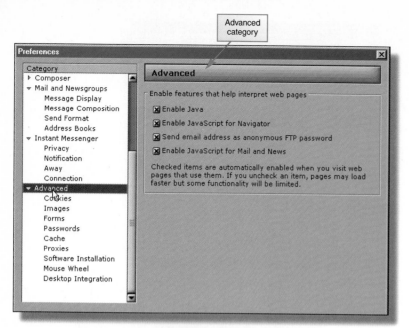

FIGURE A-10

Use the **Cookies subcategory** (Figure A-11b) to enable and disable cookies. **Cookies** are small amounts of information that are stored on your computer by a Web page so that it can use the information in the future when you redisplay it. You can use the Cookies subcategory to view and delete cookies or instruct Netscape to warn you before it stores a cookie.

The functions of the **Images subcategory** (Figure A-11c), **Forms subcategory** (Figure A-11d), **Passwords subcategory** (Figure A-11e), **Proxies subcategory** (Figure A-11g), **Software Installation subcategory** (Figure A-11h), and **Mouse Wheel subcategory** (Figure A-11i) are shown in Figure A-11.

The **Cache subcategory** (Figure A-11f) lets you set memory cache and disk cache. When you display Web pages, your system saves the pages to memory cache or disk cache so it can redisplay the pages faster. Netscape recommends you set memory cache between 1,024K and 2,000K and disk cache to 7,680K as shown in Figure A-11f. You also can use this subcategory to clear either cache.

Finally, the **Desktop Integration subcategory** (Figure A-11j) instructs Windows to use Netscape to display a variety of Web-related file types, such as HTML, XML, and XUL documents, and JPEG, GIF, and PNG images.

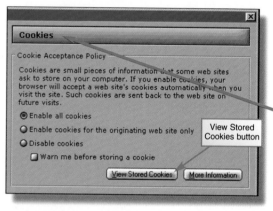

(b) Cookies

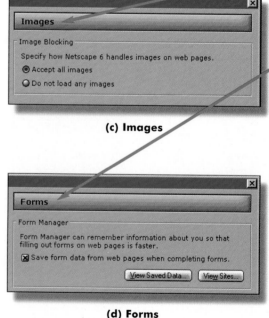

(c) Images

(d) Forms

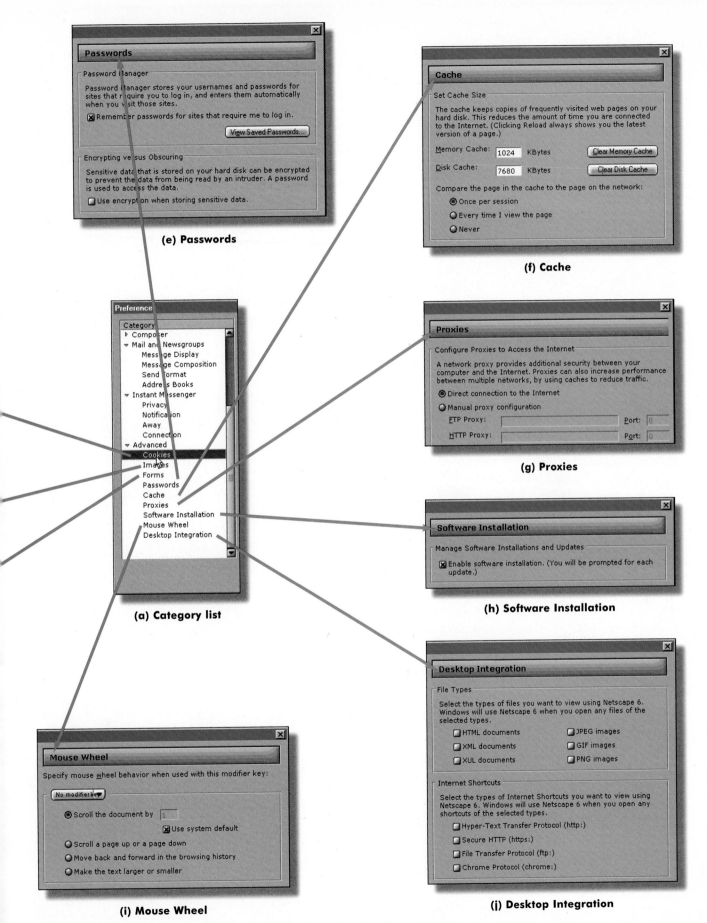

(e) Passwords

(f) Cache

(g) Proxies

(h) Software Installation

(a) Category list

(i) Mouse Wheel

(j) Desktop Integration

FIGURE A-11

Index